From Quarry to Cornfield

From Quarry to Cornfield

The Political Economy of Mississippian Hoe Production

Charles R. Cobb

THE UNIVERSITY OF ALABAMA PRESS

Tuscaloosa and London

Copyright © 2000
The University of Alabama Press
Tuscaloosa, Alabama 35487-0380
All rights reserved
Manufactured in the United States of America

1 2 3 4 5 6 7 8 9 / 07 06 05 04 03 02 01 00

Typeface: Trump Mediaeval

∞

The paper on which this book is printed meets the minimum requirements of American National Standard for Information Science–Permanence of Paper for Printed
Library Materials, ANSI Z39.48-1984.

Library of Congress Cataloging-in-Publication Data

Cobb, Charles R. (Charles Richard), 1956-
    From quarry to cornfield : the political economy of Mississippian hoe
production / Charles R. Cobb.
        p.   cm.
Includes bibliographical references and index.
    ISBN 0-8173-1050-9 (paper)
    1. Mill Creek Site (Ill.) 2. Hoes, Prehistoric—Mississippi River
Valley. 3. Mississippian culture. 4. Indians of North
America—Illinois—Antiquities. 5. Illinois—Antiquities. 6.
Mississippi River Valley—Antiquities. I. Title.
    E78.I3 C59 2000
    977'.01—dc21

                                        00-009857

British Library Cataloguing-in-Publication Data available

In memory of my grandmother, Mamie Seaton,
who would have been the first archaeologist in the
family, had she been born in another generation.

Contents

Figures and Tables

FIGURES

TABLES

Acknowledgments

The research represented in this book was carried out in two pulses. It began as my dissertation study, which was completed in 1988. After a hiatus of several years, I picked the thread up again in 1991 after I arrived at Binghamton University. I thus have had the good fortune to revisit an earlier body of research with additional fieldwork and analyses, which, not unexpectedly, altered many of the substantive conclusions in my original study. Further, my perspective on political economy has continued to evolve, resulting in theoretical changes in the original study as well. The somewhat lengthy time devoted to my study of the production and exchange of prehistoric hoes has resulted in a huge debt to numerous institutions and people who facilitated the logistical aspects of my work and who contributed to the ongoing gestation of my theoretical ideas.

High on my gratitude list are the archaeologists and related personnel associated with the Shawnee National Forest. Much of the research described here, including the excavations at the Dillow's Ridge site, was conducted on National Forest properties. Dan Haas and Mary McCorvie did everything possible to promote both the research and educational dimensions of my research, and I believe they have done a tremendous job of acquainting the public with the value of archaeology in the Shawnee Hills. Mary has wonderfully integrated the Passport in Time Program with our fieldwork, and it has been a pleasure to work with the volunteers in that program. The landowners in the research area also have been very supportive of this work, and I am thankful for their interest and patience with our recurring intrusions. I must single out Jackie and Perry Mowery as individuals who have a deep love for the landscape, prehistory, and history of the Shawnees, and I will always be grateful for their support and friendship.

The research began during my tenure as a graduate student at Southern Illinois University at Carbondale, and I had the good fortune to be associated with supportive mentors who are now good colleagues and friends. In particular, Jon Muller and Brian Butler supported all facets of my work and were more than willing to let me wander off in theoretical directions that did not always match their own. In the 1990s, Binghamton University and Southern Illinois University at Carbondale became partners in researching Mississippian life in the southern Illinois uplands, and my collaboration with Butler and Muller continues. At about the same time, Jean Stephens undertook surveys and excavations in the Dogtooth Bend region to the south, and her work and advice have been invaluable. Chip McGimsey directed the fieldschool at Dillow's Ridge in 1994 and deserves the credit for many of our insights on site occupational history. I also thank Don and Prudence Rice for marshaling the support of both the Department of Anthropology and the Center for Archaeological Investigations at SIU-C.

Numerous faculty and students (undergraduate and graduate) at Binghamton University have contributed in one way or another to the development of my research, and I regret that I cannot name every single individual. Randy McGuire, Reinhard Bernbeck, and Susan Pollock commented on various chapters in the book and have also made a major impact on my thoughts about political economy. I greatly appreciate their camaraderie and absolve them of blame for any parts of this study that may raise eyebrows. Seán Rafferty and Larissa Thomas worked closely with me on this research at various points in their careers, and Larissa performed a particularly close reading of an earlier draft of the book. Their subsequent successes have been richly deserved. The floral analysis was carried out by Lee Newsom and the faunal analysis by Emmanuel Breitberg and Peter Stahl. I trust that I have done no serious damage in my interpretation of their work.

Basic to success in any endeavor is core support from family and friends. My wife, Debby, has heard enough about chert to last anyone a lifetime, and I will forever be indebted to her for her support. My parents, John and Heloise, were a continuing source of strength throughout my graduate studies, and I thank them for giving me free rein to explore my quirky interests throughout childhood and into college.

Several funding agencies made this work a reality. I am grateful to the National Science Foundation (BNS-9120222) and the National Geographic Society (Grant #5241-94) for providing the funding necessary to sustain a multiyear project.

From Quarry to Cornfield

1   A Day in the Life

By the beginning of the second millennium A.D. human communities had been extracting metals and minerals from the earth's crust for thousands of years. Steady advances in quarrying and mining technologies had provided growing access to a broad range of raw materials widely valued as markers of wealth or as utilitarian resources. In turn, these substances—such as gold, copper, tin, and salt—were increasingly important in trade networks. In the Old World, demand for the earth's treasures was an important dimension of the global economy that was taking shape by the 1400s.

Several centuries before the development of the mercantile system that would create upheaval in the New World, a group of villagers was busy at work in the flinty hills northeast of the confluence of the mighty Ohio and Mississippi rivers in the present-day United States. Continuing a tradition that their ancestors had followed for generations, the villagers excavated into a hillside with stone spades in search of one of the most prized raw materials of their era. They pried brown, flat chert nodules from the earth and placed them in a growing pile. At the end of the day, the pile of stones was carried to the top of the hill, where a small village of 10 wattle-and-daub structures stood. Over the course of the next few days, several accomplished flintknappers from the village transformed the crude nodules into well-crafted hoes and spades. Holding a few aside for their own use, they placed the remaining two score or so into large, bark-woven bags.

The following morning a number of villagers gathered the bags and threw them over their backs. Setting off westward, they followed a well-worn path that snaked through the hills and avoided the steeper terrain. After the good part of a day, their path emerged from a break in the hills and entered the expansive floodplain of the Mississippi River. The flat relief was a sharp contrast to the hills where the men and women lived. As they continued on their now level trail, they began to approach a tight group of low prominences that interrupted the even line of the horizon. The irregularities on the landscape slowly came into focus as a series of rounded and flat-topped earthen mounds. A stockade of tall posts punctuated by square bastions every 40 or 50 paces enclosed the tumuli. The porters passed through a small opening in the stockade wall and entered a vibrant village several times larger than their own. Smoke rising from roofs marked a busy residential area consisting of about 50 houses. In the center of the village was a large plaza surrounded by five large mounds. Two of the mounds had structures on top, but timber walls around them prevented the visitors from having a clear view of the activities of the secluded priestly leaders.

The weary travelers were led into the village and made welcome by relatives and old acquaintances. After an evening of feasting and storytelling, the following day was spent bartering over the contents of the bags. The visitors passed on the stone tools to their trading partners, and in turn refilled their bags with a variety of foods and crafts. Once again, they placed the bags on their backs, bid farewell to their friends and neighboring families, and retraced their steps home.

With some variation, the stone tools continued their journey. The new owners held some aside for their own use, then placed the remainder along with other regionally procured goods, such as galena cubes and fluorite beads, into a wooden canoe that lay beached alongside a large creek running by their village. Shoving into the water, they paddled downstream several miles until they entered the Mississippi River. The canoe was turned upstream and kept close to the shore to avoid the worst of the current. After a lengthy journey northward, the canoe was pulled ashore and the group hoisted their packs like their trading partners before them; then they continued inland on foot.

After passing a number of villages, the travelers approached yet another set of artificial hills on the flat landscape. Impressive as their own village was, these mounds dwarfed their own, even towering over the remaining patches of forest that broke up the large fields of maize. They recognized many of the features of their own village in this town, but as with the gargantuan mounds, everything in this huge settlement was many magnitudes larger. Hundreds of structures were visible, grouped into neighborhoods. Mounds also seemed to be grouped into clusters, usually arranged around plazas. By far the largest grouping occupied the center of the town, dominated by a tremendous platform mound that overshadowed the entire community. Artificial lakes dotted the area, where rainwater had filled in borrow pits gouged by the removal of clay to build all of the earthworks. Everywhere life teemed. Dogs barked, people played ball games in the plazas, the smells of cooking emanated from the various barrios, and several new mounds were in the process of being erected.

Impressed as they were by these sights, the newcomers had seen them before. Replaying a scene from their own village several days earlier, they were greeted by old friends, fed, and put up for the night in preparation for a new round of trading for the goods they carried. Two days later they returned home carrying items not easily obtained in their own village: an embossed copper plate, a shell gorget, and several quartz crystals.

In the large town to the north, the stone tools entered the final stage of their journey. The collection was broken up into smaller lots and distributed among households. The tools were hafted onto short wooden handles and became workable spades and hoes, particularly useful for cultivating fields that provided the maize, beans, and squash that were the mainstays of the diet. And in an interesting twist, the tools that were crafted by the hands of men saw much of their use in the hands of women, who tended the fields and did most of the harvesting. The women considered the hoes an essential part of their daily toolkit. The edges of the tools were resharpened as they became dull or damaged to prolong their usefulness. During the seasons when the tools were not being used, special care was taken to cache them in storage pits in the floors of their houses. Sometimes the houses had to be unexpectedly abandoned due to accidental fires and the caches would be forgotten. There they would remain for centuries until they were discovered by archaeologists and put into use again; not as implements for cultivating plants, but as tools for recreating and understanding a lifeway that had long since disappeared.

This study explores the manufacture and exchange of the stone hoes that made their way into households throughout a large region of North America. They were produced in the hilly region of southern Illinois (Figure 1.1) where our story began during a dynamic time known as the Mississippian period (ca. A.D. 1000–1500), when many societies in the American Southeast and Midwest were transforming into chiefdom-style polities characterized by complex social, political, and economic relations. In undertaking this study, I argue that a political-economic framework can greatly illuminate those processes guiding the production, exchange, and consumption of stone hoes. Because the Mississippian period predates the mercantile and capitalist eras, my interpretive framework will differ in many respects from that used to understand the emergence of the world system, industrial capitalism, and related issues in political economy. Although I believe that there are qualitative differences between the way political economies are organized in small-scale versus modern societies, there are still similarities in the important questions to be asked of each: How was labor organized? What were the mutual effects between production and

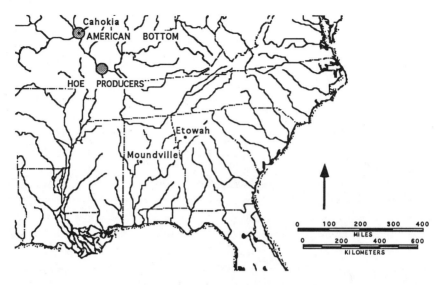

Figure 1.1. Location of sites and regions referred to in the text.

exchange? What was the interaction between production for exchange, social organization, social hierarchy, and gender relations?

In confronting these and related issues, two themes will be continually visited throughout this work—history and scale. The events occurring in the research region could be seen to have parallels elsewhere. As already noted, quarrying and mining enjoy a lengthy history worldwide. One also might be able to identify grossly similar forms of social organization between Mississippian groups and other chiefdom-style societies in Polynesia, Africa, and elsewhere. Yet, the genesis of the Mississippian period and the particular form that it took in the Central Mississippi Valley was a unique process—one that demands an appreciation from a historical perspective not only for explanatory reasons, but also for the purpose of appreciating Native American cultures from the standpoint of their everyday life, rather than reducing their features to variables on a flow chart. Consequently, how people worked and lived are just as important as the theoretical models that inform us about such activities.

Those Native American groups engaged in the extraction of chert and its manufacture into hoes may have constituted unique cultures, but they were not closed societies. Starting from the location of the quarries and moving outward, the stoneworking communities were enmeshed in an ever-widening ripple of relations that had different manifestations and impacts at varying scales. At the local level, people probably married into neighboring villages and traded foodstuffs and valuables back and forth; at a much greater scope the hoes they produced were one of the most intensively and extensively traded items during the Mississippian period and are found over a substantial portion of the American Midwest and Southeast. A major objective of this study is to explicate the nature of relations at either end of the scale, as well as points in between.

At a more basic level, I aim to provide an understanding of how the manufacture of hoes was embedded in the social relations of everyday life. In other words, how can the organization of production be viewed as a social as well as technological phenomenon? In following this pursuit, I am interested in how archaeologists bridge from the archaeological record to make statements about the social constitution of production and the mobilization of surplus. Finally, I am concerned with how the manufacture of stone digging implements can be framed as a particular manifestation of the labor process during the Mississippian period, and with what that tells us about the political economy of late prehistoric Native American societies. I am particularly interested in exploring how power relations governing the labor of stone hoe production, exchange, and consumption varied greatly depending upon which part of the economic cycle was involved. As I will argue, production appears to have involved little social asymmetry, interregional exchange shows some evidence of influence by elites, and consumption was likely impacted by gendered notions of labor. In short, the reproduction of the system of hoe manufacture entailed a multifaceted web of power and labor relations that extended far beyond the technical act of extracting chert and making stone tools.

POLITICAL ECONOMY, ANTHROPOLOGY, AND ARCHAEOLOGY

Anthropologists have been interested in political-economic studies for several decades, although interest in the topic has exploded since the 1970s (see overviews by Marcus and Fischer 1986; Ortner 1984; Roseberry 1989). In a broad sense, the term *political economy* denotes a study of power relations and how they mediate access to wealth and basic resources. Several political economy studies, such as *Europe and the People Without History* (Wolf 1982) and *Sweetness and Power* (Mintz 1985), have become classics in the field, solidifying the importance of political economy in anthropological research.

My broad definition of political economy in fact glosses over what has developed into a wide range of approaches and objectives. To list just a few of these directions, we have ambitious studies concerned with the development of the modern world system and capitalism (Wallerstein 1974; Wolf 1982); with how the production and exchange of certain commodities impacted specific cultures (Mintz 1985; Nash 1979); with relations of power from a gendered perspective (Harris and Young 1981; Sacks 1974; Silverblatt 1991; Stoler 1985); and with the role of symbols and ideology in the reproduction of relations of inequality (Helms 1988; Keesing 1987; Sahlins 1990).

There are several important common threads that unite these and related works, despite the diversity of approaches, and my research on Mississippian societies embodies these emphases. The first thread goes back to the definition of political economy offered above: underlying all of the studies is a strong concern with the nature of power relations and how they may be related to material aspects of society. Second, the studies are sensitive to historical processes and contexts. Reacting against the idea of a timeless, ethnographic present, political-economic anthropologists have strongly advocated the importance of a historical approach that lays great emphasis on how groups came to be what they are (or were). This perspective sees human communities as constantly changing and only understandable as dynamic recipients and modifiers of cultural practices. Finally, political-economic research in anthropology is usually concerned with notions of scale and scalar processes. Although individuals and communities may represent key loci in the reproduction of cultural practices, they do not exist in a vacuum. Local traditions and practices are subject to the influences of neighboring communities, encompassing nation-states, and large-scale or global economic systems that may regularly insinuate their way into everyday life, sometimes abruptly and jarringly, at other times gradually and barely noticed.

Two modifiers must be added to the general attributes of political economy as practiced within anthropology. These relate to (1) differing notions of history in anthropology and (2) various ways in which the idea of scalar relations is put into practice in case studies. Many anthropologists embracing a historical perspective primarily use it in an operational sense. Here, history involves a documentation of the long-term, that is, looking at the changing sequence of cultural practices through time rather than framing studies in terms of limited, synchronic observations. In this sense, ethnographies may attempt to "finesse" history by limiting themselves to descriptive chronicles (Marcus and Fischer 1986:95). Yet history also can imply certain theoretical and epistemological stances toward explaining or interpreting the reproduction or transformation of practices through time. With the exception of some cultural anthropologists and archaeologists (e.g., Hodder 1987; Knapp 1992; Roseberry 1988; Sahlins 1985; Trigger 1989; Wolf 1990), however, the theoretical articulation of history with political-economic topics is rarely broached.

Randall McGuire (1992:168–70) has pointed out that anthropologists and archaeologists typically adopt one of three approaches to history. The first is the ideographic history of cultural-historical archaeology that was heavily criticized by the New Archaeology for its normative and diffusionist views on culture change. Another perspective sees history as the outcome of cultural difference and is based in structural and symbolic approaches. History unfolds via the disjunctures of opposing world views between participants and interest groups. History is a gradual process because structures and symbols are presumed to be resistant to change.

A third approach, one embraced by a number of political-economic anthropologists and followed in my study, emphasizes history as a material social process. Under this model, conflict and change are products of competing interests both within and between social groups. Social inequality and power relations are key levers of historical transformations. This does not deny that ecological change, demographic shifts, and similar "external" stimuli are consequential in culture change, but the impact of such variables is conditioned through cultural meaning and social practices. It should be underscored that relations of power are not assumed to be the only driving force in history, but they do constitute an important dynamic for addressing a number of research questions with anthropological relevance.

The second qualification to my overview of political economy relates to the idea of scale. Recognition of the multitiered dimension of human relations may represent an important cornerstone of political-economic research (Marquardt 1992; Marquardt and Crumley 1987), but it is a very difficult concept to operationalize from a methodological standpoint. For this reason, research tends to emphasize some level in the continuum (e.g., communities versus world systems), while at the same time attempting to recognize and reconcile the various levels of interconnectedness. Often, this issue is construed as an "agency-structure" problematic. Thus, for example, we have studies that attempt to evaluate how households (often considered agents) in different cultures may articulate with capitalism (an economic structure) (e.g., Collins 1986; Robben 1989; Rutz 1989; Wong 1984).

Even though the bulk of political-economic research tends to be concerned with the growth and impact of world capitalism, other sources of structure are often incorporated into studies. Archaeologists have considered the Georgian world view (Beaudry et al. 1991; Deetz 1977; M. Johnson 1996) and even phases or horizons (e.g., Tiawanaku, Beaker culture, Mississippian) as forms of structural, large-scale phenomena that form the upper layer in a multiscalar framework. For reasons unknown, over large geographic areas and within limited spans of time, societies decided to reproduce similar practices and material culture. The communities sharing those characteristics were far from unitary cultures, yet they did seem to impart some broad conception of identity. At the same time, individual communities continued to follow practices and create material culture with long-standing local histories. We still have a poor grasp of what the widespread collectivities represent (ritual systems, polities?), and how and why they became intertwined with local communities to forge new identities that combined the new and the old. But this synthesis does seem to be fundamental to the process of social reproduction.

Giddens (1976) observes that social reproduction occurs at three levels: (1) the actor, (2) a field of interaction and meaning, and (3) structures relating to collectivities. Whereas the first and third levels broadly correspond with the agency and structure dyad, his second level seems to incorporate a notion of immediate sociality that transcends the individual. In other words, human beings reproduce their culture as members of social groups, not as completely autonomous individuals (McGuire 1992:134). Thus, while it could be argued that archaeologists have a difficult time accessing the individual actor or agent (M. Johnson 1989), it could be countered that an appropriately fine level of resolution is one that involves a notion of the social group above the individual—the household or community, for example.

While notions of history and scale are essential for framing political-economic research, they do not necessarily imply a theoretical stance. For this, many anthropologists conducting political-economic research have strongly relied upon the writings of Marx and the large corpus of Marxism-influenced research that has been produced over the past century. Such an emphasis is not surprising when one considers that a major focus of the Marxist literature has been the growth and ramifications of capitalism, concerns that anthropologists have transferred to non-Western settings: the historical development of capitalism; the incorporation of traditional anthropological study areas into the capitalist world system; the impacts of the commoditization of labor on indigenous societies; the export and effect of Western technologies on traditional practices and beliefs; and so on.

Many historical archaeologists have been moving in this direction with their research, but when we consider societies that existed long before the capitalist era, many of the key issues involving labor, power relations, and the economy assume qualitatively different proportions (Cobb 1993; Dalton 1977; Feinman and Neitzel 1984; Saitta 1994; Schneider 1977). Exchange no longer involves the neutral transactions of a money economy, but entails the forging of alliances and obligations that may endure for many generations. Rarely are people alienated from the means of production, and the mobilization of labor is not necessarily a matter of tribute or taxes; the transfer of surplus may be bound up in a complex network of reciprocity, expectations of social positions, and debt manipulation. The extreme differences between capitalist and non-capitalist societies have led many researchers to question the very applicability of concepts that may be taken for granted in modern situations. What is surplus? How broadly can the idea of "class" be applied? What is the basis of exploitation when access to basic resources is unrestricted and economic differentiation is not pronounced?

LABOR AND THE SOCIAL CONTEXT OF PRODUCTION

One avenue of addressing such questions in a context that is not tied to a specific historical era is to focus on the labor process. One of the advantages of emphasizing labor—particularly for a study such as this, which is concerned with the organization of production—is that this concept allows us to focus squarely on issues of differential access, social inequality, and the mobilization of surplus. It also urges us to move down from grand issues of scale and regional syntheses and to consider in more detail the daily lives of peoples living beyond the scope of written history.

The relationship of individuals or groups to the labor process typically defines their relationships to one another (Marx and Engels 1970:42–43, passim). Labor involves not only technology and energy expenditure, but also the social mechanisms that prescribe or proscribe relative access to resources between individuals and interest groups. Labor is the social framework of work; it implies not only production, but also relations of production and the web of beliefs and meaning that may structure work. From this perspective, labor is a linchpin between political and economic activities and involves "culture" as well as "practical reason."

The political economy of societies may be characterized and differentiated (internally and comparatively) by their institutional arrangements for the appropriation of surplus, which in turn are defined by variation in the allocation and extraction of labor (Godelier 1972:273–74; Pearson 1957:334; Saitta and Keene 1990; Wolf 1966). And it is the nature of surplus mobilization that in large part defines asymmetrical access to wealth and power. Importantly, there are myriad ways in which labor and surplus may be mobilized, and they do not easily fit into traditional categories that, for example, dichotomize elites and commoners (Paynter and McGuire 1991; Saitta and Keene 1990:211–12) or argue for predictable relations between political and economic

realms (Bernbeck 1995). In short, surplus flow is dictated by heterogeneous relations of power rather than just hierarchical ones.

A now popular view of conceptualizing power in archaeology is
the "power to" and "power over" duality, largely deriving from Foucault's (1980) work (e.g., Bender 1990; Paynter and McGuire 1991;
Tilley 1984). "Power to" implies the self-endowed capability to initiate
as well as resist actions, whereas "power over" refers to the more common notion of the ability to circumscribe or dictate the actions of others. Eric Wolf (1990) employs an even more diverse approach to power
relations with a fourfold definition: (1) endowed power, or the potency
of an individual; (2) the ability to impose one's will in interpersonal
relations; (3) tactical power, wherein individuals have the ability to
control the settings in which others work; and (4) structural power,
which refers to the ability to mobilize and allocate labor. Although
care must be taken to avoid reducing power relations to labels or categories, these approaches are useful for thinking about variability in
power relations and the settings in which they occur.

Here is where archaeology can hope to make some very real contributions to research in political economy. The broad scope of human
history with which we deal encompasses a dizzyingly broad array of
societies. Among all of this variation, is it possible to chart out broad
regularities in the political economy of small-scale groups that somehow resemble those documented for the political economy of capitalism? Are there, for example, parallels to the concepts of commodity or
capital or surplus labor—or can these concepts themselves be applied
outside of capitalist contexts? For instance, some would argue that a
term like *commodity* is best reserved for market or money economies
(e.g., Muller 1997:15–16). On the other hand, Appadurai (1986:11–15)
claims that the differences between gift exchange and commodity exchange have been exaggerated. Not only do we have a tendency to ro-
manticize the very calculating ways of small-scale groups, but also
commodification itself is not a purely impersonal dimension of market
forces—it involves a complex configuration of cultural as well as economic factors.

These perspectives do not constitute mere quibbling over nomenclature. They also represent important differences in the way that we both
view and attempt to explain the organization of the political economy
in non-capitalist contexts. Although I am not explicitly concerned in
this project with resolving variability in our use of political-economic
concepts, I am interested in whether we can develop any kinds of generalizations that are appropriate for small-scale political economies. If
so, can we use these broad themes or generalizations judiciously, in a

manner that does not overshadow the importance of agency and the reproduction of local systems?

From the view of many North American archaeologists, at least, the answer to this last question would seem to lie in the realm of research framed in the neo-evolutionary paradigm that has waxed and waned (and waxed again) in the twentieth century. As we enter the twenty-first century, the critiques of neo-evolutionism are well rehearsed, and even those who continue to use evolutionary taxa usually do so with a clear understanding of the shortcomings that such categories entail. Knowing this, many archaeologists still continue to be concerned with chiefdoms, and the continuing strength of this concept suggests that the political economy of chiefdoms may be one avenue toward generalizing about some forms of pre-capitalist societies. In a general overview of power and labor in chiefdoms, Jeanne Arnold (1996:60) observes that "there is substantial cross-cultural variability in the degree to which elites are active in managing others' labor, but it appears that common to all is the regular—as opposed to temporary—power to draw upon labor from the relatively stable position of higher offices." This approach toward chiefdoms, which focuses on the links between power and labor, seems especially appropriate for Mississippian period societies because they display evidence for the well-established social ranking, organization of labor at the community level, and economic differentiation that are traditionally cited as hallmarks for chiefdom societies.

THE MISSISSIPPIAN PERIOD IN NORTH AMERICA

In the first millennium A.D., Native American societies in eastern North America were undergoing great changes that represented a major shift from the multitude of hunting and gathering life-styles that had typified the region for the preceding eight to 10 thousand years. Particularly important ecological and demographic trends included increasing sedentism, growing dependence on cultivated plants, and expanding population levels. Other major phenomena documented by archaeologists for this interval are the widespread adoption of a new portable storage technology in the form of ceramic vessels, the development (or reappearance) of sophisticated long-distance exchange networks, and a growing emphasis on public construction, particularly earthworks (Smith 1986; Steponaitis 1986). Certain aspects of the archaeological record, such as mortuary practices, also point to growing social differentiation.

These changes were felt to varying degrees and manifested in dif-

PERIOD	INTERVAL
Paleoindian	10,000-8,000 B.C.
Early Archaic	8,000-6,000
Middle Archaic	6,000-3,000
Late Archaic	3,000-1,000
Early Woodland	1,000-200
Middle Woodland	200 B.C.-A.D. 400 A.D.
Late Woodland	400-800
Emergent Mississippian	800-1,000
Mississippian	1,000-1,500

Figure 1.2. General periods of the Southeast and lower Midwest.

ferent ways across the eastern United States. Indeed, documenting the interrelationships between these variables has been a major challenge for archaeologists working in the larger region as we have come to appreciate the often surprising combinations in which they occur. For example, while received wisdom might dictate that the construction of substantial earthworks would require sizable populations supported by cultigens, the Lower Mississippi Valley displays a strong tradition of mound building for some 4,000 years without any appreciable archaeological evidence for domesticated plants—from Middle Archaic (ca. 3000 B.C.) to Coles Creek (ca. A.D. 900) cultures (Figure 1.2). In contrast, one of the strongest early surges toward a reliance on cultigens can be found in the Illinois River Valley of west-central Illinois, where domesticated plants such as chenopod and little barley became important components of the Middle Woodland or Hopewell (ca. 200 B.C.–A.D. 400) diet. Yet the scale of mound building in the Illinois Valley is relatively modest, particularly when compared with contemporary developments elsewhere, such as southern Ohio where, again, impressive Hopewellian earthworks occur with the near absence of cultigens.

From a synchronic perspective, the important trends I have enumerated for the first millennium A.D. often occur in bewildering combinations across the landscape of eastern North America. From the diachronic perspective, archaeologists generally agree that these traits gradually became widespread with much variation and occasional reversals along the way. In the latter regard, the Late Woodland period (A.D. 400–800) is a particularly intriguing instance of an actual decline in mound construction and long-distance exchange across much of the midwestern and southeastern United States, while population levels and a dependence on cultigens continued to rise (Nassaney and Cobb 1991).

During the interval A.D. 800 to 1000 in southeastern and midwestern North America, things began to change dramatically. Mesoamerican domesticates, particularly maize, became increasingly important in the diet. Along the Central Mississippi River Valley and its tributaries, shell-tempered ceramics, new forms of storage technology, and wall-trench houses of wattle-and-daub construction became common. By around A.D. 1000, these trends had coalesced into a general widespread pattern that lasted until about A.D. 1500, an interval referred to as the Mississippian period. There is some disagreement over the exact boundaries of the distribution of sites that can be called Mississippian (Smith 1986): the most liberal interpretation would see the western margin around the Oklahoma-Arkansas border; the northern edge in the lower portion of the Midwest states of Illinois and Indiana; and the eastern and southern boundaries represented by the Atlantic Ocean and the Gulf Coast. From about A.D. 1000 onward, earthen mounds and other large-scale constructions appeared in many communities, accompanied by substantial population increases. True towns appear on the landscape, in some cases with populations possibly numbering in the thousands, although small hamlets and farmsteads were much more common. Importantly, mortuary evidence demonstrates the development of pronounced differences in social status and the emergence of what has been interpreted as chiefdoms. The Mississippian period is best known for the truly impressive mound centers located in the rich floodplains of the drainages fingering throughout the Southeast and Midwest. To North American archaeologists, names such as Moundville and Etowah evoke images of grand platform mounds, large plazas, and rich burial assemblages (Figure 1.1).

At the very apex of the scale sits Cahokia, the huge town that figures in the beginning of this chapter, representing an outlier even among the many very large Mississippian centers. The site is located in southwestern Illinois in a portion of the Mississippi River floodplain known as the American Bottom. It consists of a lozenge-shaped arrangement of more than one hundred mounds of varying shapes and functions segregated into several sets of plaza groupings spread out over an area of some 14 square kilometers. The largest cluster in the middle of the site was set off by a palisade and is distinguished by Monk's Mound, which stands 30 meters high and represents the largest single monument in North America north of central Mexico. Recent studies of Cahokia indicate that massive efforts were made by its inhabitants and neighbors to produce an artificial landscape charged with political and ceremonial significance (Emerson 1997; Holley et al. 1993; Pauketat 1994).

Numerous other major sites mirror the central features of Cahokia on a much reduced—but still impressive—scale throughout the Midwest and Southeast. But the Mississippian lifeway extended far beyond the reaches of the spectacular mound centers; the many farmsteads and hamlets that are found scattered across the landscape are probably much more representative of everyday life for the majority of people. It is problematic to what degree the rural Mississippians were incorporated into the polities that are presumed to have existed around the mound centers. Many mound centers appear to have had subsidiary mound sites and numerous satellite communities that we presume were articulated into dynamic, yet often fragile, polities. Many communities existed in hinterland areas well away from mound centers, and their isolation hints that they may have been relatively autonomous politically, if not socially.

Researchers are still struggling over how best to characterize the Mississippian phenomenon. On the one hand, it cannot be denied that a number of key traits were shared across a large area of North America. On the other hand, if one focuses on specific regions in more detail, considerable diversity is also evident. It has become very apparent that "Mississippian" is not a monolithic entity or culture that was imposed across a vast area; instead, local regions incorporated a number of traits and ideas, and modified them according to local traditions. Thus we see a strong pattern of ongoing regional idiosyncrasies coupled with a regular interaction between regions that seems to have accounted for many of the similar features and artifacts that we place into an essentialistic Mississippian category.

In addition to the widespread styles and types that characterize the Mississippian period, archaeologists have documented that many kinds of raw materials and finished goods crisscrossed the Mississippian culture area for several centuries (Brown et al. 1990; Dye 1995; Lafferty 1994; Muller 1995). The picture they paint is one of a steady flow of goods over a huge network of rivers and well-developed trails. Particularly valued raw materials included marine shell, copper, galena, fluorite, mica, and a variety of stones. In many cases, these materials were rendered into a variety of finished artifacts displaying widely shared symbolic and iconographic styles, a phenomenon commonly referred to as the "Southern Cult" or the Southeastern Ceremonial Complex (Brown 1976; Galloway 1989; Howard 1968; Waring and Holder 1945). In a very general sense, the peoples making and trading these items constituted a Mississippian "world system," albeit a very different one from that described for the modern era (King and Freer 1995; Peregrine 1992).

The problem with characterizing Mississippian interaction and economic activities as a "world system" is that this perspective describes broad structural trends, but it does not account for the variety of cultural ways in which labor may have been mobilized. To achieve this goal, we must move to a "bottom-up" perspective that privileges the actions of actors, lineage groups, households, and communities. It is from this vantage point that I undertake my own study on the production and exchange of chert hoes.

THE MILL CREEK QUARRIES

One of the major raw materials in the larger Mississippian exchange sphere was a variety of chert located in an unassuming setting in the hills of southern Illinois. As early as the mid to late nineteenth century, scholars and antiquarians in the Midwest recognized an impressive prehistoric quarry known as the "Indian Diggings" in the far southwestern corner of the state (Morse 1881; Perrine 1873). These investigators discovered scores of pits scarring a large ridge system, and thousands of excavated nodules and broken blanks scattered over several acres around the pits. With the heightened interest in the sites and artifacts of the "moundbuilders" during this time, it quickly became apparent that one of the more impressive artifact types recovered from such sites as Cahokia—large stone hoes—was most commonly made from the chert deriving from the Indian Diggings in southern Illinois (Figure 1.3). Mill Creek chert, named after a nearby village and stream, thus became recognized early on as a very important raw material to the mound builders, and the quarry was explored by prominent archaeologists from the Smithsonian Institution and the Field Museum of Natural History (Holmes 1919; Phillips 1899, 1900; Thomas 1894).

The early research in southwestern Illinois also established the presence of a small mound center that was engaged in hoe manufacture, the Hale site, in the floodplain southeast of the large quarry. In addition, researchers discovered smaller quarries dotting the hills as well as numerous sites referred to as workshops scattered throughout the hills and floodplains of the small creeks that run through the area (e.g., Hudelson 1938; Snyder 1910). It became apparent to archaeologists by the turn of the century that here, in the hinterlands of southern Illinois, existed one of the greatest quarry systems and production centers in prehistoric North America. Not only was the regional evidence of quarrying and hoe manufacture impressive, but also the thousands of

Figure 1.3. Mill Creek chert hoe.
(Courtesy of the Center for Archaeological Investigations, Southern Illinois University at Carbondale.)

Mill Creek chert hoes turned up by farmers' plows and archaeological
excavations at sites in Illinois and surrounding states pointed to a
heavy trade in the tools over a large geographic area.

One of the key points made by James Brown and co-workers (1990)
in their study on Mississippian trade is the relative lack of systematic
attention paid to this subject prior to the 1980s given our long-standing
knowledge about the interaction that must have occurred between
Mississippian sites. As a corollary to this point, the various loci and
types of production that made trade possible also have not received the
amount of attention that one might expect, although it can fairly be
said that in the past 10 years Mississippian production systems have
become a topic of increasing interest, and the imbalance is rapidly being redressed.

The Mill Creek chert quarry system provides a particularly suitable
entry point into issues of Mississippian production and exchange. It
represents one of the largest extractive and production efforts recognized for the Mississippian period and provided one of the most widely

exchanged items. In sum, the quarries and workshops constitute an important window into Mississippian period political economy.

The remainder of this study will continually engage the issue of what is meant by a political economy of chiefdoms. The following chapter delves into the broad implications of this question, particularly as it ultimately affects our interpretation of Mississippian societies. An area of particular concern is the contrast between the generalizing aspects of thinking about the organization of chiefdoms and the particularizing aspects of dealing with specific societies. In other words, if we are ultimately concerned with concrete human societies and the relationships between actors and interest groups, how far can such a broad category as "chiefdom" take us in achieving this kind of understanding? Yet one can hardly build from the ground up without blueprints of any kind. As much as we might like to think otherwise, interpretations and explanations about the actions of specific societies or their constituent subgroups are guided by generalities we extract from previous anthropological research. I thus argue that the interplay between the particular and general modes is essential for arriving at the kind of conclusions in which I am interested—statements about real and unique societies living in a real past, but which may share some commonalities with other societies that may be removed in space and time.

Because of these ultimate aims, the notion of chiefdom does have serious limitations for the interpretive process. Despite the heuristic usefulness of the concept, it is ultimately impossible to escape the essentialistic dimensions of the idea of chiefdom. Neo-evolutionary categories represent a point of departure for analysis, rather than an end point. To make headway toward addressing the kind of variation one might expect under the chiefdom label, it becomes necessary to use analytical concepts that are more concerned with process (Wolf 1982) and relations (Resnick and Wolff 1987). Toward these ends, anthropologists have advocated the use of such analytical units as mode of production (Roseberry 1989; Wolf 1982), class analysis (Resnick and Wolff 1987), social reproduction (Friedman and Rowlands 1978; Harris and Young 1981), and gender (Leacock 1978; Sacks 1974), among others, and the relative usefulness of some of these constructs is considered in the second chapter.

I next consider the exchange and consumption of hoes (chapter 3). Key questions include defining the evidence for the demand and use of Mill Creek chert hoes in terms of (1) their broad distribution, (2) their differential occurrence between sites, and (3) their actual use and disposal within individual communities. Fortunately, because of the efforts of other scholars, a substantial amount of research has already been carried out on these questions, particularly the first, and we know as much about the distribution of Mill Creek chert hoes as any other artifact type from the Mississippian period. We know much less about the actual mechanisms of exchange.

Chapter 4 sets forth an overview of approaches to the organization of lithic technology. The widely used framework of organization of technology is also used to structure my own methodology toward lithic analysis. Yet such studies often suffer from their lack of articulation between social theory and lithic analysis; thus chapter 4 serves as a critique of the traditional organization of technology framework, and it works toward a model more concerned with labor and the social construction of technology.

The quarrying of Mill Creek chert was done in a small corner of extreme southern Illinois. The geological and geographic context in which this unique resource was found is of special interest, not only for the obvious economic reasons, but also because this interior, hilly region provides a major contrast to the riverine settings that are usually considered "classic" Mississippian environs. Chapter 5 provides background on both the source area and adjoining regions that were home to important Mississippian period occupations.

In the following two chapters (6 and 7) I move on to analytical aspects of production and the economy of the Mill Creek study area. I first look at the regional structure of stone tool manufacture, comparing production at a number of workshops. In chapter 7, the analytical lens is focused on a single, extremely well-preserved village and workshop site known as Dillow's Ridge. The study of this community provides a more detailed look at the broad range of economic activities carried out in conjunction with hoe production. Finally, I conclude with an attempt to synthesize the presented knowledge in a way that is true to the themes of scale and local history (chapter 8). The Mill Creek case is promoted as a case study that contributes to our understanding of the general political economy of chiefdoms as well as the political economy of those chiefdoms occupying Mississippian North America. Even more, it represents an attempt to say something about living communities and the relations that bound them during a very volatile period of history in North America.

2 Specialization, Exchange, and Power in Small-Scale Societies and Chiefdoms

Archaeological studies of chiefdoms have now matured to the point that there is much less concern with whether one is dealing with a chiefdom and more interest in general issues such as: How did this polity come to be? How was it organized? or How does its political economy compare with those of other chiefdoms? Certainly, the issue of assessing characteristics of chiefdoms continues to be a matter of interest, but archaeologists broadly concur that there are certain overt material signatures that allow one to move on to matters more theoretical than taxonomic. Public and monumental architecture, elaborate burials, long-distance exchange, and production specialization are some of the correlates archaeologists typically rely upon to infer the presence of a chiefdom (e.g., Earle 1987a; Peebles and Kus 1977; Renfrew 1973).

A recent School of American Research (SAR) collection of essays (Earle 1991a) sums up very well the current thinking on chiefdoms, particularly with regard to those processual attributes that underlie the physical manifestations or correlates used by archaeologists. Earle's (1991b) useful overview presents valuable insights into the issues with which conference participants were grappling. Generally speaking, they agreed that a chiefdom is a polity that is centrally organized at a regional scale and encompasses a population in the thousands. A chiefdom also has a degree of heritable social ranking and economic strati-

This chapter revised and expanded from Cobb 1996.

fication. Kinship may be an important organizing principle, but in some instances it may serve to promote certain individuals or lineages rather than to constrain hierarchy. The typological issues in the SAR seminar dealt not so much with the definition of a chiefdom as with the nature of variability within chiefdoms. Scale of development, financing (staple versus wealth) of polities, and structure (group-oriented versus individualizing) were seen as three key axes of variability. One of the interesting divides among the participants was over the means by which chiefly elites maintained power: some argued for economic coercion, others for ideological mechanisms.

One may quibble over finer points in the summary of chiefdoms achieved by the SAR participants, having a disagreement with some aspect of their definition, perhaps, or asking whether there are other ways to view a chiefdom's structure. Nevertheless, the groundwork laid by the likes of Oberg (1955), Service (1962), Fried (1967), and others in thinking about the nature of "intermediate" societies has been developed sufficiently so that archaeologists can make sophisticated studies of the trajectories of individual chiefdoms, as well as insightful comparisons between chiefdoms (see, e.g., Drennan and Uribe 1987; Earle 1991a).

For all of these reasons, I shall not provide an exegesis of chiefdoms, tracing the history of the concept and providing my own model of how they came to be or changed over time. I have strong reservations with the typological implications of "chiefdom," but then, so do other people who continue to use the term (see Blitz 1993a; Earle 1987a). Nevertheless, it remains difficult to ignore the power of some of the general structuring principles that have led to the classifications and sub-classifications of chiefdoms. Therefore, although this study adopts a historical stance, I find myself in agreement with those who believe that it is possible to wed generalizations with historical contingency in our explanations of the past (Bender 1990; Trigger 1989); in this case, with reference to chiefdoms. My particular interest is a certain Mississippian period polity in North America (ca. A.D. 900–1400) that I believe has a number of unique characteristics, yet comparison with other chiefdoms provides some broad ways of thinking about the articulation of those characteristics.

I take as my point of departure an observation made by Kristian Kristiansen (1991:17): despite all of the work done on chiefdoms, insufficient attention has been paid to the organization of production— and, by extension, to a very fundamental component of the political economy. If we accept the thesis that the channeling of surplus production toward elite activities is fundamental to the development of chiefly hierarchies (Carniero 1981; Earle 1987a; Sahlins 1972), then variability in the organization of production represents a critical link in understanding diversity in chiefdoms. Building on this foundation, I wish to explore the issue of whether there is anything truly distinctive about the organization of production—with particular reference to specialization—and the political economy of chiefdoms in the same sense that capitalism, for example, exhibits distinctive features (e.g., commoditization of labor). The careful reader will have observed by the title of this chapter ("small-scale societies and chiefdoms") that I am already hedging my bet because the issue is difficult to resolve for the chiefdom taxon itself. Nevertheless, I believe our understanding of pre-capitalist political economies has advanced sufficiently to enable us to build some very general models describing processes of production and surplus flow for intermediate societies. Furthermore, a number of empirical studies on the Mississippian period in North America allow us to use these models to generate useful statements about Mississippian political economy.

To many archaeologists, the Mississippian period groups of southeastern North America represent classic archaeological examples of chiefly societies (Peebles and Kus 1977; Smith 1978b, 1986; Steponaitis 1986). Evidence for social hierarchy and some degree of centralization includes widespread monumental earthwork and plaza complexes, elaborate mortuary assemblages with fancy imported objects, and other signs of control over goods and labor. Rapid population growth and the emergence of a widespread system of sedentary hamlets, villages, and towns were closely tied to the emergence of maize as a dietary staple. The material evidence for social hierarchy is further buttressed by sixteenth-century accounts of the Southeast by Spanish explorers, who describe powerful chiefs living in settings that mirror the archaeological record (Clayton et al. 1993). In effect, the expeditions of Hernando de Soto, Tristan de Luna, and others stumbled upon groups who were still living a Mississippian lifeway.

Unfortunately, the primary accounts of the North American Southeast tell us little about the nature of the economy and how chiefs may—or may not—have controlled production, surplus labor, and material wealth. Later eighteenth-century accounts are more plentiful and detailed (e.g., Adair 1930; Bartram 1955; Lawson 1967), but the transformations that must have occurred during the two-century interval after contact urge caution in extrapolating from these later descriptions back to prehistoric Mississippian societies. Despite the sketchiness of the historic record, archaeologists have made great headway in recent years toward unraveling the variability in Mississippian political economies and production systems (e.g., Anderson 1994; Blitz 1993a; Muller 1987; Pauketat 1994; Steponaitis 1991). These studies have adopted a wide variety of theoretical perspectives, although one issue they hold in common is an interest in the nature of social differentiation within Mississippian societies, particularly with regard to the emergence (or lack thereof) of distinct socioeconomic groups with preferred access to wealth and power.

CLASS REDUX

A class analysis is a common entry point used by anthropological political economists to address the differential acquisition of wealth and power. Most studies invoking a class analysis are concerned with the rise of capitalism, in which the class process is framed in the context of wages and exploitation. For example, with capitalism, some would see the class process as unpaid surplus labor taken from producers (Resnick and Wolff 1987:115). Although this might serve as an adequate general definition, political economy studies frequently have foundered in attempting to bridge between general concepts and case studies. Resnick and Wolff (1987) voice the frustration that many scholars have experienced in attempting to resolve ambiguities in Marx's work, particularly with regard to his apparent cycling between essentialistic and historical applications of his key concepts such as class and capital. These authors point out that Marx advocated a class analysis in his theoretical works, but often resorted to a more static perspective in his case studies. For example, toward the end of *The Eighteenth Brumaire of Louis Bonaparte*, Marx (1990:124) comments that "in so far as millions of families live under economic conditions of existence that separate their mode of life, their interests and their culture from those of the other classes, and put them in hostile opposition to the latter, they form a class." Resnick and Wolff (1987) suggest that, from a methodological viewpoint, Marx found it difficult to avoid talking about class as both a thing and a process, and this is a problem that continues to plague studies by modern scholars as they move from the world of ideas to the actual application of these ideas to concrete settings.

One can clearly see this same dilemma in anthropological writings. Roseberry (1989:161ff.) refers to class *formation* at the same time that he discusses class as a process. In advocating an extension of the notion of class beyond the capitalist sphere, Terray (1972) calls for a class analysis that distinguishes primitive from capitalist economies. Entry to primitive classes is closed on the basis of age, sex, and similar divisions, whereas capitalist classes are open and constitute separately from preexisting political and economic conditions. Here Terray uses Marx's well-known distinction between classes in themselves (primitive) and classes for themselves (capitalist). One can see, however, that in defining these differences he begins to characterize classes as things— there is an uneasy balance struck between seeing class as a relation and class as a group.

Ultimately, most Marxism-influenced scholars would maintain that class is a process, although in empirical studies there might be an understandable tendency to conflate units of analysis with the process itself. E. P. Thompson's (1966) classic study of the English working class can fairly be said to summarize the views of many: "I do not see class as a 'structure', more even as a 'category', but as something which in fact happens (and can be shown to have happened) in human relationship. More than this, the notion of class entails the notion of historical relationship" (Thompson 1966:10). Nonetheless, his title *The Making of the British Working Class* betrays the common tendency to see class as a thing despite our protestations to the contrary.

But the resolution of the dichotomy of class as a thing versus class as a process is not so clear-cut as correcting a misplaced emphasis or doing away completely with the typological notions of class. In fact, it could be argued that class has three dimensions in its usage, and from a dialectical perspective it is problematical as to whether any single one should be considered solely appropriate for a study of the mobilization of surplus. Two of the dimensions consider class as a process; the third considers class as a thing.

Class as a *historical* process is epitomized by the views of E. P. Thompson in the preceding discussion. With this approach, we bring the greatest clarity to an understanding of the class process when we address the appropriation of surplus labor within finite spatial and temporal boundaries. In its most refined application, a class analysis might make important distinctions not only between steelworkers and capitalists, but also between twentieth-century North American and British steelworkers, or even between steelworkers in Pennsylvania and Illinois.

The use of class as a *general* process can be seen in the works of individuals who have worked within a mode of production framework. Defining modes of production and their articulation was one of the key thrusts of the Structural Marxism that saw its heyday in the 1960s and 1970s (e.g., Althusser and Balibar 1970; Hindess and Hirst 1975). Despite the general critiques of that paradigm, there are those (e.g., Roseberry 1989) who argue that it is still productive to use modes of production to refer to specific sets of class relations, a position also endorsed by a number of archaeologists (e.g., Bernbeck 1995; Muller 1997). Wolf's (1982) influential work, *Europe and the People Without History*, made distinctions between capitalist, tributary, and kinship

modes of production based largely on the relationships between producers and the means of production, as well as the ways in which surplus was extracted. In effect, a mode of production framework tends to
equate a class with a generic entity with the goal of making generalizations about class processes. While Wolf, Roseberry, and others go to
great lengths to emphasize that modes of production are best understood as historical constructs, their discussions and applications have
retained a generic sense of modes as well. This approach to a class analysis is not necessarily inconsistent with the historical one. It merely
recognizes that some aspects of class processes may cross-cut societies
(e.g., the commoditization of labor in capitalist societies), whereas
other aspects will be more restricted to specific historical settings (e.g.,
the fusion of Bolivian tin mining and indigenous ideology).

Although some might disagree with the viability of a "generic" class
analysis, both generic and historical approaches still tend to view class
as a process. Customarily, more troublesome to political economists
is the practice of viewing class as a thing, not least because of the
ahistorical implications of an essentialist stance. However, argument
can be made that issues of class formation and the coalescence (however temporary) of interest groups are intrinsic elements of interest to
the study of political economy.

One of the critiques of the Structural school in Marxism was that
class was often construed as epiphenomenal; in other words, class
emerged from the contradictions between structures and was not sufficiently viewed as a problem in its own right. Paradoxically, if carried
too far, if we view class merely as a process, then we threaten to make
real human groups and their lived experiences epiphenomenal. In this
case, we tread too closely toward focusing on interactions at the expense of the people who initiate and experience them. Moreover, we
ignore the reality that people do create categories for themselves and
for others. In other words, class is a process, but it can either take a
material form or be manifested as cultural categories. Further, cultural
categories and notions of identity direct experience, structure power
relations, and channel the flow of surplus labor (Wolf 1990). Consequently, human groups and the objects they create do not exist as separate entities from the relations they create.

Focusing on class primarily as a process hinders the completion of
the cycle of returning to thinking about real social groups rather than
abstractions. It is impossible to consider issues such as the emergence
of the American labor movement while ignoring the realities of daily
life for the black lung–ravaged coal miners of Pennsylvania, how they
viewed themselves as a group, and how others may have attempted to
impose categories on miners for their own self-interests. In the same

way, we cannot disregard the emergence of social groups with self-defined interests who existed among prehistoric communities. Admittedly, individuals can belong to more than one interest group or class, and groups themselves vary greatly in their membership, ideologies, and goals through time. But to deny that the definition and understanding of such groups are an important focus of our studies is to weaken immensely the historical dimension of our pursuit. This perspective does not deny the porous boundaries of classes or social groups, their constantly changing nature, or the different perceptions of the same class that may be held by other groups (or even by those within the same class). It does suggest, however, that classes may exist as historical moments, and their identification as both entities and the outcomes of processes is a fundamental component of any political economy project.

Moreover, to deny that class has—and should have—both essential and processual attributes is to practice a manichaean Marxism that is clearly at odds with the dialectic. The reproduction of classes and class relations is sustained not only by overt political and economic strategies implemented by opposing interest groups, but also by a social and concrete milieu that may involve shared housing styles, dress, physical behavior, speech, and myriad other culturally mediated traits that create a sense of identity. While classes and the class process are not static entities, there are thematic regularities that bind classes and their reproduction that should be visible to both the historian and the archaeologist.

We can take this a step further. A relational view of the dialectic would argue that there is a fundamental relationship not only between human groups and human actions, but also between things and relations. Ollman (1976), for example, maintains that in a theory of internal relations the conditions of existence are taken to be part of what something is: things not only sustain relations, things *are* relations. This has important ramifications for archaeologists, because it implies that material culture serves as a vehicle for the active reproduction of class relations, and that our studies have the potential to identify both classes and the class process. Of course, the view that material culture is an active agent in social reproduction has frequently been touted by those adopting poststructural perspectives, as well (Hodder 1987; Shanks and Tilley 1987). Whether objects actually embody relations or are perceived as relations by people is an interesting phenomenological question, but either instance would not necessarily change the actions or views of agents with regard to material culture.

Taken in sum, a class analysis must not focus on relations only. It must also consider defining the interest groups who both initiate and are defined by those relations. Ultimately, a class analysis must consider those things and processes (physical capital, alienated labor, inalienable goods, etc.) that constitute the currency of and for surplus labor. Such an approach recognizes that social groupings are more than just a sum of their parts—that they are constituted by people and their relations—and are not easily reduced to discrete elements.

If one's premise is that a class analysis also incorporates a notion of class as a group, can one conclude that classes and the class process preceded the capitalist era? Marx's work and that carried out by subsequent political economists on the rise of capitalism have never relied upon the assumption that classes are unique to capitalism in the same way that capital and commodified labor are. Instead, the argument has been that capital and wage labor lead to a distinctive form of surplus extraction that defines *capitalist* classes. There seems to be a general consensus that class does have some relevance, in the absence of capitalism, under conditions of economic and political stratification, wherein elites represent coercive surplus takers. There are numerous examples of this process in history, ranging from the tributary empires of Eastern Asia or the Mediterranean world, to the paramount chiefs of Hawaii. Marx and Engels recognized classes in the feudal and other modes of production that preceded capitalism (e.g., Marx and Engels 1970). One challenge for political-economic studies rooted in periods preceding the rise of the modern world system is to define simultaneously the class processes structuring surplus flows and the coalescence of interest groups around different forms of surplus labor.

Nevertheless, when considering chiefdoms or kin-based societies, the issue of class becomes much more controversial. While I will not review in great detail the discussion, suffice it to say that the issue of classes in non-capitalist societies was heavily debated among the French Structural Marxists in the 1960s and 1970s with no real resolution. Much of the debate centered on the idea that, in order for class divisions to exist, exploitation must be present—exploitation being defined as the appropriation of surplus in order to reproduce the conditions of the appropriation or extortion of surplus labor (Kahn 1981:71). The issue is still a matter of concern among anthropologists. Many maintain that the idea that all societies participate in a class struggle serves to deny the large qualitative differences between interest groups in intermediate societies and state formations (Lee 1990; Trigger 1990; Tuden 1979). A key principle underlying this viewpoint is a reluctance to see the presence of classes when social control is still closely tied to the kinship structure (Kristiansen 1991:21; Muller 1997).

In this light, can the framework of kinship be considered exploitative? Some would think so. Meillassoux (1972), for instance, argued that cohorts of older males could act as classes in some African societies through their control of social reproduction, which allowed them to exploit younger males. In contrast, Godelier (1972) viewed the appropriation of surplus labor through the kin network as more functional than exploitative. Similarly, Hindess and Hirst (1975) have maintained that exploitation and appropriation do not represent the same processes. More recently, anthropologists have explored the idea that in kin-based economies, elders or lineages may exploit others through ideology and ritual rather than through overt coercion or economic control (e.g., Keesing 1987:166; McGuire and Saitta 1996). Nevertheless, it can be argued that, if labor mobilized through ritual serves to reproduce a position of privilege, it still represents a form of subtle surplus appropriation if not outright economic exploitation.

In short, ethnographers, archaeologists, and ethnohistorians have amply demonstrated that significant social and economic differences may occur between interest groups in non-capitalist societies. Whether one wishes to refer to these differences as class-based is not without importance, but more important still is the idea that the differences can be understood by analyzing how surplus labor is organized and manipulated, and what types of interest groups coalesce around this process. Very different forms of surplus-labor appropriation exist in different societies, and one of our tasks as anthropologists is to explore that variability and how it is historically situated. The term *class* is laden with so much baggage that one's skepticism is probably justified when the concept is used in reference to small-scale political economies. On the other hand, bland terms such as *interest group* do not carry the immediate appeal to issues of labor and surplus that are intrinsic to class. Alternatively, some archaeologists have argued that, no matter how we refer to economic interest groups, it is still possible to use a class analysis for groups traditionally described as chiefdoms and small-scale societies (Cobb 1993; McGuire 1992; Paynter 1989; Saitta 1994; Saitta and Keene 1990). Quite simply, a class analysis refers to the study of the mobilization of surplus labor regardless of time or place. That said, the question then arises, What is distinctive about surplus appropriation in non-capitalist economies?

Using an approach toward class analysis developed by Resnick and Wolff (1987), Saitta (1994) maintains surplus flow in small-scale societies may be mobilized by "subsumed classes," that is, individuals or interest groups who accumulate power by controlling the distribution of goods rather than their production. In his conception of the communal political economy (see also McGuire and Saitta 1996), producers may communally appropriate their own labor in a process that may benefit the welfare of the group; thus, the movement of surplus from producers to elites is not always an exploitative enterprise. Consequently, the identification in the archaeological record of a linkage between distribution and elites does not have to imply sharply uneven power relations, nor should we focus solely on the actions of elites and forego notions of agency and resistance involving non-elites. As I argue in the following section, there is considerable evidence to suggest that subsumed classes are a distinguishing feature of political-economic control in most small-scale societies, in which a number of mechanisms serve to inhibit privileged access to the means of production. However, there do seem to be instances in which privileged access to distribution may involve exploitation and overt struggles over surplus production.

PRODUCTION, DISTRIBUTION, AND SURPLUS APPROPRIATION

One of the great tensions in chiefly societies centers on the desire by leaders to accumulate material wealth to enhance the economic basis of inequality, on the one hand, and two kinds of constraints on these demands, on the other. First, there is a recurring pattern whereby producers tend to own the means of production, and aspiring leaders often must mobilize surplus through charisma and wiles, rather than extortion. Second, a lineage system may bind leaders through kinship to potential provisioners of surplus, and familiarity may breed both contempt and the ability to resist demands on labor. These social and economic dimensions of pre-capitalist societies have led many anthropologists to argue that one of the key transformations toward more complex political economies involves the ability of leaders to usurp traditional constraints on the alienation between producers and the means of production (e.g., Earle 1987a; Fried 1967; Haas 1982; Wolf 1982).

Some have promoted the idea that "complex" chiefdoms may represent this transition, whereby leaders have gained the right to amass wealth through tribute and extortion even in cases in which they may still not have gained direct control over the means of production. Earle (1987b), for example, describes the "moveable feasts" of Hawaii, where chiefs traveled around the islands and were feted by subjects in grand displays of surplus consumption. Even in less complex economies, however, some individuals may have the ability to accumulate wealth and power, even in the absence of direct control over the means of production or a right to exact tribute (Feinman and Neitzel 1984; Sahlins 1963).

One useful way to think about the political and economic differences between various forms of societies is to use the mode of production distinctions that Wolf (1982) has drawn (Figure 2.1). In addition

Modes of Production	Means of Surplus Extraction
Capitalism	ECONOMIC • Wage labor • Producers are alienated from the means of production
Tributary State	POLITICAL • Surplus is exacted by political-military means • Some producers may be alienated from the means of production
Kin (includes Chiefdoms)	KINSHIP • Surplus is mobilized through kin obligations • Producers typically own the means of production

Figure 2.1. Wolf's (1982) modes of production in relation to means of surplus extraction.

to the capitalist mode, he defines a tributary and a kin-based mode of production. He makes these distinctions by using mode of production as a way of viewing strategic relations, to wit, the way human beings transform nature through their labor and the entire web of social relations involved in that process. In the tributary mode, producers typically maintain access to the means of production and subsistence, and ruling groups rely on the political process to extract labor. In the kin mode, it is kin ties that allocate labor to the transformation of land.

Wolf (1982) places chiefdoms within the kin mode of production, with the caveat that there is great diversity in the way that kin relations can structure production and exchange. He sees kinship as having multiple social roles in chiefdoms, but a central one is the rationalization of surplus extraction; in other words, lineages in some chiefdoms are appropriators of surplus, and kinship can act as both infrastructure and superstructure (see also Kahn 1981; Paynter 1989:377). Taken at face value, this perspective would suggest that the production of surplus through the reproduction of kin relations, despite the myriad forms in which kinship may structure this process, is the distinctive political-economic feature of non-capitalist societies. Asad (1987) has criticized Wolf (1982) in part because he believes kinship ties existed before the development of the political and economic functions to which Wolf attributes kinship—although making an argument over the historical precedence of conditions belonging to an era that probably predates *Homo sapiens* is problematical.

Wolf (1982:89) himself cautions about focusing too narrowly on kin relations when he observes that, in some cases, residence may be a more important structuring principle for group organization than kinship. Nevertheless, the general relationships between kinship and the political economy posited by Wolf have had great staying power because the processes categorized into his different modes have been so widely documented by others (see Kahn 1981).

Asad (1987) has taken the stance, which I find somewhat pessimistic, that there is nothing that unifies non-capitalist societies, and thus there is no basic key to understanding them. He is probably correct in asserting that one cannot make deductions about the structure and development of particular economies on the basis of the notion that kinship is the basic means of organizing labor (Asad 1987:602). However, if there is one recurrent theme in the political economy of small-scale groups, it is that *distribution* and *exchange* assume a prominent role in social control and the manipulation of labor (see Bender 1985; Dalton 1977; Hindess and Hirst 1975; Sahlins 1972; Tuden 1979). Where producers own the means of production and political mechanisms for ensuring a continuity in the appropriation of surplus goods and labor are absent, individuals and interest groups build economic and political ties through the strategic accumulation and bestowal of goods on the basis of exchange and alliance networks.

One could see this as a distinction between moveable wealth and immovable wealth (Dumont 1977). Certainly, exchange is an important dimension of economic inequality in state formations, but there is more of a premium on controlling fixed resources and sources of production than exists in "primitive" economies. In an advanced expression of this pattern, we see the development of private property, which Engels (1972) found critical to the emergence of capitalism. In contrast, because access to the means of production and immovable wealth is much less restricted in small-scale societies, interest groups frequently turn to moveable wealth as a form of power. Furthermore, commodities associated with the alienation of producers from the means of production become alienable possessions; inalienable possessions, on the other hand, often retain an "exclusive and cumulative identity with a series of owners through time" (Weiner 1992:33). Such items can be used to control others who are eager to gain their possession, leading to a pattern whereby some individuals use exchange for underwriting relations of inequality instead of altruistically sharing their dividends at large. Even for those societies in which sharing may be a mandated feature of leadership, distribution still may be used to forge delayed debt obligations (Sahlins 1963; Trigger 1990).

Many archaeologists have been influenced by the idea of a prestige-goods economy that shares some similarities with the trade of inalienable goods described by Weiner (1992; see also Brown et al. 1990; Cobb 1989; Frankenstein and Rowlands 1978; Welch 1991). In a prestige-goods economy, elites manipulate exchange not merely to gain status-related objects, but also to mobilize labor when they are unable to control the means of production. Through prestations, loans, feasting, and other mechanisms, elites distribute food and valued possessions in order to gain the allegiance of others, who may repay through labor, goods, or other means.

Prestige goods as most commonly interpreted seem to represent a wider category than do inalienable goods. Weiner (1992) defines inalienable possessions as having a well-defined association with specified individuals and histories. Prestige goods may be imbued with distinction not merely by their association with individuals, but also by the kinds of relationships that they facilitate; also, there is often a strong association between types of prestige goods and specific ceremonies or rituals. Some objects may be used for bride-wealth, others for puberty rites, while yet others may serve as badges of office. As suggested by these diverse activities, the ownership of prestige goods does not have to be restricted to elites; these goods in fact may be important for daily rituals or rites of passage among the populace.

The notion of prestige-goods economies has been criticized on several fronts. One concern is that prestige-goods models pay too little attention to the role of ideology and how material culture may be meaningfully constituted (Hodder 1991:63). Saitta (1994) maintains that such models do not sufficiently distinguish between exploitative and nonexploitative ways in which surplus may be mobilized, whereas Pauketat (1994) believes prestige-goods models overemphasize the movement of nonlocal goods at the expense of defining control of the distribution of locally important goods. These critiques do not undermine the importance of exchange as a central means for mobilizing labor in chiefdoms and small-scale societies. What they do reveal is that researchers have not fully addressed (1) variation in exchange as a function of both scale and social relations and (2) the ideological and symbolic dimensions of exchange that explain *why* it may occur.

EXCHANGE AND DISTANCE

Archaeologists have adopted a wide range of opinions about the types of wealth that may be important to exchange and social inequality. Earle (1987b) believes that "staple finance" (control of basic products such as foodstuffs) was the most common foundation for complex societies, but notes that the movement of bulk goods often posed major logistical problems. Thus, spatially "compact" complex polities were more suited to this form of economic leverage. "Wealth finance," on the other hand, had the advantage of relying on the exchange of portable valuables as a means of economic power, and the high value to weight ratio of valued goods permitted their movement across great distances (see also Schneider 1977).

For small-scale political economies, there is a real question as to whether sufficient demand for basic products, such as foodstuffs, existed to provide the basis for a system of social inequality based on staple finance, even if the polities were socially or politically compact (Muller 1987). Although periodic shortfalls in foodstuffs likely occurred, the high degree of self-sufficiency typical of small-scale, agrarian communities makes a dependence on staples controlled by elites unlikely. That is not to say that food items may not have been regularly exchanged to provide items that were valued for their taste, ritual purposes, and so on. Malinowski (1961), for example, notes that foods typically accompanied the well-known Kula valuables on their trade cycle.

With the increasing importance of food production and stored surplus in more complex polities, control over staple goods assumes a much greater importance to the political economy. Further, the immovable nature of staple-goods production may offer greater opportunities for localized control that often may not be possible with nonlocal valuables. At the same time, attempts to control local means of production are much more likely to engender social tensions than control over the exchange of valuables, because local access to and use of the corresponding means of production are defined by indigenous traditions and norms. Attempts to usurp social constraints on surplus labor represent one of the ongoing struggles between aspiring leaders and their kin and neighbors in small-scale societies (Sahlins 1963; Wolf 1982).

As a result, small-scale societies are more actively involved in the movement of portable prestige goods as a means of status building than they are in staple finance. Ironically, however, elites may have no say over the immediate procurement or production of prestige goods because they derive from locations outside of the immediate social realm. Indeed, the ultimate source of prestige goods may be shrouded in mystery, which adds to the allure and power of their possession— particularly since objects from distant places may demonstrate the power of their possessors to control esoteric knowledge and act as intermediaries with the forces of the universe (Helms 1988, 1993).

Elites are able to obtain such items mainly by virtue of strategic positions they hold in society, which allow them to participate differentially in external exchange networks.

At the same time, the ritual power or authority associated with such objects can be very fragile, precisely because there is no direct control over their production. Uncontrollable events abroad—warfare, social collapse, natural disasters—may dictate the abundance and frequency of arrival of valuables. Moreover, elites in intermediate societies often lack the means to act as cohesive peer groups for sustained periods to dominate external exchange networks to their own advantage. Primitive logistics and communication systems are major obstacles in this regard. In short, for a variety of reasons, the long-distance ties among elites that may form primitive world systems typically do not involve the exploitation of distant areas that typifies the modern world system (see Chase-Dunn and Hall 1991; Kristiansen 1987; Schneider 1977; Wallerstein 1978).

Yet, Earle's (1987b) vision of wealth finance is not predicated solely on valuables obtained from distant sources, and he uses the Inka as an example of a case in which elites controlled valuables within the reach or immediate control of a polity. It is possible that for more complex societies absolute distance and mystification are no guarantee of economic or ritual value for objects or raw materials; there must be a broader consensus on the meaning attached to valuables to transform them into effective media for social control through distribution and exchange (Pauketat 1994).

As will be seen for Mississippian polities, elites in different regions appear to have used varying strategies for influencing distribution and exchange. These strategies were structured by a number of factors, including degree of political centralization, relative access to nonlocal finished goods and raw materials, and ecological and geographic constraints.

SYMBOLS, IDEOLOGY, AND EXCHANGE

To argue that individuals or interest groups mobilize labor through exchange and distribution, merely because production is closed as an avenue of control, verges on being overly economistic if one does not take into account the relationships and symbolism embedded in trade goods. In other words, the political economy must be wedded to symbolic and ideological dimensions to fully appreciate social asymmetry and the unequal distribution of power (Ortner 1984; Roseberry 1989). This requirement becomes particularly salient when the whys and wherefores of the mobilization of surplus are considered. As Saitta

(1994) has argued, too many studies of surplus flow focus on what happens to surplus once it has been appropriated, and not enough attention is devoted to the strategies by which it is extracted.

Herein lies the real potential strength of research on inalienable goods and prestige economies. If the manipulation of labor is strongly tied to the strategic distribution of material goods, it is necessary to understand the role played by those goods in a society, and why they were so desired. It is only by considering symbolic behavior and meaning that we can bridge the difference between those who point out that inequality emerges with the differential access to strategic resources (Paynter 1989) and those who argue that wealth does not automatically lead to power, particularly in small-scale societies (Crumley 1987). This divide exists only if we view resources as strictly material. If knowledge is also viewed as a resource, then privileged access to ritual and ceremony also represents an important source of power (e.g., Bloch 1989; Godelier 1973; Keesing 1987). From this perspective, the political economy is intimately tied to conflicts over meaning and symbols (Marcus and Fischer 1986:85), and we can think in terms of symbolic as well as material capital (Bourdieu 1977).

We have numerous intriguing examples from the archaeological record of apparent attempts to control knowledge and belief systems, even among very small-scale groups. For instance, Barbara Bender (1989) observes that European cave art shows a trend through time of more restricted placement and, presumably, more restricted access. She argues that a movement toward art related to male hunting and initiation ceremonies reflects a process of social power rooted in female control over biological reproduction being subsumed by male control over social reproduction. Archaeologists have been turning with increasing frequency to such concepts as hegemony and ideology to deal with the type of power conflicts that are not rooted solely in materialist bases, such as seen in Bender's (1989) work (e.g., Miller and Tilley 1984; Parker Pearson 1984; Pauketat 1994; Paynter and McGuire 1991).

With good reason, a fundamental aspect of archaeological methodology involves the classification of artifacts, features, site types, and so on. Few would argue against the idea that interpretation and explanation benefit greatly from rigorous typologies. Yet, types that are too broadly defined, or defined for other purposes (e.g., chronology), can hinder an understanding of the social and symbolic roles that particular types of material culture may have played in the reproduction of unequal power relationships. All too often, for instance, one sees burial studies lumping different artifact classes on the basis of subjective assessments of relative value. In Eastern North America, copper artifacts may be grouped as high-prestige items alongside marine shell artifacts, whereas whole pots may occupy a position somewhere between mundane items, such as lithics, and higher-level prestige goods. However, cultures attach widely different meanings and values to different classes of goods, including objects made from the same raw materials. It is necessary for the archaeologist to examine the context and consumption of goods to achieve this kind of understanding and appreciate why demand existed in the first place. To fully grasp the entire political-economic cycle, we must know how objects were used and where they ended up, as well as how they were produced and exchanged.

SPECIALIZATION AND THE DIFFERENTIATION OF LABOR IN SMALL-SCALE GROUPS

Just as the recurrent core features of capitalism may be associated with an incredible diversity of cultural, social, and political practices, the manipulation of labor through distribution in non-capitalist societies may be manifested in a wide variety of cultural forms. Consequently, one must frame an understanding of the class process within the historical conditions under which it emerged and operated. Yet, despite my own examples of exchange and distribution as class processes, it must be emphasized that production cannot be disregarded or perceived as homogeneous in small-scale societies. I do not want to leave the impression that labor is undifferentiated in small-scale societies and determined by exchange. This notion tips the scale too far away from production (and leaves one open to the epithet of "circulationist"). Producers in small-scale societies are not all equal controllers of the means of production (Godelier 1973; Saitta 1994), and the role of production in inequality and power relations must be considered alongside exchange.

Archaeologists in particular have been concerned with variation in production as manifested in specialization (see Brumfiel and Earle 1987; Evans 1978; Muller 1984; Tosi 1984; Yerkes 1983). Specialization reflects the differentiation of labor, and it has long been held that the differentiation of labor is tied to political complexity (see Durkheim 1933; Engels 1972; Marx and Engels 1970). Many archaeologists continue to see a broad correlation between degree of specialization and complexity, although there is now a recognition that a wide variety of forms of specialization occurred in the past, and categorizing them is difficult (Brumfiel and Earle 1987; Clark 1995; Clark and Parry 1990; Costin 1991). Despite the variability evident in specialization, some archaeologists would still see full-time specialization outside of the realm of subsistence pursuits as being primarily a trait of state formations (e.g., Muller 1984). Yet, even in many small-scale societies, staple or prestige goods were produced by a restricted segment of the populace. The nature of elite influence or control over specialists among such groups is a critical issue in the political economy, given the traditional constraints on differential control over the means of production.

Given that different types and degrees of specialization may occur within any one society, it is dangerous to extrapolate from the social relations of production of one class of items to the overall political economy of a society. At the same time, different types of production cannot be seen as unrelated, even if they represent different types or degrees of specialization. For small-scale groups in particular, the demands of the domestic economy cannot be understood apart from the production-for-exchange economy. Indeed, it can be questioned how distinct the two are. Although it may be useful as a point of departure to examine the two economic spheres separately, ultimately they must be considered as part of the larger whole.

Just as important, one cannot analyze specialization without focusing on surplus labor (Cobb 1993). Because specialization is a form of production, it must be examined within the wider arena of social relations that constitute the labor process. To assess degrees of specialization or demarcate different types of specialization without using labor as a cornerstone of analysis is to objectify specialization. Specialization is a relational construct, and attempts to categorize this concept must be seen as a point of departure for penetrating its historical manifestation within a given context. Consequently, one must closely examine the underlying relations that structure production as it may be manifested by specialization. These deeper relations involve a complex articulation of production, distribution, exchange, and consumption at an economic level, as well as the mediation of these processes through social and symbolic realms.

From a methodological standpoint, specialization and labor cannot be fully comprehended by focusing primarily on indices of production as a technical activity. As a practical necessity, one must begin by looking at workshops, standardization, specialized tools, and the like in order to begin the process of understanding the differentiation of labor. To reach that understanding, though, one must also look at exchange and consumption. Furthermore, different types of production should be considered at the same time. How, for example, do the relations underlying production for exchange of a category of goods articulate with the relations of production of the domestic economy? Finally, one must hope to achieve some grasp of the social meaning attached to categories of goods produced by specialized labor.

MODELS OF MISSISSIPPIAN PRODUCTION, SPECIALIZATION, AND LABOR

Studies of Mississippian production and exchange have begun to flourish. Brown et al. (1990) have remarked that there was a curious lack of interest in Mississippian trade and economy until about 15 years ago or so, which is surprising, given the prominence those topics achieved during the rise of processual archaeology. This is not to say that archaeologists were unaware that Mississippian groups participated in long-distance exchange networks; it has long been recognized that marine shell, copper, and other valued materials were moved substantial distances across the landscape. Nevertheless, sophisticated source analyses, stylistic studies, and other systematic approaches to evaluating production and trade relationships have been relatively spotty until the past decade or so (e.g., Muller 1989; Phillips and Brown 1978; Walthall 1981). It is well documented that certain individuals often had special access to prestige goods (as reflected in mortuary assemblages), but we are still uncertain of the mechanisms of exchange and how the manufacture of these objects was structured.

In contrast, the ecological parameters of Mississippian adaptations and the subsistence economy have been widely studied (see Smith 1978a, 1978b, 1986; Steponaitis 1986). Broad-scale regional efforts (e.g., Bareis and Porter 1984; Blitz 1993a; Muller 1978; Steponaitis 1978) have led to a sophisticated appreciation of diversity in Mississippian settlement patterns. Furthermore, the settlement data have been complemented by numerous studies documenting a great range of variability in subsistence practices across the Southeast, revolving around a core of maize agriculture (see Fritz 1990).

These kinds of ecological knowledge are very important for establishing a baseline for subsistence production, and for relating this baseline to production and exchange in other realms of Mississippian life. There is little debate among researchers that all Mississippians, including chiefs, were probably engaged in subsistence production to some degree. Moreover, groups appear to have had the capability for subsistence autonomy, although periodic shortfalls appear to have been a continuing problem (Anderson et al. 1995). Consequently, subsistence production was presumably sufficiently intensive to guarantee surpluses for bad years as well as for social obligations.

Much of the recent research on Mississippian nonsubsistence production has been structured in terms of specialization. Notwithstanding my critiques of the use of this concept, these studies have gone a long way toward building a much broader perspective on the nature of

Mississippian production and its link with exchange networks. I will now turn to this work as a way of framing my research in the Mill Creek region of southern Illinois.

HOUSEHOLD AND COMMUNITY PRODUCTION

Along with food remains, the best evidence of production for use on Mississippian sites probably derives from lithic assemblages. Following a widespread pattern in late prehistoric North America, Mississippian societies relied heavily on an expedient tool technology (Koldehoff 1987; Parry and Kelly 1987; Teltser 1991). Expedient stone tools typically are flakes that have been removed through an informal core technology and are put directly to use with little or no modification. A formal biface technology is most frequently seen in the manufacture of small arrow points, and even those required a modicum of skill, and many researchers view them as expedient tools, as well.

Mississippian groups acquired their stone from both local and distant sources, depending on geological conditions. Although there is little question that the production of most domestic stone tools could have easily been accommodated within the daily round, some areas lacked good-quality raw materials. Thus, exchange networks were an important conduit of stone for sedentary Mississippian groups in many regions. American Bottom communities in southwestern Illinois, for instance, did have access to local low-quality cherts, but they also relied heavily on Burlington chert acquired from quarries in Missouri, about 40 kilometers to the southwest (Ives 1984; Kelly 1984).

There is strong evidence that much of Mississippian production for exchange was organized at the level of the community or household. In the Central Mississippi River Valley, one of the most widespread forms of nonsubsistence production involved shell beads. Hamlet and farmstead sites frequently yield bead blanks, partially manufactured beads, and chert microdrills used for perforating beads (Koldehoff 1990; Pauketat 1994; Prentice 1983). Shell-manufacturing debris at these sites is usually present in small amounts, suggesting that beads were produced in small to moderate numbers. Where species identification is possible, the shell can often be attributed to a marine origin, indicating that even rustic Mississippian groups were able to benefit from the larger Mississippian exchange sphere. Historical accounts document that shell beads were extremely popular among Southeastern groups for clothing and display, and it is likely that bead production in small Mississippian communities was oriented toward both personal use and small-scale exchange with neighbors (Prentice 1983, 1985; Thomas 1997).

A range of other goods appears to have been produced at the household level, as well. In the Black Bottom region of southeastern Illinois, Muller (1987) has found evidence for the working of fluorite and cannel coal ornaments throughout the smaller sites in the settlement hierarchy. Downriver at the mound site of Wickliffe, Drooker's (1992) innovative reconstruction of textile manufacture from fabric-impressed ceramics has found that the skill and effort devoted to weaving could have easily fit into the round of everyday activities. Furthermore, despite my characterization of lithic manufacturing as production for use, it is likely that some small-scale production of stone tools for local exchange also occurred. Mortuary studies have inferred flintknapping specialists who likely were involved in this process (Cobb and Pope 1998; Seeman 1984).

None of the examples provided above—and many more could easily be cited—necessarily make surprising statements about the organization of production in Mississippian societies. Most production in small-scale societies and chiefdoms is conducted at the household or community level. Although there is great similarity in the activities conducted within Mississippian households and farmsteads (Blitz 1993a:104; Muller 1986:204), that is not to say all groups embedded identical activities within the domestic economy. A recent systematic comparison of Mississippian domestic assemblages at three small sites in Illinois indicates that there is important variation in tool assemblages and subsistence remains, which may reflect important differences in the way in which household labor was organized (Thomas 1997). As Bruce Smith (1995:245) has noted:

> Rather than yielding any clearly and consistently identifiable pattern of household unit integration within Mississippian societies, excavation of a growing number of short-term homestead settlements has underscored both the variety of different frameworks of social cohesion that could have existed and the difficulties inherent in attempting to describe such social networks with any degree of specificity.

REGIONAL SPECIALIZATION

Muller (1984) has cautioned that the procurement and modification of spatially restricted resources may give the superficial appearance of production specialization, when the underlying relations of production were in fact structured no differently from those of other rural Mississippian communities. He refers to the phenomenon of people taking advantage of a nearby and localized resource as "regional specialization." His own case study involved the Great Salt Springs in southeastern Illinois, an impressive salt-extraction site characterized by brine reduction kilns, thick deposits of burned shell and clay, and huge quantities of salt-pan sherds. Taken as a conglomerate, the site looks like a large special-use facility for reducing and exporting salt in large amounts. Yet, Muller's study found that the site was composed of innumerable small episodes of salt reduction over a period of several centuries, reflecting a pattern that easily could have been the result of repeated short-term occupations (see also Muller 1997; Muller and Renken 1989). The Great Salt Springs looks like a good case for intensive specialization, but only because the regional restriction and exploitation of this resource make for an impressive archaeological site that belies the more unassuming relations of production that led to its creation.

Similar arguments could be made for many of the raw materials valued during the Mississippian period. Conch shell, highly prized for cups, gorgets, and beads, could have been acquired by small groups scanning Florida beaches at optimum times, such as after heavy storms. The well-known copper sources of the Great Lakes were exploited well back into Archaic times, although Mississippian groups appear to have relied heavily on Appalachian sources (Goad 1978). In either case, the metal was available in relatively pure surface deposits, thus eliminating the need for mining or smelting technology. Much of the galena found in the Central Mississippi River Valley can be traced to southeast Missouri sources, but there is no evidence of major production centers in that region (Walthall 1981).

Although there is little to suggest the monopolization of source areas by Mississippian elites or the development of sophisticated systems for raw material procurement, neither can one assume that the relations of production are the same for all cases of regional specialization (a point that Muller does not deny). As in the case of domestic production, we must consider variation in regional specialization, particularly as that variation relates to the diverse forms of social organization in which production may be embedded.

ATTACHED SPECIALISTS

A number of archaeologists have argued that some Mississippian producers appear to have been making goods under some form of tributary or patron-client relationship with elites, similar to the "attached specialists" defined by Earle (Brumfiel and Earle 1987; Earle 1981). Paul Welch's (1991) study of the economy of the Moundville chiefdom in Alabama found that most nonutilitarian and some utilitarian classes of goods were produced only at the paramount site of Moundville. In contrast, most utilitarian items were manufactured throughout the entire spectrum of the site-size hierarchy. The production of prestige goods at Moundville appears to have been restricted to certain areas of the site. Manufacturing debris from greenstone axehead production, for example, is largely found in one locale, while shell bead production appears to be mainly located in another tract. While Welch does see a centralization of some production reflected in these data, he doubts that the producers possessed skills beyond those of ordinary Mississippians. Nevertheless, the fact that the production of some items was restricted to the paramount site of Moundville itself within the Moundville polity suggests attempts by elites to control the fruits of production for some categories of goods.

Some of the best evidence we have for specialized work areas derives from the American Bottom region, although researchers have arrived at varying conclusions about what these areas may represent in terms of relations of production. Richard Yerkes (1983, 1989) was an early proponent of shell bead specialization in the American Bottom. As opposed to the widespread evidence for shell bead manufacture found in small sites elsewhere in the Central Mississippi Valley, Yerkes documents a trend toward the restriction of production to a few communities during the height of Cahokia, ca. A.D. 1050 to 1150, with a subsequent decentralization during Cahokia's decline. What this says about elite intervention in production is uncertain, but the evidence is certainly suggestive of some form of attached specialization.

Timothy Pauketat's (1994) work at Cahokia evokes Moundville in his descriptions of workshops and centralized production of valued items. A particularly important finding in his research is a pattern whereby valued raw materials were imported into the American Bottom, then manufactured into finished items with a symbolism that could be locally grasped. This stands in contrast to the idea that finished goods bearing panregional symbols of Mississippian cosmology were especially desired by elites. Pauketat argues that elite sponsorship of local specialists making objects (megalithic axeheads, fireclay figurines, copper-covered ornaments, and other items) that were comprehended and desired by a broad spectrum of the surrounding population would have been much more successful in harnessing the support of labor than would a policy of importing items finished outside of the American Bottom, because nonlocal objects may have been imbued with a more alien symbolic meaning.

ELITES AND POWER

The difficulty with many of the attempts to explain diversity in specialization is that variability is construed in terms of such factors as technology or time devoted to an activity. While useful for some purposes, such taxonomies do not necessarily address a political economy of specialization. In other words, how do historic cases of production

involve unequal power relations or dominance? As the data from Cahokia and Moundville, as well as other Mississippian centers, demonstrate, some individuals and factions were able to take special advantage of the opportunities afforded by long-distance exchange networks.
Much of the power of Moundville elites appears to have been tied to
their abilities to control the flow of prestige goods in and out of the
paramount center. Mound building and population seem to have declined at the site at the same time that control over long-distance exchange was faltering (Welch 1991). Cahokia elites also appear to have
taken advantage of nonlocal materials to enhance their own positions
of power, but they favored the importation of raw materials that could
be molded into items bearing localized symbols of power and authority.
Mississippian power relations thus may have involved the negotiation
of symbols and beliefs, as well as the appropriation of wealth. This
theme seems to be gaining a wider currency in Mississippian studies
(Knight 1986; Steponaitis 1991). Bruce Smith (1992) has interpreted
Cahokian "woodhenges" as vehicles for controlling the timing of ritual
events, and Thomas Emerson (1997) has viewed the American Bottom
settlement system as a landscape of Mississippian beliefs and ideologies that were closely linked to power and economic control.

In contrast to the class-based societies that Pauketat, Emerson,
and others would see for Cahokia and possibly other mound centers,
Jon Muller (1997) and others (e.g., Milner 1990) have recently reacted
strongly against models of highly centralized and powerful Mississippian polities. Muller's position is derived in part from his reading of
the ethnohistoric evidence for Southeastern Indians, in which accounts
typically indicate that chiefly elites were held in strong check by governing councils and social constraints on power. Further, surplus most
often was appropriated as subsistence goods through a form of socially
expected tribute, far short of institutionalized appropriation. Muller
also points out that historical accounts show that goods were frequently redistributed by leaders through feasting, an activity that appears to be supported in the archaeological record by heavy concentrations of food remains around mounds at certain sites (e.g., Belmont
1983; Michals 1981; Rudolph 1984; Welch and Scarry 1995). With regard to the archaeological record, Muller (1984, 1987, 1997) has long
contended that more simple models of social organization could, through
the course of several centuries, account for the impressive buildup of
earthworks and accumulations of fancy objects that we so often take
as evidence for entrenched authority.

Even where Mississippian chiefdoms may have achieved some degree of marked centralization, it is questionable whether elite interest
groups were able to sustain their power beyond a few generations. Mis-

sissippian polities were somewhat fragile entities, and their coalescence underwent periods of cycling rather than the gradual rise and fall
curve we often associate with the life span of political systems (Anderson 1994; Anderson et al. 1995). The cycling behavior was due to
myriad factors, including social constraints on the mobilization of surplus, intrapolity competition among elites, frequent warring between
chiefdoms, and climatic fluctuations impacting food supplies. Even
those archaeologists who argue for more complex models of Cahokian
development believe that this site maintained its peak only for a maximum period of 150 years or so (Emerson 1997; Pauketat 1994).

Debates over the mobilization of surplus also extend beyond the
confines of the mound centers. One of the major unresolved issues in
Mississippian studies is whether rural farmsteads contributed to the
support of elites (Smith 1995:245-46). If so, such a pattern would attest
to a much larger physical range of elite influence. The ethnohistoric
accounts leave little question that sixteenth-century chiefdoms could
encompass substantial areas; the boundaries of Coosa, one of the largest chiefdoms visited by the De Soto expedition, have been estimated
to extend as far as 300 kilometers on a north-south axis, although it
was considerably narrower east to west (Hudson et al. 1985:733). But
did such political expanses in fact represent integrated economic entities? The eponymous paramount town of Coosa apparently had the
ability to exact tribute from outlying towns, sometimes resorting to
force, but settlements on the margins of the polity often sought to escape control from the core (Hudson et al. 1985).

The large size of the Coosa territory may be open to debate, given
its reconstruction from the less than reliable recollections of sixteenth-
century Europeans, who spent relatively little time in the region. Even
if accurate, it is likely that Coosa's size was an exception for Mississippian chiefdoms. David Hally's (1993b) analysis of the distribution
of mound centers in northern Georgia suggests that chiefdoms in that
region were usually less than 40 kilometers across. The Apalachee
chiefdom in the Florida panhandle, for which we have fairly extensive
documentation, appears to have measured about 75 by 75 kilometers
at the time of European contact (Scarry 1996). Still, even for the "average" polity, it appears that centralized power was unstable and the
economic reach of elites uncertain.

In a spatial analysis of the Moundville polity in west-central Alabama, Vincas Steponaitis (1978) proposed that satellite centers seemed
to be distributed so as to distance themselves from the central center
of Moundville, presumably to lessen the onus of tribute demands from
paramount chiefs. Likewise, the wide dispersal of Mississippian hamlets and farmsteads may represent a compromise between ecological

adaptation and people "voting with their feet" to avoid demands on
their surplus production (Muller 1987). Yet a number of archaeologists
contend that some small sites were unable to escape these demands,
and demonstrate evidence for the processing of goods for other locations. In one such case, H. Edwin Jackson and Susan Scott (1995) argue
that the differential representation of mammalian faunal remains at
the small site of Yarborough and the downriver center at the Lubbub
Creek Archaeological Locality in the Tombigbee drainage indicate that
outlying areas were provisioning elites with preferred cuts of meat.
While their conclusions are intriguing, there are many issues in ta-
phonomy and sampling bias to overcome in order to determine whether
marked variation in faunal assemblages reflects tribute flow.

Many Mississippian centers appear to contain surprisingly low levels of domestic structures and debris. This has led to a widely held
model whereby "semivacant" centers served as both refuges for defense
and seasonal locations of ceremonial activities (e.g., Blitz 1993a; Clay
1976; Muller 1987). Populations from dispersed sites may have contributed to a central granary to promote the general welfare, but leaders also could withdraw differential proportions for their own use. Yet
to maintain their own status, these very same leaders often used the
surplus for feasting and similar activities that benefited the general
populace. This model also generally conforms to Saitta's (1994) earlier
arguments about Cahokia, in which he would see many leaders as
"subsumed" classes; that is, more involved in communal appropriation
of their own labor and the manipulation of power through the distribution of goods than in the appropriation of surplus goods and labor
from exploited "fundamental" classes.

Past research on Mississippian political economy and labor was
often framed in the context of vertical complexity; the mobilization of
surplus and tribute flow was envisioned as moving up the scale in a
settlement system, and in turn the structure or hierarchy of the settlement system (often combined with mortuary data) was used as a proxy
for reconstructing a structural or layer-cake model of power relations
(e.g., Peebles and Kus 1977; Steponaitis 1978). At the level of the site,
it was assumed that surplus flowed from outlying residential areas toward the mound areas and the elites who occupied them.

Yet it has to be asked whether we are posing the right questions
about surplus flow in the right ways. Can the argument be advanced
only in a manner that asks about degree of hierarchy or centralization,
or are there other ways of viewing the structure of power, labor, and
surplus? The ethnohistoric record clearly indicates that power was a
heterogeneous essence among Southeastern Indians. Many groups were
divided into red and white factions related to separate functions of war
and diplomacy on the one hand, and trade and civil activities on the

other (Hudson 1976:234–39). Leaders or chiefs for each faction assumed dominance as their spheres of activity came to the fore in daily life. A complex web of political and economic powers also existed between men and women (Swanton 1946:709–33). Cross-cutting these dimensions, there could still be hierarchical notions of status, as exemplified by the four strata of society associated with the Natchez. All of this variation demonstrates that the organization of Mississippian political economies was likely multifaceted.

This bring us back to the point that extreme caution must be urged in linking political and economic processes. Not only are relations of power heterogeneous and complex, but also there is not necessarily a predictable relationship between political and economic development. As Muller (1997:271) warns with an ethnohistoric example:

> On the eve of the American Revolution, Native American societies such as the Creek and Choctaw had arguably transformed themselves into secondary states capable of challenging some aspects of the local power of the intrusive colonial societies. What is lacking from the accounts are efforts of individual chiefs to exert personal control of resources of any kind, even with the examples set by the Europeans in front of them!

Granted, we are talking about an era marked by broad changes in Native American societies, but they were drawing upon long-standing indigenous institutions even as they underwent major transformations. One of those institutions involved strong checks on the centralization of control over production and labor. The question remains as to how we can formulate models for alternative forms of political economies that are not strictly hierarchical.

CONCLUSION

Research in the Mississippian Southeast has been greatly influenced by general models of chiefdom political economy, and in turn offers great potential for refining those models. Perhaps most important for this study, there is strong evidence for great diversity in the organization and relations of production among and within Mississippian communities. The concept of specialization, even if broken down into such types as attached or nonattached, does not seem to do justice to that diversity. Although we can question the power of Mississippian elites to structure production, we also do not seem to see complete productive autonomy at the level of the household. Household production of durable goods like shell beads and fluorite objects was probably intended for local exchanges as well as personal use, and this form of exchange presumably was critical for the maintenance of relations that governed the social reproduction of communities. As a result, small communities had to maintain external links to obtain the marine shell and other raw materials so important to the maintenance of local ties. It is this multiscalar web of relations that seems to account, in part, for the panregional phenomenon that we recognize as "Mississippian."

That web of relations also incorporated a dialectic of power that played out in different ways at various scales. For instance, elites may have needed nonlocal goods to cement their authority through prestige transactions, but were hindered by their weak control over the local production necessary to sustain external trade relations and institutionalize relations of inequality. Alternatively, producers near source areas may have recognized the opportunity for economic leverage offered by their proximity to desirable resources, but found that an unstable interregional exchange system hindered their ability to translate their potential wealth into power. These structural limitations on regional Mississippian political economies are what make it so difficult for me to envision a Mississippian world system, even if it is one with only general analogues to the modern world system. The interregional patterns of exploitation and inequality that are possible with even archaic states just did not exist during the Mississippian period—at least in terms of the material economy.

There are two key implications of this argument. First, whatever "glue" there was that bound the Mississippian world, it surely involved symbolic and ideational phenomena, perhaps more so than material goods strictly speaking. This idea is hardly original on my part. But what I will argue in later chapters is that the cycle between production and exchange that was manifested in widespread areal similarities in art, architecture, and basic goods also involved a process of reproduction of identity that included households as well as mound centers, and commoners as well as elites.

Second, we must remain open to the possibility that, from a bottom-up perspective, novel ways of structuring labor can be gleaned from the archaeological record—ways that are not explained by models that view power relations as stratigraphically ordered. Power relations may involve dimensions of heterarchy as well as hierarchy, and they may differ between the production, exchange, and consumption of the same category of goods. To begin the process of achieving an understanding of the multifaceted and dialectical dimensions of power and the political economy, it becomes necessary to move to historical cases and strive for an accommodation between the general and the specific, and between structure and agency.

3 Exchanging Chert, Consuming Chert

In the absence of earthworks, Mississippian sites are most readily identified by ceramics. Shell-tempered sherds in particular serve as an important diagnostic artifact for survey crews walking plowed fields searching for sites. Over a substantial portion of the lower Midwest and Midsouth, there is another useful way to identify Mississippian sites from surface assemblages, and that is the sheen of the mirror-like polish on Mill Creek chert hoe resharpening flakes. Indeed, Mill Creek chert is so common on late prehistoric sites in the midcontinent that hoe fragments and flakes are often some of our best diagnostic types, particularly because shell-tempered pottery is subject to rapid decomposition in the many locales characterized by acidic soils.

Mill Creek chert hoes are now recognized as one of the most widely traded objects in prehistoric times, and certainly one of the most numerous (Brown et al. 1990; Winters 1981). Through the years various models have been proposed to account for their distribution. In this chapter I present an overview of the range of tools made from Mill Creek chert and what we know (and do not know) about their distribution and mechanisms of exchange. I also consider the functions of the tools and the contexts in which they are found at sites that imported them. Function and context are particularly useful for clarifying consumption, a topic that often does not receive equal weight to production or exchange in models of political economy. Yet one cannot fully appreciate either the social or technological dimensions of production or exchange without some understanding of the agents and communities who were using imported goods. It is my contention that women were most likely the consumers of hoes, although elites (of both sexes) may have been responsible for disseminating hoes within a given locale. It is still unclear as to how the large bifaces were distributed throughout the larger Mississippian world.

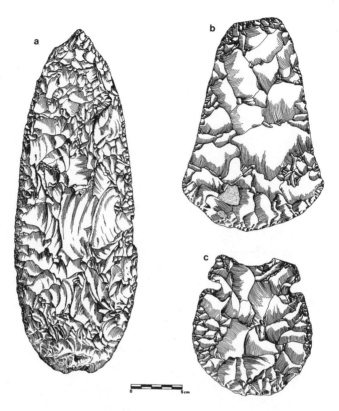

Figure 3.1. Hoe varieties: *a*, oval; *b*, flared; and *c*, notched. (Courtesy of the Illinois Transportation Archaeological Research Program, University of Illinois.)

MILL CREEK CHERT ARTIFACT TYPES

Mill Creek chert is most often associated with the manufacture of digging implements. Early researchers distinguished hoes (agricultural implements) from spades (excavating tools) on the basis of shape, although there were no clear criteria for this separation. Winters (1981:28) argues that the oval and flared-bit forms were probably hafted in the traditional hoe shape, but the side-notched forms lent themselves to being hafted as a spade. In either case, no use-wear studies have been carried out with the purpose of discriminating between hoes and spades. The term *hoe* is most frequently applied by contemporary archaeologists to all of the morphological types, with the understanding that they were probably multipurpose digging tools. Of the various hoe types that have been described in the literature (Fowke 1894; Holmes 1919; Rau 1864; Titterington 1938; Winters 1981), by far the most common are oval, notched, and flared (Figure 3.1). The hoes are bifacially made and

Figure 3.2. Birgir figurine. (Courtesy of the Illinois Transportation Archaeological Research Program, University of Illinois.)

are often quite large, up to 60 centimeters in length. On utilized specimens, the bit end typically displays a very high gloss from use.

In addition to their size and use-polish, there are other lines of evidence that support the functional interpretations for the large Mill
Creek chert tools. Early Euro-American accounts provide descriptions
of Native Americans in the Eastern Woodlands tilling fields with L-
shaped digging tools (e.g., DeForest 1964:5; Le Page du Pratz 1975:360).
A well-known statuette known as the Birgir figurine provides an even
more compelling line of support for the use of hoes during the Mississippian period (Emerson 1982:fig. 3-4; Prentice 1986). The figurine
depicts a kneeling woman holding a hafted hoe in her right hand (Figure 3.2), indicating that (at least some) Mississippian hoes were short-
handled and could be wielded in one hand. The woman also is associated with other striking motifs such as a snake with a feline head and
a gourd plant running up her back. I will return to the symbolic elements of the Birgir figurine later in the chapter.

While there is little question that Mill Creek chert hoes were important for agricultural practices, it should be kept in mind that Mississippian groups were involved in a variety of other earth-moving
practices for which digging tools would have been useful. The most
obvious is the erection of the mounds and embankments that are found
throughout the Mississippian world. In addition to piling up earth,

Mississippian groups were regularly involved in a number of excavating tasks. Many sites are surrounded by moats. The construction of Mississippian houses often entailed digging a shallow basin for the main part of the structure and excavating trenches for the placement of wall support posts. In short, Mill Creek hoes presented useful tools that potentially served a number of traditional tasks in the Mississippian lifeway.

Although digging implements constitute the bulk of the recovered Mill Creek chert tools, a number of other utilitarian and ceremonial types were produced from this raw material as well. They include chisels, adzes, picks, and small, triangular projectile points. Little has been done in the way of functional use-wear analyses on these tool types, and their prehistoric use is assumed in large part by the similarity of their shape to modern counterparts. The working ends of the smaller utilitarian tools exhibit abrasions and macroscopic polishes that presumably are associated with woodworking and other domestic activities.

Certain Mill Creek chert biface types are considered ceremonial or display items because they exhibit a high degree of craftsmanship and often occur in burials (Figure 3.3). Spatulate celts are unusual in that they were frequently ground smooth after being flaked into the shape of a large axehead, with a long stem and a bit end that may be barbed, flared, or rounded (Pauketat 1983; Titterington 1938:6). Most of the ground chert maces in the American Bottom region are made from either Mill Creek or Kaolin chert (Pauketat 1983). Maces possibly represent ceremonial war clubs (Phillips and Brown 1978:plate 56). Like spatulate celts, maces may exhibit signs of flaking and grinding done to achieve their final shape, which is characterized by a flared bit and a handle-shaped poll. So-called swords in the Duck River style (Brehm 1981) are narrow and extremely well-crafted bifaces that may be up to 50 centimeters in length. It is unlikely that they were functional swords because they are relatively delicate and would have likely broken in combat. A somewhat more common type of finely made blade is the Ramey knife. These are lanceolate shaped and average about 20 to 25 centimeters in length. Ramey knifes frequently exhibit use-wear, indicating that in some instances they may have been a regular part of the domestic toolkit.

Why Mill Creek chert? Within the Mississippian Southeast there were literally hundreds of different lithic source areas. They encompass a great variety of cherts, quartzites, rhyolites, and other stones that are amenable to flintknapping. Some tools made from these raw materials were traded widely, but most were used regionally or locally. For those that did enter exchange networks, it is assumed that they were

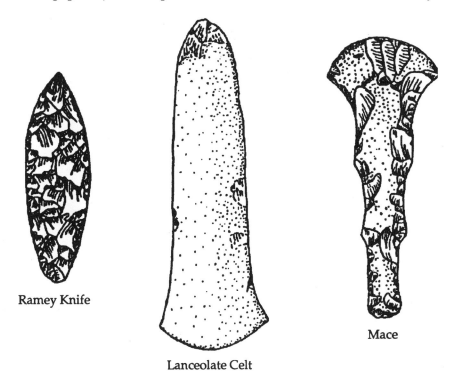

Ramey Knife

Lanceolate Celt

Mace

Figure 3.3. "Exotic" Mill Creek chert bifaces.

valued for natural properties such as their texture or color. Likewise, Mill Creek chert has special properties that made it uniquely suited over other available raw materials for the manufacture of large, durable tools.

Mill Creek chert is associated with the Ullin limestone formation, near the base of the Carboniferous Mississippian sequence (Devera et al. 1994). It occurs as nodules with a coarse and thick brown cortex. The texture is grainy and the stone displays a variety of colors, predominately brown, gray, and blue-gray. Mill Creek chert also is fossiliferous, giving it a speckled effect. Two qualities in particular were remarked upon by archaeologists who worked in the Mill Creek region early in the twentieth century (Holmes 1919; Hudelson 1938; Phillips 1900). First, the chert nodules can be very large, naturally lending themselves to the manufacture of sizable tools. Second, they occur in lenticular shapes that are natural preforms. After edge trimming and removal of the cortex from a Mill Creek chert nodule, one already has a well-advanced biface. Furthermore, as Dunnell et al. (1994) point out, Mill Creek chert has a "material toughness" not found with many

Figure 3.4. Scanning electron microscope view (100×) of
Mill Creek chert. (Courtesy of Robert M. Dunnell, Department of Anthropology, University of Washington, Seattle.)

other cherts. This quality makes Mill Creek chert particularly well
suited for heavy-duty tools such as hoes.

Finally, Mill Creek chert may have physical advantages that are apparent only at the microscopic level. Scanning electron microscope
analysis has demonstrated that the chert is riddled with the casts of
leached dolomite and/or calcite crystals (Figure 3.4); the voids likely
absorb energy and offset the propagation of fractures that would potentially break a hoe (Dunnell et al. 1994:82). In other words, major impacts are likely to shear off large fragments from—or even demolish—
implements made from "purer" cherts, whereas impact forces in Mill
Creek chert are deflected upward by the casts, resulting in the removal
of smaller flakes that leave the tool intact. This reasoning is hypotheti-

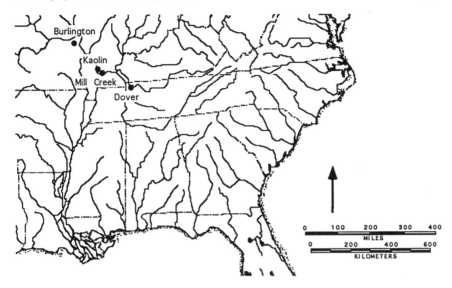

Figure 3.5. Major chert sources for Mississippian large biface production.

cal, but the edges of surviving hoes well demonstrate their ability to
weather heavy battering.

All of these properties combined made Mill Creek chert particularly
amenable to the production of large agricultural tools, but it was not
the only chert so used. Dover chert, native to western Tennessee (Figure 3.5), also was a popular chert for hoes and large, ceremonial bifaces
(Gramly 1992; Winters 1981). Not surprisingly, it has very similar
macroscopic and microscopic attributes to those of Mill Creek chert
(Dunnell et al. 1994). Despite the wide variety of stone useful for toolmaking in the Southeast, very few types fulfilled the same suite of attributes as did these two cherts: "This set of conditions taken jointly
eliminates most sources of raw material from consideration and served
to localize hoe manufacture to the Mill Creek and Dover localities"
(Dunnell et al. 1994:87). Nevertheless, a small percentage of hoes in
the Midwest and Midsouth are made from Kaolin chert, also found in
southwestern Illinois, and Burlington chert, from eastern Missouri
(Figure 3.5). Besides cherts, other raw materials were used for hoe
blades in some areas, including large shells and deer and bison scapu-
lae. What made Mill Creek chert hoes particularly distinctive is that
they were traded in far larger numbers and over a much greater area
than tools made from the other raw materials, including Dover chert
(Winters 1981).

It is apparent that digging implements of various raw materials,
shapes, and sizes were useful for a wide range of tasks carried out by

Mississippian groups. Those activities ranged from the mundane—the building of houses—to the grandiose—the construction of huge earthen monuments. It is debatable how much of a sustained demand for stone hoes or spades would have been fostered by many of these activities. Houses probably had a life span of at least five to 10 years, while larger earthworks were usually built in stages that may have been separated by decades or longer. Furthermore, most Mississippian sites are not even characterized by earthworks. The one important activity requiring earth-moving labor on a frequently recurring basis in the Mississippian world was agriculture. Before one can fully appreciate the consumption and exchange of stone hoes, then, it is first necessary to understand the role of agriculture in Mississippian societies. There is strong archaeological and historical evidence that Mississippian political life and ceremonial beliefs were intimately tied to the cultivation of a number of New World cultigens, especially maize. At the same time, the intensification of farming practices associated with a growing dependence on domesticates paved the way for a strong demand for agricultural implements.

MISSISSIPPIAN AGRICULTURAL SYSTEMS

To dispense with definitional issues first, I should point out that I am using *agricultural* in a loose sense with reference to Mississippian societies. For good reason, researchers tend to distinguish between horticulture and agriculture. Horticulture usually implies a simple form of cultivation that relies on hand tools, whereas agriculture denotes a field system that is based on a more labor-intensive technology, ranging from the recurrent field clearing associated with swiddening, to the use of draft animals or the construction of canals. In many respects, the form of cultivation practiced by Mississippian groups has elements of both horticulture and agriculture, so I will refer to their farming practices as agricultural for ease of reference.

One of the common sights recorded by the De Soto chroniclers throughout their Southeastern expedition was impressive fields of maize, beans, and other crops, so it is clear that by the sixteenth century Native American groups were strongly dependent on cultigens. The large maize surpluses were particularly critical for provisioning the De Soto expedition, which in its four-year journey was reliant upon the stores provided by the various chiefdoms it encountered. Yet the technology involved in tending fields by all accounts was relatively simple, mainly involving digging sticks or hoes in combination with substantial physical labor.

Although dates for domesticated plants in the East go as far back as ca. 5,000 to 3,000 B.P. with cucurbits (Fritz 1990), it is not until the Middle Woodland period (200 B.C.–A.D. 400) that we see strong evidence for a considerable use of cultigens, and even that is restricted to a few locations such as the Illinois Valley in central Illinois (Asch and Asch 1985). The important domesticates during the Woodland era are native to North America and include sunflower (*Helianthus annuus*), goosefoot (*Chenopodium berlandieri*), and little barley (*Hordeum pusillum*), and several plants that were cultigens and possible domesticates, such as maygrass (*Phalaris caroliniana*), knotweed (*Polygonum erectum*), and sumpweed (*Iva annua*). These plants were valued for their seeds, which are rich in starch (goosefoot, knotweed, little barley, maygrass) and oil (sumpweed, sunflower). The starchy-seed complex in particular seems to have been favored by Woodland groups, who possibly used them to make broths or porridges (Braun 1983).

The earliest dates for maize in the Eastern Woodlands go back to a few Middle Woodland contexts, ca. A.D. 400 (Chapman and Crites 1987; Riley et al. 1994). Its rare occurrence at that time suggests that it was a very minor supplement to a wide-spectrum diet. The importance of maize across the Southeast appears to have grown slowly during the Late Woodland period, then greatly accelerated during the Emergent Mississippian period to the point that it had become a staple during the Mississippian period. This transition is well documented in the American Bottom, where the amounts of maize found at Late Woodland sites indicate that it was probably a protected garden plant, but by the Emergent Mississippian period had assumed the importance of a key storable good (Kelly et al. 1984:154).

Despite the importance of maize to Mississippian groups, it cannot be emphasized enough that they made use of a wide variety of cultivated and wild resources. The indigenous North American cultigens continued to be used, although their importance diminished after the Woodland era; beans became important sometime after A.D. 1000 (Fritz 1990), and nuts, berries, fruits, and seeds contributed greatly to the diet. Faunal resources were also very important, particularly white-tailed deer, a number of small mammals, fish, and birds. Indeed, the broad Mississippian subsistence base is contrasted from the preceding Woodland diet not so much by the addition or deletion of resources, but the growing reliance on a few cultigens, with maize being the centerpiece. Nevertheless, the growing dominance of maize coupled with increasing population levels led to a field agriculture that by the time of the Spanish entrada probably looked very different—and had different social and technological requirements—from the small plots that are presumed to have been maintained by Woodland horticulturists.

Without question, there was considerable regional variability in Mississippian cultivation practices as well as differential reliance on the main cultigens. The recovery of hoes from rockshelters in Illinois points to the maintenance of small garden plots in hilly regions (Winters 1981), while larger groups in the uplands likely practiced a slash-and-burn agriculture (Lopinot and Woods 1993; Oetelaar 1993; Winters 1981). Those settings contrast greatly with expansive floodplains, where it may have been feasible to open up sizable plots of arable land to continuous cultivation for generations. There also is evidence that some bottomland regions may have had ridged fields, reflecting a labor-intensive effort to sculpt the landscape into tracts with long-term agricultural potential (Riley 1987).

Cahokia provides one of the more striking examples of the amount of land that may have been cleared for agriculture and to provide wood for fuel and construction. Using wood charcoal from a sample of domestic structures, Lopinot and Woods (1993) have documented that at its population peak during the Lohmann and Stirling phases (ca. A.D. 1000–1150), extensive use was made of imported tree species, mainly from the uplands to the east, with a subsequent return to a greater localization and generalization of tree use during Cahokia's decline. Lopinot and Woods estimate that during the Stirling phase timber resources may have been exhausted within a 10- to 15-kilometer radius of Cahokia.

It is within this context that the benefits of a hoe technology become apparent. The scale of clearing and cultivation during the Mississippian period reached unprecedented levels for prehistoric eastern North America. It would be stretching the case to say that Mississippian farming could not have been carried out without stone hoes, but they were apparently highly prized where available. In regions like the American Bottom, for example, there were tremendous increases in the amount of Mill Creek chert (often as polished flakes) through the Emergent Mississippian and Mississippian periods (Kelly et al. 1984; Milner et al. 1984). As Howard Winters (1981:25) observed, "Mill Creek hoes, and to a lesser extent hoes fashioned from Kaolin chert from Union County, Illinois, and from Dover chert from Stewart County, Tennessee, were apparently *de rigeur* [sic] for the properly equipped Mississippian farmer."

Because agricultural produce fuels the human body, it also has the potential to fuel the political economy. The control of food stores is an important dimension of power for elites aspiring to attract fealty and labor, a point made by Earle (1987b) with his notion of staple finance. Muller (1987, 1997) argues that Euro-American historic accounts show the obligations and opportunities provided by maize surpluses were a two-way avenue; families donated a portion of their harvest to a communal granary in the nominal control of leaders, but in turn leaders were obligated to make supplies available to the populace in times of hardship. This form of redistribution was accomplished through feasting, prestations, and other special occasions. It is uncertain how widely the model of generalized reciprocity can be applied to all Mississippian groups, particularly whether it can be extended back several centuries before the European Colonial period when many of the well-known Mississippian traditions were at their zenith (ca. A.D. 1200s). Some archaeologists argue that leaders did receive preferential types and/or amounts of plant and animal foods (e.g., Blitz 1993b; Jackson and Scott 1995; Welch and Scarry 1995), although they also emphasize that social obligations for distribution were likely complex and not easily subsumed under a simple notion of domination.

Even if there were periods during the heyday of major centers like Etowah or Moundville in which elites extracted and controlled a substantial percentage of the annual harvest, we still have no solid evidence to suggest that farmers lacked the means to provision themselves adequately (excepting chronic shortfalls caused by droughts and other climatic factors [Anderson et al. 1995]). In the final analysis, despite the uncertainty over the political power that may have been afforded through control of agricultural stores, the fact remains that maize and its cultivation were important themes in Mississippian life.

The centrality of farming to Mississippian groups was not restricted to subsistence and politics: it assumed a major role in ceremonial life as well. Historic Native American groups of the Southeast conducted a Green Corn or Busk ceremony, an annual fertility rite for maize. This was not merely an agricultural ceremony, but a larger arena for regenerating the sacred fire, promoting group solidarity, glorifying deeds in battle, and placating spirits (Howard 1968; Swanton 1928). In lieu of monopolizing agricultural surplus, scheduling of the agricultural cycle (and attendant events) may have provided elites with some measure of social control. The so-called woodhenges of Cahokia offer a possible example in this regard (Smith 1992; Wittry 1969). In the western portion of the site there is evidence for circular arrangements of red cedar posts that were rebuilt several times. The woodhenges range in diameter from 80 to 160 meters. Additional posts in the interior of the circle may have assisted in the tracking of annual sunrise cycles. Bruce Smith (1992) suggests that Cahokia elites may have used the woodhenges to schedule feasting and ceremonial days—particularly those associated with agriculture. In turn, those events were critical for controlling goods, services, and labor that promoted the position of elites.

The woodhenge hypothesis rests on the notion that the power of

Mississippian elites may have been rooted more in ideology and ceremony rather than outright coercion. Further support for this idea comes
from the Southeastern Ceremonial Complex (SECC). This medley of
iconography, ceremonial objects, and regalia was often rendered from
exotic materials (marine shell, copper). It also has a strong association
with burials that are attributed with elite status, although caution
must be used to avoid the circular reasoning of assuming SECC goods
are elite related because they show up in burials, while arguing that
the burials are elite because they have SECC objects (Muller 1997).
Nevertheless, if the meaning—and even definition—of the SECC is
open to debate, few question the ceremonial connotations of many of
the recurring motifs and symbols.

Howard (1968) traced historical motifs of the Busk ceremony to
many of the elements of the SECC and argued for a strong connection
between the two. The Birgir figurine from the BBB site in the American
Bottom provides the best example of a hoe within the larger symbolic
world of agriculture. There are many characteristics of the statuette,
particularly the symbols of life and death, that suggest that it is a
mythological female entity related to agricultural fertility (Emerson
1982; Prentice 1986): the serpent has a strong association with death
in the Southeast; the woman's facial expression, particularly the curled
lips and bared teeth, is one often associated with trophy heads and
death in Mississippian art; and the hoe and gourds have obvious links
to agriculture. Furthermore, the context of the figurine may have a link
with death. It was found ceremonially "killed" in the courtyard of a
site interpreted as a temple-mortuary complex (Emerson 1997:115–24;
Emerson and Jackson 1984).

On the basis of the links between the motifs on the Birgir figurine
and historical accounts of Native American beliefs, Prentice (1986)
suggests that the statuette is a representation of the Earth-Mother,
who is an embodiment of life and death and a cycle-of-life cosmology.
While few if any Mississippian archaeologists would deny the inextri-
cable links between agriculture and Mississippian belief systems, it
should nonetheless be emphasized that the Birgir figurine presents an
unusual co-occurrence of a stone hoe with the symbolic realm of fertility (a stylized hoe may also occur with the Schild figurine [Emerson
1997:206–7]). One does not find this tool as a regular feature of Mississippian art, and, except for the Birgir figurine, there is nothing to
suggest that hoes held any strong symbolic associations for Mississippian peoples. Digging implements seem to have been prized mainly for
their usefulness as agricultural tools. Yet, Mill Creek chert hoes were
so sought after in the Central Mississippi and Lower Ohio valleys that
it is rare to find a Mississippian site in those regions without the pres-

ence of these tools. Clearly, communities were quite proficient at providing farmers with the tools of their trade, even if hoes are not the type of object we normally associate with Mississippian long-distance exchange.

EXCHANGE

Most studies of Mississippian period exchange have focused on fancy objects that tend to be viewed as prestige goods. Aside from the eye-catching appeal of these fancy artifacts, this emphasis reflects the reality that many of the trade goods that have survived in the archaeological record are the sort of items that show up in burials, mounds, and other contexts that have been a focus of archaeological investigations. Marine shell was widely valued for the production of beads and shell gorgets, and was even used in its natural form (often with engravings) as a drinking cup (Brain and Phillips 1996; Muller 1987; Phillips and Brown 1978). Most of the marine shell appears to derive from Florida, where it presumably could be gathered from beaches. Copper was another highly desirable material that was manufactured into earspools, used to cover headdresses, rendered into embossed plates, and rolled into beads (Goodman et al. 1984). Much of the copper used by Native Americans was available in a fairly pure, raw form from the Great Lakes region and the Appalachians, with Mississippian groups making heavy use of the latter source (Goad 1978).

The demand for copper and shell has a lengthy history in North America and may be related in part to natural qualities of these materials, such as color. Red and white, for instance, were very important colors in Native American cosmology. Yet Mississippian exchange systems embraced a wide variety of other finished objects and raw materials too. At sites like Spiro and Moundville, nonlocal ceramics may have been imported from distances of several hundred kilometers (Brown 1983; Steponaitis 1983:49–50, 1986:391–92). Galena was traded from southeast Missouri to Spiro and Moundville, as well (Walthall 1981). Mica, fluorite, bauxite, and greenstone are but a few of the materials that can be added to the list of important trade goods. Yet most, if not all, of these materials and artifacts are assumed to have had some form of ceremonial or other special status. The one widely traded—and surviving—artifact type with a utilitarian function is the stone hoe.

Howard Winters's (1981; Brown et al. 1990) pioneering work on the distribution of chert hoes has provided archaeologists with one of the best-documented exchange goods in North America. His research took him to numerous museums and institutions throughout the Eastern United States where he recorded hoes by raw material type and provenience where possible. Although archaeologists working in the Central Mississippi Valley were already aware of the importance of Mill Creek chert hoes in that region, Winters's systematic collections survey revealed a truly surprising scope of exchange.

> In its broadest aspects, the distribution of Mill Creek hoes extended from the Aztalan area of southern Wisconsin on the north to the northern counties of Mississippi on the south, and from Blennerhassett Island in easternmost Ohio on the east to eastern Oklahoma on the west. Thus, the distribution sphere encompassed an area of some 200,000 square miles in the Midwest and South. The heaviest concentration of hoes is in the Illinois and Missouri counties that flank Cahokia and the American Bottom, but there are substantial quantities in western Kentucky and Tennessee, northeastern Arkansas, southeastern Illinois, and southwestern Indiana. (Winters 1981:29–30)

As more archaeologists learn to recognize Mill Creek chert, it is possible that these boundaries may be stretched even farther. Mill Creek chert has recently been reported from the Moundville area (Welch 1991), where it had not been documented at the time of Winters's study. Only a small number of flakes have been found at Moundville satellite sites (Welch 1991:174), but the fact that some of them display the distinctive use-polish suggests that the hoes retained their primary function even at locations distant from the source area.

The amount of Mill Creek chert moving across the landscape far surpassed by many orders of magnitude the quantities of ceremonial goods. Within the Central Mississippi and Lower Ohio valleys—the major consumer regions of stone hoes—hoes and hoe flakes are ubiquitous on Mississippian sites, ranging from the smallest hamlets to the largest mound centers. No matter one's station in life or location in the settlement system, access to Mill Creek stone hoes seems to have been a given for people living along those drainages and their hinterlands.

The logistical task of transporting hoes across the Southeastern landscape was facilitated in great part by an extensive system of rivers and trails. Many of the largest rivers in North America are found within the Southeast, and the topography of the region lends itself to travel by watercraft. Falls and rapids are common at higher elevations, but rivers such as the Mississippi, Ohio, Arkansas, Tennessee, and Cumberland would have afforded easy canoe travel for lengthy distances. Much to its chagrin, the De Soto expedition found that the Mississippian adaptation to waterways included very large war canoes and sophisticated battle tactics. There is little question that the aptitude for riverine travel witnessed among Native Americans of the sixteenth century reflects a long acquaintance with watercraft (likely on the order of millennia) and the capability to move significant amounts of goods over considerable reaches.

The major overland routes have been fairly well documented, demonstrating that the entire Southeast was linked by numerous trails (Myer 1928). Not surprisingly, many of the largest Mississippian complexes, such as the Nashville Basin in Tennessee and Moundville in Alabama, had numerous trails radiating out in all directions. Many small, interior settlements were also located along trails (Butler and Cobb 1996; Koldehoff 1996). Thus, even for those communities that would have been difficult to reach by water, overland travel still presented a means of interaction and communication with the larger Mississippian world.

Although the focus of this discussion is on hoes, it should be emphasized that it is unlikely they were being transported separately from other items. Once they were removed from the source area, presumably the hoes joined piles of other objects in canoes or bags that were being carried across the midcontinent. Many of the accompanying goods were likely the prestige items that have gained so much attention in the literature. As Malinowski pointed out for the Kula ring, it was the norm rather than the exception for goods with different values and meanings to travel together:

> The ceremonial exchange of the two articles [necklaces and bracelets] is the main, the fundamental aspect of the Kula. But associated with it, and done under its cover, we find a great number of secondary activities and features. Thus, side by side with the ritual exchange of arm-shells and necklaces, the natives carry on ordinary trade, bartering from one island to another a great number of utilities, often unprocurable in the district to which they are imported, and indispensable there. (Malinowski 1961:83)

We need not rely on analogy alone to support the idea of the multifaceted nature of exchange in southeastern North America. The sixteenth-century Spanish castaway, Cabeza de Vaca, spent a number of years as a trader among Native Americans in the Southeast and describes himself trafficking in sea snails, shells, hides, red ochre, and flint, among other items (Cabeza de Vaca 1993:65). One can only assume that he was entering into a long-established set of exchange relations along well-traveled routes.

Because Mill Creek chert hoes were so widely exchanged, the question naturally turns to how the exchange was managed, assuming it was not a completely haphazard affair. Given the great number of hoes recovered from the American Bottom, some archaeologists in the past raised the possibility that Cahokia itself controlled the Mill Creek chert quarries, or at least the trade of hoes (e.g., Morse 1975:65). Winters (1981:31) speculated on this possibility, but felt that insufficient research had been carried out in southwestern Illinois to rule out the idea that regional centers closer to the quarries played a strong role in the chert trade.

What these models hold in common is the notion that mound sites (and elites at these sites) were central to the movement of hoes as well as other goods during the Mississippian period. This idea can be attributed in part to the reality that mound sites quite simply contain more objects of foreign origin than do other site types—although Muller (1987, 1997) warns that this pattern may be a function of scale. In other words, large sites had more people and thus were more likely to contain more of everything, no matter how exchange was organized. But it has also been pointed out that mound sites usually occupy strategic locations on drainages that likely were major trade routes (Brown 1975; Fowler 1975).

Given the scale of Cahokia, this site has often been implicated as a major player in the movement of goods along the Mississippi River Valley, and even over large portions of eastern North America. The more extreme interpretations see Cahokia as a highly influential center within a Mississippian "world system" that was able to attract or extort substantial amounts of raw and finished durable goods and foodstuffs (Dincauze and Hasenstab 1989; Goodman et al. 1984; Peregrine 1992). A more moderate perspective concedes that the creation of the built environment at Cahokia was very impressive by any standard, but it did not require the control of extensive tributary relations; the resources and population within the American Bottom were more than sufficient to the task (Milner 1990; Muller 1987; Pauketat 1994).

A fall-off curve based on Winters's Mill Creek chert hoe distribution data indicates a relatively normal fall-off from the source areas, with the American Bottom representing a major aberrancy in terms of its high numbers (Figure 3.6). As Brown et al. (1990) emphasize, however, the hoes do not follow a normal fall-off south of Cahokia, even if one eliminates the source area data. They interpret this pattern to mean that Cahokians probably exerted a major influence on pulling hoes toward themselves—and possibly disseminating hoes north of the American Bottom—but that the source areas themselves were probably under the control of local centers.

Jon Muller's (1997:368-70) reanalysis of the same Mill Creek hoe data indicates that Cahokia's role in hoe exchange may be overstated

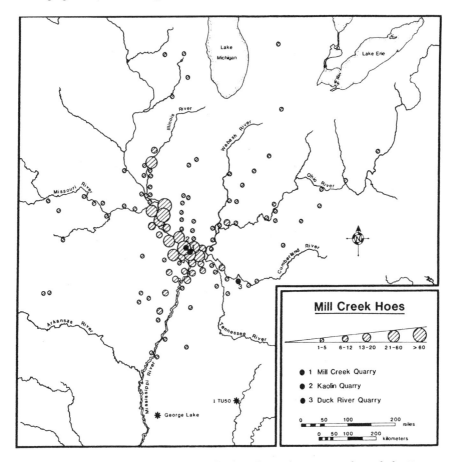

Figure 3.6. Distribution of Mill Creek chert hoes. (From "Trade and the Evolution of Exchange Relations at the Beginning of the Mississippian Period," by James A. Brown, et al. In *The Mississippian Emergence* edited by Bruce D. Smith; published by the Smithsonian Institution Press, Washington, D.C.; copyright © 1990. Used by permission of the publisher.)

(Figure 3.7). He maintains that the number of hoes from regions near the American Bottom fits into a fall-off curve that best approximates distance from the source areas in southwestern Illinois rather than distance from the American Bottom. The large quantities of hoes in and around Cahokia can thus be accounted for by proximity and population density; the region is only about 160 kilometers northwest of the quarries and contained one of the densest population concentrations in Mississippian times. Mill Creek chert is not necessarily more abundant by site or household in the American Bottom than in other regions, but the cumulative weight of a very high number of sites leads

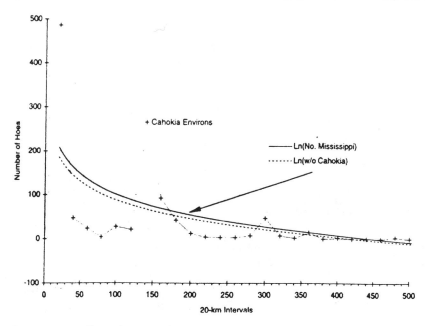

Figure 3.7. Muller's distance-decay model of hoe exchange. (From *Mississippian Political Economy,* by Jon Muller; published by Plenum Press, New York; copyright © 1997. Used by permission of the publisher.)

to a proportionately high number of hoes. In fact, those researchers who have closely examined Cahokia's external ties consistently remark on the fact that they are much stronger with northerly regions than with southern ones (Fowler and Hall 1978; Harn 1975; Kelly 1991a). Mill Creek chert hoes do point to one strong southern connection for the American Bottom, but that does not mean outright control over the quarries by Cahokia elites.

Another possibility that has been forwarded is that one of two mound sites—Ware and Linn—in the Mississippi River floodplain west of the Mill Creek area may have controlled either the quarries or hoe exchange (Fowler and Hall 1978; May 1984; Winters 1981). It is not possible to evaluate this possibility for Ware because of the paucity of data from the site. A restudy of surface collections from the Linn site does make this center a plausible player in the exchange of hoes (Cobb 1991). The collections are characterized by high amounts of Mill Creek chert artifacts, including early-stage reduction debitage and broken preforms. Without modern excavations at the site, however, it is not possible to assess the significance of these data. The Linn site clearly had concentrations of Mill Creek debris related to hoe manufacture, but without chronometric data we do not know whether its occupants were exporting hoes throughout the Mississippian period or for only a short interval, or were merely making hoes for internal consumption. No known quarries are near this mound center, and its relationship to the source areas is unknown.

A final possibility, and one that will be forwarded here and developed in later chapters, is that some form of localized control over chert procurement and hoe production was maintained throughout the Mississippian period. Earlier hypotheses for external control over the Mill Creek chert source areas seem to be grounded mainly in the idea that economic control radiated out of mound centers, and the larger the mound center the more economic power likely was wielded by elites. Following this reasoning, the impressive lithic production system seen in the Mill Creek region could have flourished only under the guidance of elites. The lack of major mound centers in the source region led researchers to look elsewhere for that kind of power. Yet there are no firm data to back that model. Barring evidence to the contrary, a scenario of political autonomy of the Mill Creek region remains the most plausible alternative.

CHRONOLOGY

Because of the scarcity of modern research in the Mill Creek region proper, the best evidence for the dating of the exchange network historically comes from consumer regions. Small hoes were often made from Mill Creek chert (as well as other raw materials) during the Middle Woodland period when starchy-seed horticulture became important in some regions. The small Woodland hoes are oval and about 10 to 15 centimeters in length. There has been no systematic study of their distribution, but they are mainly found in southern Illinois and some nearby regions such as the Illinois Valley in central Illinois. The scale of Woodland hoe exchange appears to have been minuscule compared with that in the Mississippian period.

There was a veritable explosion in the exchange of large Mill Creek chert hoes during the Emergent Mississippian period, corresponding with the intensification of maize agriculture. All of the regions adjoining southern Illinois began importing hoes in large numbers during this time, as reflected by a relatively sudden upsurge in Mill Creek chert debitage and hoe fragments. For example, Mill Creek chert flakes and hoes are first documented in the terminal Late Woodland phase (contemporaneous with Emergent Mississippian elsewhere) in western Kentucky (Sussenbach et al. 1986); in the Black Bottom region in southeastern Illinois the amount of Mill Creek chert represented in the debitage assemblages increases from 2.8 percent to 8.2 percent between the Late Woodland and Mississippian periods (Lafferty 1977:118); and the terminal Late Woodland Big Lake phase in the Malden Plain of southeast Missouri sees the first appearance of Mill Creek chert on a regular basis (Dunnell and Feathers 1991). In the American Bottom, where there is a rich amount of data on chert type frequencies, the amount of Mill Creek chert relative to other types increases greatly during the Emergent Mississippian period and makes an even greater leap with the advent of the Mississippian period (Kelly et al. 1984; Milner et al. 1984).

There are few chronometric dates for the Mill Creek chert ceremonial objects, although they are consistently recovered in Mississippian contexts. The Mill Creek chert sword found at the Hazel site in Arkansas was dated to ca. A.D. 1050 to 1150, while the burial with the mace from the Lilbourn site in southeast Missouri is believed to date to about A.D. 1100 (Morse and Morse 1983:247, 249). These two examples suggest that the exchange of chert ceremonial objects was taking place early in the Mississippian period.

Although the beginnings of the larger exchange system can be identified, the demise is more difficult to pinpoint. The heaviest consumers of hoes were those regions located in the "Vacant Quarter," a large area in the midcontinent with its epicenter at the Mississippi and Ohio rivers confluence, which seems to have witnessed large-scale abandonment in the A.D. 1400s (Williams 1990). While the scale and even reality of the abandonment is open to debate (Lewis 1990; O'Brien and Wood 1998:331–33; Wesler 1991), there is no question that Mississippian ceased to flourish in this region, and prehistoric sites dating to the late fifteenth and sixteenth centuries are very rare. The cessation of the hoe trade followed this decline. That Mill Creek chert artifacts are still recovered from sites dating to the final Mississippian Sand Prairie phase (ca. A.D. 1250–1400) in the American Bottom suggests that the exchange network was still operating until the end of recognizable Mississippian activities in the Central Mississippi Valley.

Within the Mississippian time span there is some variation in the introduction of hoe types. The notched and oval varieties occur early in the Mississippian sequence (ca. A.D. 900–1000), whereas the flared-bit form does not seem to appear until around A.D. 1200 (Lewis 1982:39; Milner et al. 1984:175). In the American Bottom, the flared form is the most common type during the Sand Prairie phase at the end of the Mississippian sequence, while notched forms are not known to occur at sites of this time period (Milner et al. 1984:181). It is uncertain whether the later, flared type offered an advantage over other types or represented a stylistic variation.

It is intriguing that later in the Mississippian period Dover chert hoes from Tennessee seem to displace some of the trade in Mill Creek hoes in parts of the Lower Ohio Valley (Cole et al. 1951:134; Winters 1981). Yet, this pattern is not universal. A recent analysis of variation of lithic types through time at Wickliffe Mounds in western Kentucky indicates that a reliance on both Mill Creek and Dover cherts grew through time, although Mill Creek chert is far more common in all time periods (Carr and Koldehoff 1994). It is fascinating to ponder the reasons behind, and implications of, a rivalry between two source areas in the hoe trade. At this time, we only have very general empirical data demonstrating a broad overlap between Dover and Mill Creek cherts.

As more evidence comes to light on the timing of Mississippian exchange, it is apparent that a number of classes of goods rose and fell in their abundance and distribution. Many of the items we associate with the Southern Cult appear to have achieved their distributional peak sometime around A.D. 1250. Yet, some objects, such as shell masks, appear to be very late (post–A.D. 1350), whereas other objects, such as long-nosed god maskettes, occur very early (pre–A.D. 1200) (Kelly 1980; Williams and Goggin 1956). Shell gorgets also display stylistic changes through time (Muller 1997:370–78). Our ability to make preliminary statements about fluctuations in Mississippian exchange is a relatively recent phenomenon, but it promises to be a lucrative direction for tracing the duration and nature of ties between regions.

From the chronological data we have on hoes, which is heavily biased toward the American Bottom, it appears that there was a great upsurge in the trade starting in the Emergent Mississippian and early Mississippian periods that was maintained for a period of several centuries. Sometime in the 1200s to 1300s, Dover chert hoes made inroads on Mill Creek chert hoes in some areas of the Lower Ohio Valley and Confluence region, but Mill Creek chert hoes still enjoyed a widespread popularity. From the long-term perspective, Mill Creek chert hoes may have fluctuated in supply and demand, but overall appear to have been fairly plentiful throughout the Mississippian period.

If large portions of the Central Mississippi and Lower Ohio valleys were abandoned in the 1400s, the Mill Creek region presumably followed the same path because we have no later sites (post–A.D. 1400s) elsewhere with secure contexts for Mill Creek chert. Apparently, Mill Creek chert hoes occur at sites dating to the Parkin phase in eastern Arkansas (McNutt 1996:244), a period that extends into the era of European contact. However, the earliest dates for the Parkin phase are mid-fourteenth century (Morse and Morse 1983:295), and it is likely that Mill Creek chert dates to components from the early part of that phase. Those few individuals who do make mention of Mill Creek chert at sixteenth-century sites, do so in reference to its absence (e.g., Mainfort 1996:178).

CONSUMING HOES: ARTIFACTS

Although elites from nonlocal mound centers such as Cahokia may have had little control over the Mill Creek chert sources, they may have played a major role in the dissemination of hoes. This idea is supported by the distribution and nature of hoe caches among Mississippian sites. The frequent occurrence of hoe caches was remarked upon by several archaeologists in the late nineteenth and early twentieth centuries:

> The agricultural implements are frequently found in caches. One cache of 4 spades and another of 9 notched hoes are known to have been found in the immediate vicinity of Monk's Mound. A cache of 2 oval spades . . . was found near the Powell Mound, and one of 8 was found near the Mound Group 7 miles north of Cahokia, at Mitchell . . . it has been noted that in most of these caches the implements show no evidence of use. (Titterington 1938:5–6)
> The chipped stone implements known as spades are frequently found buried in large numbers. (Fowke 1894:134)

Where chert descriptions are available, Mill Creek chert hoes constitute the great majority of the cached specimens.

I have elsewhere argued that caches can be separated into two types, *domiciliary* caches and *distributional* caches, on the basis of the number of hoes and their condition (Cobb 1989). Domiciliary caches are associated with residential structures and contain a small number of hoes, usually between two and 10 examples. They typically are buried in pit features in the floor. Most or all of the hoes in a domiciliary cache exhibit evidence of use, either by being broken or having the characteristic bit-polish. Their context suggests that they were being stored for future use when they entered the archaeological record, and they were not discards. Domiciliary caches are commonly found in the American Bottom, where we have what is probably the largest record of excavated structures in the Southeast (e.g., Hoehr 1980; Latchford 1984; Milner 1984; Throop 1928), but they have been recorded in other areas as well, including southeast Missouri (Walker and Adams 1946:90). Small caches even have been found at upland rockshelters (e.g., Klein 1981:345), demonstrating that the storage of agricultural implements was a widespread and common practice during Mississippian times.

Distributional caches have a large number of hoes, usually several dozen or more, and they are in pristine condition. Furthermore, these caches tend to be associated with mound centers. One of the best known examples was recovered in the mid-1800s at the East St. Louis site, where 70 to 75 unused hoes were found in a pit (Rau 1869). This feature was near two other pits in a triangle arrangement. The second pit held a large number of perforated marine shells, while the third contained several chert and greenstone boulders. Another cache of 63 pristine blades was discovered at a mound group in Perry County, Missouri, in the late 1800s (McAdams 1895). Other accounts of distributional caches include two separate ones (57 and 75 hoes, respectively) from a site near Caseyville, Kentucky (Fowke 1894). The attributes of the distributional caches suggest a form of holding or "banking" at mound centers before eventual distribution to satellite communities. Further support for this model is found in the distribution of Mill Creek chert hoe fragments and resharpening flakes in the American Bottom, which decline noticeably in frequency as one moves south from the Cahokia area (Kelly 1991b:76). This suggests that, while all communities in the American Bottom could obtain Mill Creek chert tools, those closer to mound sites had easier access.

The nineteenth-century dates for the discovery of most of the large hoards coincide with the destruction of mound centers by the growth of cities and great expansion of farming. No very large pristine caches have been described by archaeologists in more modern times, and the older discoveries were rapidly broken up and are not available for restudy. Nevertheless, they appear very different from the caches found in domestic structures.

It has been proposed that valued objects during Mississippian times were often interred with burials, both as a status marker and as a way of removing the valuables from circulation to prevent their debasement from oversupply (Brown 1975:27). Hoe caches do not seem to fit neatly into this logic. They were made from a relatively abundant, if spatially restricted, raw material and could be replaced fairly rapidly assuming lines of exchange remained open. Furthermore, hoe accumulations are not associated with burials. Thus, the caches seem to fit a separate realm of behavior from that found with mortuary practices. It is plausible that periodic spurts of oversupply may have led to the storage of hoes in more secular contexts. If caches do represent a form of storage prior to dispersal, it is also possible that burial may have helped to maintain moisture in the chert, delaying the onset of brittleness.

Every classification scheme has its exceptions, and so it is with the cache typology. Two reported caches have a sizable number of both utilized and nonutilized specimens. One large hoard of 108 hoes has been reported from a site near Big Lake in northeast Arkansas, and a photograph depicts several broken specimens (Anonymous 1973). Morse and Morse (1983:255) describe this cache as an "alleged" find, but if genuine it represents one of the largest known. A smaller cache of 44 hoes was recovered from the Mound Lake site in Illinois (Miller 1958). Four are noted as having wear from use, and "a few" were broken. It is difficult to say what is represented by these mixed caches. Were people storing their own, used hoes with a supply of new hoes for the upcoming agricultural season? Were they offerings of some sort? Even with the other cache types it cannot be argued that they always neatly fit into the distributional/domiciliary taxonomy. The East St. Louis find, for example, seems to have elements of a votive deposit of some sort, given its association with caches of other objects.

On the basis of the available evidence, it is possible to forward the following conclusions about hoe caches in the Mississippian Southeast: (1) the regular occurrence of large, often pristine, caches with mound sites suggests that individuals at these centers enjoyed a preferred access to the regional hoe trade as a function of their status and of the strategic placement of centers along major waterways; (2) the regular occurrence of small caches of used hoes with houses indicates the large caches were broken up and disseminated to smaller communities as part of local exchange systems; and (3) a few of the hoe caches may have been ceremonial deposits.

The distribution and use of the Mill Creek chert "ceremonial" blades were quite distinct from those of the hoes. Maces seem to be the rarest item in this category, and finds include the burial interment at the Lilbourn site and one from the Craig mound at the Spiro site in eastern Oklahoma (Bell 1947). Spatulate celts are somewhat more common and occasionally occur in caches at mound sites (Titterington 1938:6–7), although Mill Creek chert is not always the predominate material represented. Duck River–style swords made from Mill Creek chert also have been found at the Great Mortuary at Spiro (Hamilton 1952), but the recovery of one from the wall trench of a structure at the Hazel site also indicates they were not restricted to elite contexts (Morse and Morse 1983). The eccentric types made from Mill Creek chert and other silicious materials often have pigment residues, primarily in red, green, and yellow; in some cases the implements may have been painted, in others the residues may have rubbed on as a direct result of tool use (Sievert 1994).

The bifaces known as Ramey knives are the most common Mill

Creek chert "display" lithics recovered, although their contexts suggest they found their way into utilitarian uses as well. For instance, in the American Bottom they occur singly and in caches in domestic structures and with burials (Milner 1984:92; Pauketat 1983; Perino 1963:96). Outside of the American Bottom, large Mill Creek chert knives often occur as mortuary goods (e.g., Conrad 1991; Santeford 1982:254–58).

Except for Ramey knives, all of the Mill Creek chert ceremonial implements are relatively rare. Their ceremonial use has been inferred from their frequent inclusion in burials, although, as described earlier in this chapter, they occasionally are found in secular contexts. Long knives and maces are also found depicted in the hands of individuals on shell gorgets and engravings, as well as on copper plates (Lewis and Kneberg 1946:115; Phillips and Brown 1978:177, plate 56; Thurston 1897:98), which is taken as further support for their special role in Mississippian society. Beyond the idea that these unusual items were highly valued in late prehistoric times, however, we have little understanding of how the different categories of ceremonial objects fit into the Mississippian world view. Such studies are hampered by our small sample size.

Although there is a tendency to collapse all bifaces other than hoes into a ceremonial category, there does seem to be some variation among the individual types that is worthy of further study, if the sample sizes can be increased and the proveniences secured. This variation may relate to ceremonial and practical uses that are specific to individual tool types. It also may be affected by different perceptions of the same tool types by various Mississippian traditions. It is possible that the inhabitants of Spiro, for instance, may have had very different views on the significance of a mace than did those of Lilbourn.

A final, key point about the exchange network is that it involved *finished* Mill Creek chert hoes and exotics. Outside of the source region in Illinois, there is little evidence from Mississippian sites of the debitage categories (e.g., smaller reduction flakes and bifacial thinning flakes) or bifacial preforms associated with stone tool manufacture (Dunnell et al. 1994; Kelly 1980:133; Lafferty 1977:26; Winters 1981:26). What debitage is found consists predominately of resharpening or rejuvenation flakes. Yet the number of Mill Creek chert bifaces moving to consumer regions, combined with the recycling of the tools, often leads to a pattern whereby Mill Creek chert represents a significant portion of both the debitage and tool assemblages. For example, an analysis of a sample of the lithic artifacts from the Wickliffe site in Kentucky demonstrated that about 36 percent of the debitage was Mill Creek chert, as were 38 percent of the tools (Koldehoff and Carr 2001).

At the Julien site in the American Bottom, Mill Creek chert comprised approximately 9 percent of the analyzed debitage sample (Milner 1984:78). The smaller amounts from the Julien site likely are a
function of the greater distance to the source areas, but the amount of
Mill Creek chert is nonetheless significant.

Many of the Mill Creek chert hand tools recovered from consumer
sites, such as adzes, appear to have been made from broken hoes (Dunnell et al. 1994). Consequently, some of the Mill Creek chert debitage
in consumer regions is likely related to retooling and recycling, rather
than just resharpening. This evidence suggests that small implements
made from Mill Creek chert were not necessarily widely traded out of
southern Illinois, but were manufactured locally. Finally, Mill Creek
hoes also served as cores that were sometimes reworked into amorphous or bipolar cores, which, in turn, were used for the production of
flake tools (Koldehoff and Carr 2001).

Excavations at the Bonnie Creek site, a Mississippian farmstead in
south-central Illinois (Koldehoff 1986), have provided a general model
for the manner in which Mill Creek hoes typically were recycled at
consumer sites (Figure 3.8). Broken hoe fragments could easily be reworked into several different technological directions. Freehand or bipolar cores could be used for the production of expedient flake tools or
small projectile points; microlith cores could be used to manufacture
microblades; and flakes in general could be applied to tasks to which
their shape was suited. Alternatively, large fragments of broken hoes
could be converted into celts, adzes, and other bifacial tools. Although
Mill Creek chert may have been most desired in the form of agricultural implements, consumers found the raw material extremely useful
in a wide variety of technological settings.

CONSUMING HOES: PEOPLE

My suggestion that elites may have had differential access to imported
stone tools with the aim of strategically disseminating them indicates
a form of consumption oriented toward reproduction of social position,
rather than consumption for practical value. Yet this kind of demand
by elites was only intermediary: it may have constituted an important
stimulus to hoe production, but the ultimate demand was represented
by the thousands of households that desired Mill Creek chert hoes for
their everyday excavating tasks. Without this widespread desire, there
would have been no hoe trade to take advantage of.

Who were the people who used Mill Creek chert hoes on a daily
basis? All evidence points to the probability that women were the primary consumers. We have the example of the Birgir figurine to show

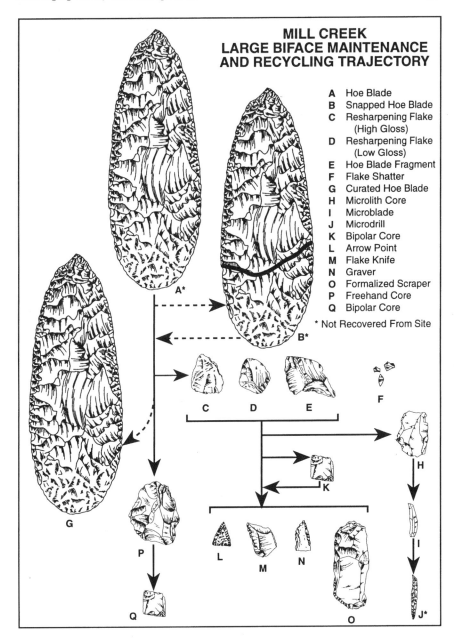

MILL CREEK
LARGE BIFACE MAINTENANCE
AND RECYCLING TRAJECTORY

A   Hoe Blade
B   Snapped Hoe Blade
C   Resharpening Flake
      (High Gloss)
D   Resharpening Flake
      (Low Gloss)
E   Hoe Blade Fragment
F   Flake Shatter
G   Curated Hoe Blade
H   Microlith Core
I   Microblade
J   Microdrill
K   Bipolar Core
L   Arrow Point
M   Flake Knife
N   Graver
O   Formalized Scraper
P   Freehand Core
Q   Bipolar Core
* Not Recovered From Site

Figure 3.8. General model of hoe recycling. (Courtesy of Brad Koldehoff.)

us the physical and metaphorical links between women and agricultural practices. The ethnohistoric record for the Southeast is replete with examples of the central role played by women in the agricultural cycle. Use does not necessarily imply ownership in the Western sense. It is more likely that households possessed many tools in common, particularly those mundane ones that were used for a number of tasks. Under these circumstances, it would not have been unusual for a man to use a hoe to assist in the construction of a neighbor's house. Nevertheless, the documented importance of hoes for agriculture, and the centrality of women's labor in plant cultivation, suggest very strong links between women and hoes.

At a basic level, this observation becomes yet another piece of the growing amount of evidence contradicting the notion that stone tools were the province of men (e.g., Gero 1991; Sassaman 1993). Yet, what were the technological and social reasons underlying the preferential selection of stone hoes by women in many regions? The relative abundance of large bifaces (assuming lines of exchange were not interrupted) and the superiority of Mill Creek chert as a digging material may have combined to provide an ideal product to an interest group feeling historically unprecedented demands on labor. Given the major upsurge in the exploitation of domesticated plants associated with the Mississippian period, it may be surmised that the technological transformations associated with that shift were accompanied by changes in the organization of labor. Presumably, the work requirements entailed by field cultivation could be offset to some degree by more efficient hoes. Whether this led to more "free" time is doubtful, but it is very possible that, at least in some small way, Mill Creek chert hoes may have contributed to the freeing of women's labor to other tasks. It is still unclear as to what these other tasks or roles may have involved.

Claassen (1991) and Sassaman (1993) have observed that women's subsistence activities may have promoted their prestige during the Archaic era in eastern North America. During the Mississippian period, agricultural technology may have constituted a dialectical role with regard to women's status. On the one hand, it may have been tied in to a larger idealized view of women and their importance to fertility as well as social reproduction (embodied in the Birgir figurine), which in turn may have been played out in the Green Corn ceremony and similar rituals. On the other hand, the potential for intensified subsistence production—permitted by a growing reliance on tropical cultigens and more efficient cultivation technologies—may have led to expanded demands on women's labor. Such demands may not have been clearly demarcated by lines of gender, either. The authority to exact tribute demonstrated by the female captive cacica of Cofitachequi, who guided

De Soto in South Carolina, emphasizes that leaders—regardless of their background—often had preferential access to the fruits of others' labors.

Mill Creek chert hoes do not appear abruptly on the archaeological landscape. As I have noted, in southern Illinois there are Middle Woodland and Late Woodland examples of digging implements made from the same raw material. It is the scale of production and exchange, and new types of biface morphology, that are distinctive during the Mississippian period. Additionally, it may be that increased demand by women may have been a major force in spurring and shaping late prehistoric exchange networks involving hoes and other items. This idea moves us away from androcentric or elite-focused rationales for exchange, to more complex models. If we consider that all individuals in a society had something to gain from long-distance exchange, it becomes easier to reconcile the wide range of goods that were traded and consumed.

CONCLUSION

Based on patterns of exchange and consumption, my model of Mill Creek chert hoe exchange does not depart in great detail from the one forwarded by Muller (1997), except in emphasis. He downplays the role of elites in the movement of goods across the Mississippian Southeast, arguing that down-the-line exchange fostered by kinship and other ties can account for the patterns of goods recovered archaeologically. I would agree with this position insofar as it relates to the mechanics of daily exchange, but I still believe that access (social as well as geographic) placed elites in a somewhat favorable position with regard to the fruits of exchange.

The fall-off data do make it seem unlikely that elites did much to shape the general structure of hoe exchange. Yet the distribution and nature of hoe caches suggest that elites may have had "first dibs" on goods unloaded from canoes. This right may have accrued from a number of reasons, including the privileged economic position of elites within a community and their participation in alliances extending outside of the community. The ultimate dispersal of hoes to a region surrounding a mound center (or nodal community) presumably followed a familiar route alongside other goods through prestations, feasting, and similar means. At the same time, it is conceivable that the next canoe laden with goods bypassed that particular center and downloaded 20 kilometers upstream. That particular batch of hoes and other materials may have entered into a network of exchange ties relatively unaffected by those at the first site. Nevertheless, it is important that the consumption of hoes by elites may have varied from the consumption of hoes by the rest of Mississippian society. For elites, the acquisition of hoes was directed toward the reproduction of positions of status as the digging implements were distributed alongside other goods. For the occupants of households, the consumption of hoes was more directly tied to immediate biological reproduction, but may also have had important ramifications on gendered dimensions of labor.

The varying manner of participation in exchange and consumption by different segments of society underscores the multiplicity of power relations enveloping a class of goods as they move through their use-life. Some researchers of prehistoric technology have advocated a *chaîne opératoire* approach (Lemonnier 1992; Sellet 1993), which examines the transformations that tools undergo throughout a technological sequence, as well as the concepts and knowledge related to manufacture. Turning our attention to how relations of production undergird this system may in fact require the notion of a *chaîne de travail*, in which the organization of labor (as opposed to work or craft) may vary between procurement, production, exchange, and consumption. In the following chapter, I examine in some detail how the concept of labor may be articulated more closely with the organization of technology.

4 Rethinking the Organization of Lithic Technology

The cumulative weight of over a century of archaeological research on the exchange and consumption of Mill Creek chert hoes has amply demonstrated the capability of prehistoric communities to sustain chert quarrying and tool manufacture for hundreds of years. Yet inferences about production are mainly either indirect, based on the distribution of hoes, or broad, qualitative statements from short-term studies now a century old. For these reasons, further insights into the organization of hoe production have naturally necessitated a return to the Mill Creek region itself.

Lithic studies traditionally were not a major focus of Mississippian research until the past decade or so. This bias can be attributed in part to the aesthetic appeal and data potential of other artifact categories, such as copper plates, shell gorgets, ceramics, and the like, which upstage Mississippian lithic assemblages. Simply stated, formal stone tool types in the late prehistoric era are relatively few in number compared with the carefully crafted bifaces that we take for granted for the Archaic period. Instead, Mississippian households carried out a wide range of tasks with mundane flakes detached from bipolar and amorphous cores (Koldehoff 1987; Teltser 1991). The paucity of bifacial technology at Mississippian sites does have its exceptions, however, notably in the case of Mill Creek chert hoes.

My approach to the analysis of hoe production is greatly influenced by the technological organization (TO) framework. In the past 15 to 20 years there has been a veritable explosion of lithic research under this rubric, much of it originating with hunter-gatherer studies; recently it has expanded to more complex societies as well. In this chapter, I consider both advantages and shortcomings of the TO perspective, exemplified by a mini–case study on the role of stone tools in the Southeastern fur trade of the Colonial era and concluding with a consideration of the place of quarry studies in the TO paradigm. Following the political-economic bent of my own work, I hope to demonstrate that a more explicit emphasis on the social dimensions of labor is a vital ingredient to any anthropological study purporting to be interested in technology. The groundwork then will have been laid for moving to the Mill Creek case in following chapters.

THE ORGANIZATION OF TECHNOLOGY AND LITHIC STUDIES

Lithic studies of the organization of technology emphasize the manufacture, use, discard, and recycling of tools; relationships between raw materials, production, and consumption; environmental impacts on technology; and the human behaviors that structure the complex interplay of these variables. The theoretical perspectives that most frequently inform the organization of technology framework tend to be adaptationist or selectionist, although there is considerable diversity within these approaches. At a broad level, TO studies tend to focus on three strategies: curation, expediency, and opportunism (Nelson 1991:62). From Darwinian or adaptationist viewpoints, these strategies may be manifested in the organization of technology through efficiency, risk-avoidance, or ecological imperatives. In other words, a specific technology is often seen as the best solution to a given problem, within known constraints such as available raw materials, sophistication of manufacturing capabilities for the technology in question, and degree of social complexity. "In all definitions, technology is viewed as a means to solve problems posed by both the physical and social environments . . . since particular environmental conditions will favor choosing and organizing one technological strategy or strategies over others" (Carr 1994:1).

Among the various successes enjoyed by TO analyses, two that particularly stand out are (1) evaluating the relationship between settlement mobility and lithic procurement and reduction strategies and (2) documenting and explaining the worldwide (although not synchronous) shift from a reliance on formal tools to expedient tools.

Experimental lithic studies have greatly clarified the nature of reduction sequences, particularly for biface technologies and the characteristic types of waste flakes that occur at different points in the manufacture of stone tools—although there is by no means universal agreement (cf. Callahan 1979; Crabtree 1972; Magne and Pokotylo 1981; Mauldin and Amick 1989; Newcomer 1971; Patterson 1990; Stahle and Dunn 1982). Building upon this work, lithic analysts have formulated a number of generalizations to account for systematic variation in the occurrence of portions of the reduction sequence across settlement systems (e.g., Ammerman and Andrefsky 1982; Jefferies 1982; Raab et al. 1979; Ricklis and Cox 1993). For instance, in a simplified application of these principles to hunter-gatherer groups, it is held that long trajectories (i.e., the presence of early reduction to bifacial thinning debitage) are more likely to be associated with base camps, while short trajectories distinguish temporary-use sites. Considerable variation is conceivable with the latter pattern; a short trajectory dominated by early-stage debitage might typify initial reduction near quarry areas, while a short trajectory dominated by late-stage debitage might indicate special-use sites located far from source areas or base camps, where tools were being resharpened and rejuvenated in order to prolong their use-life.

Lewis Binford's (1979, 1980) ethnoarchaeological research has been highly influential on lithic TO studies concerned with settlement mobility and curation among hunter-gatherers. Lithic analysts have integrated his foraging and collecting models with patterns of lithic procurement and production, and added an explanatory robustness from an ecological perspective to the burgeoning field of TO studies. For instance, since "patchy" environments are more likely to be associated with collecting groups, this same type of environment presumably would be conducive to the kind of lithic reduction strategies reflecting base camp and special-use site adaptations.

The flurry of research over the past 10 years devoted to the transition from formal to expedient technologies in North America and elsewhere exemplifies the maturation and sophistication of TO studies. Parry and Kelly (1987) note that the transition occurred around A.D. 500 in eastern North America, when there was a dramatic change in emphasis from standardized core reduction for the manufacture of blades and bifaces to a nonstandardized and situational technology characterized by bipolar and amorphous (multidirectional) cores. This transition coincides with a long-term shift from the mobile hunting and gathering of the Archaic period (ca. 8000–1000 B.C.) to the more sedentary life-style of the Woodland period (ca. 1000 B.C.–A.D. 900). Archaic hunter-gatherers often (although not always) relied on formal, well-made biface technologies based on high-grade stone because the tools were easily curated, resharpened, and amenable to a variety of tasks—qualities well suited to mobile groups who needed reliable, portable tools when access to new raw materials was not always predictable (Andrefsky 1994; Goodyear 1979; Kelly 1988).

The technological move to expedient flake tools is attributed to a growing reliance on cultigens, increasing sedentism, and the declining requirements for high-quality portable tools. The underlying cause of this transition is often related to efficiency, but others have argued that risk also was a factor in the technological transformation (Kelly and

Todd 1988; Torrence 1989). In other words, hunting-gathering economies require the dependability offered by formal and complex stone
tools, whereas groups more dependent on cultigens (such as Mississippian societies) have less of a need to offset the risks of hunting and
gathering with a formalized stone tool technology. Sedentary groups
are more likely to maximize their productive investments in storage
(e.g., the construction of granaries), the processing of vegetal foods (e.g.,
ceramics), and related technologies.

Nevertheless, neither formal nor expedient technology ever completely displaces the other: Paleoindians also used expedient technologies and sedentary Woodland groups still used formal biface technologies. Although there is a transition in the dominance of expedient over
formal technologies through time, they remain interdependent, and
that interdependence is governed by such factors as the local abundance of raw materials, group mobility, and subsistence practices (Bamforth 1986; Cobb and Webb 1994; Custer 1987; Johnson 1986).

In addition to research that has shed light on the formal to expedient
transition and the relationship of lithic technology to settlement patterns, the continuing efforts of a number of scholars working under
selectionist and adaptationist paradigms have provided a much better
understanding about the effects of such variables as raw material availability, mobility, and resource distribution on the organization of lithic
technology. Such approaches have been, and likely will continue to be,
crucial to TO research. Nevertheless, there have been expressions of
dissatisfaction from some of these very same researchers about the
small number of ambitious lithic studies that advance the cause of
explicitly integrating social dynamics with the organization of technology (Carr 1994; Kimball 1996; Nelson 1991:88; Torrence 1994).

Recently, the role of stone tools in political-economic relationships
has drawn increasing attention from researchers interested in the organization of chiefdoms and states (e.g., Brumfiel 1986; J. Johnson
1996; Koldehoff 1987; McAnany 1989; Nassaney 1996; Pope and Pollock 1995; Yerkes 1983, 1989). One important conclusion drawn by
scholars working in central Mexico and Mesoamerica is that impressive lithic manufacturing areas characterized by millions of artifacts
and tons of debris may in fact represent the result of relatively unso-
phisticated organizational systems. John Clark's (1986) review of the
Teotihuacan obsidian industry does suggest that specialists under the
eye of the state were manufacturing tools, but the specialists were
small in number and not all confined to Teotihuacan, as formerly
thought. He believes that groups near the source areas were producing
the well-known blades that were made in such large quantities, while
Teotihuacan workers emphasized obsidian luxury items. Teotihuacan

elites were apparently more interested personally in the latter items, which entered the prestige goods network with other centers in Meso-america. Although Clark believes that elite sponsorship and organization were central to the maintenance of blade technologies (see also Clark 1987), he argues against the emergence of the highly specialized blade factories that have become so widely assumed for Teotihuacan.

Farther south, the impressive Mayan chert workshops at Colha, Belize, have yielded thick deposits of debitage attesting to the manu-facture of impressive quantities of bifaces for exchange. Debitage esti-mates for some of the workshops are on the order of an incredible 960,000 grams of waste flakes per cubic meter (Shafer and Hester 1986:160). Despite these impressive deposits, Shafer and Hester (1983; Shafer 1985) posit that production could have been accommodated within the daily or seasonal round of part-time specialists, although they believe it likely that elites played a major role in the exchange of the tools.

It is noteworthy that in both the Teotihuacan and Mayan examples researchers propose that elites were much more involved in the distri-bution rather than the direct production of tools. These conclusions lend more weight to the argument (see chapter 2) about the difficulty faced by elites in monopolizing the manufacture of basic goods even within complex societies.

Although research devoted to various permutations of specialization continues to represent a major thrust in some of the more ambitious organization of lithic technology studies, there have been some intrigu-ing attempts to link lithic technology with ceremonial and symbolic behavior. In the North American midcontinent, several models have been proposed to account for the emergence of a lamellar blade tech-nology during the Middle Woodland period (ca. 200 B.C.–A.D. 400). George Odell (1994) has proposed that Middle Woodland bladelets from the Illinois Valley in some instances may have been special tools for skeletal dismemberment in Hopewellian burial ceremonialism. Carol Morrow (1987) has argued that, at a broad scale, Middle Woodland blade technology was important for displaying and reproducing re-gional identity.

The focus on social and ceremonial contexts for Hopewellian blade manufacture is due in large part to the fact that the presumed efficien-cies associated with blade manufacture (e.g., Clark 1987:260) do not seem to make sense for the entirety of the American midcontinent. This region is characterized by numerous high-quality lithic source areas and the need to produce great amounts of cutting edge from a restricted supply of raw material does not appear to have been a wide-spread concern. The blade technology associated with the Middle Woodland period does not easily fit into models of TO based upon natural selection or adaptationist criteria, leading some researchers to seek social factors to account for its brief florescence.

If there is one thing that unites research attempting to link lithic technology to issues of broader theoretical interest such as ceremonial behavior or political-economic organization, it is the recognition that the study of lithic technological organization alone is not likely to lead to major advances in anthropological knowledge. Instead, the most successful TO studies explore the ways in which lithic technological organization can dovetail with other, independent lines of evidence (often nonlithic in nature) to make inferences relevant to an anthropological archaeology. For instance, Morrow's (1987) work with Hopewell blades and social interaction finds support in regional ceramic stylistic studies (Braun 1985; Braun and Plog 1982). Recommendations that TO studies be more firmly linked to other lithic analytical approaches within the *chaîne opératoire* method may have merit (Kimball 1996:108; Simek 1994), but they do not go far enough. One can only go so far in understanding the past through microwear studies, new avenues of debitage analysis, or examinations of tool design, no matter how well these lithic approaches may be articulated with one another. Furthermore, stone tool technologies must be explored with respect to issues besides mobility, settlement, and raw material distribution— even for hunter-gatherer societies—if we hope to place lithic analyses firmly within the realm of archaeological theory that goes beyond adaptation or natural selection.

LITHICS, LABOR, AND TECHNOLOGY

My dual interests in political economy and lithic studies have led me to ask: In what other directions can we take the organization of technology? As exemplified by case studies in the previous discussion (e.g., Clark 1986; Morrow 1987; Shafer and Hester 1986), can stone tools and debitage further illuminate issues involving notions of power, inequality, historical contingency, and human agency? What are the different ways in which lithic studies inform us about both anthropological theory building and the day-to-day lives of past communities?

I would like to pursue these questions with particular reference to processes of production and the organization of labor. Part of my inspiration stems from a little-noticed, two-decade-old commentary by Scott Cook (1975) on Payson Sheets's (1975) seminal study "Behavioral Analysis and the Structure of a Prehistoric Industry." Cook took a different tack from the other commentaries following this *Current Anthropology* article, most of which dealt with topics such as behaviorism versus cognition, or the role of technology in behavioral models. Cook pointed out that stone tools and debitage are not mere reflections of human behavior, but are the "product and by-products of the socially necessary labor of prehistoric artisans" (Cook 1975:380). Moreover, when we use terms such as *technology* and *industry* in conjunction with lithics, we must bear in mind that we are talking about a central component of the economy, and by extension the means of production, the organization of production, and the mobilization of surplus labor.

The broadening of perspective that Cook called for demands a different take on technology than often seen in lithic studies. Yet this shift does not entail a questioning of the methodological foundations of organization of technology studies; instead, it asks that they be placed in a context that systematically links lithic analyses with other realms of material culture and more holistic research questions—particularly questions that address the organization of labor. This restructuring is based on the premise that labor is a concept that involves work and technology, but also transcends it. As Eric Wolf (1982:74) has observed:

> Labor is always social, for it is always mobilized and deployed by an organized social plurality. Marx therefore drew a distinction between work and labor. Work represents the activities of individuals, singly or in groups, expending energy to produce energy. But labor and the labor process was for him a social phenomenon, carried on by human beings bonded to one another in society.

I made the point in the second chapter that specialization is best understood as a broad term that in fact refers to a variety of ways in which labor can be organized. For lithic studies, the end point is not to measure degrees of specialization or to create an ever-expanding typology of specialization based on technological correlates such as workshops or tool standardization, but to evaluate how surplus labor may be mobilized under different historical circumstances and under different technological constraints. In what different ways are specialists drawn into the labor process? Is their labor coerced? Is it manipulated? Is it subsumed (see Saitta 1994)? How can we distinguish these and other aspects of labor from the archaeological record?

In historical and archaeological research, gender studies seem to be at the forefront of the push to situate technology within its social setting (e.g., Dobres 1995; McGaw 1996). Marcia-Anne Dobres (1995:26) observes that technology represents a dialectic between (1) the social relations of production and things produced and (2) the intersection of social dynamics and material realities. From her perspective, gender relations are inscribed into the material world, and technology is central to the reproduction of the sexual division of labor. The sexual division of labor also may have been a crucial variable in the organization of lithic technology. The increasing reliance on expedient lithic technologies associated with the shift to agriculture and sedentism may also embody a growing importance of women in lithic tool manufacture and use (Gero 1991; Sassaman 1992). Women are more likely to have used expedient flake tools that could be easily manufactured and replaced with locally available materials, because many of their manufacturing activities occur within fixed loci such as households or settlements. These changes also may be related to tensions in the allocation of labor and the distribution of surplus. Similarly, the rise of groundstone technologies may have in some instances signaled the growing importance of women in processing activities, and the growing institutionalization of a gendered division of labor (e.g., T. Jones 1996).

What are the implications of studies emphasizing the labor process in our conceptions of technology? First, the variables structuring the organization of lithic technology are not limited to selection, adaptation, efficiency, and risk avoidance. Technology is socially constituted (Dobres and Hoffman 1994; Edmonds 1990; Gero 1984; McGuire 1992:103–6), and its organization is structured by exploitation, competition, factionalism, gender and age relations, and competing objectives. Second, labor and the relations of production are not limited to the manufacturing process alone. Relations of production, exchange, distribution, and consumption are intimately tied to one another and to technology in a recursive relationship. Demand may stimulate production, or constraints on production may dampen exchange and consumption. Third, the material manifestations of technology not only reflect sociocultural systems, they also reproduce the labor relations that underlie the political economy. As such, technology is not only a thing; it is also a practice that contributes to social reproduction. Finally, labor relations are historically contingent. While we may find convergences or analogies in lithic technology that speak to common patterns of procurement, manufacture, and use, the historical development and social context of similar technologies may be vastly different. It is thus highly questionable whether there are strongly predictable relationships between the organization of technology and social systems.

These conclusions do not deny the contributions that selectionist arguments may have to make to the understanding of the organization of lithic technology, but they do relegate Darwinian insights to a different order of explanation. The independent recurrence of certain tool forms and manufacturing techniques at different places and times around the world seems to argue that there are optimal solutions to design and manufacture. Underlying this commonality, however, is the fact that very different social systems may be using very similar tools and technologies—and it is much more difficult to relate the social uses of technology to such variables as efficiency of tool design or raw material procurement. Yet, how do we ascertain the role of tools in their larger social world, and is there any correlation whatsoever between the social purposes of tools and their functional ends? What really matters? Origin, function, or context? Selective pressure or historical contingency?

This quandary has taken the form of a well-known evolutionary debate in the natural sciences concerning the architectural spandrels of St. Mark's cathedral in Venice. Stephen J. Gould and Richard Lewontin (1979) used spandrels (right-angled intersections of domed arches) as a metaphor for questioning certain tenets of selectionism, such as whether all aspects of form have immediate utility and what other attributes of form may be left out of traditional evolutionary arguments. They pointed out that nonengineering aspects of the spandrels, in particular the space they allowed for religious frescoes, may have represented important justifications for using this architectural form. Other architectural solutions for supporting large domes did exist at the time, but they did not provide the large stone canvas for display found with spandrels. Although other evolutionists and even architectural historians have joined in debate about the points made by Gould and Lewontin (e.g., Mark 1996), St. Mark's remains a powerful metaphor for questioning the respective roles of selection, adaptation, and history in evolutionary explanations.

What does an evolutionary debate about the design of an eleventh-century Byzantine-style cathedral have to offer those of us interested in the organization of lithic technology? I believe the point is clear: we must be aware of historical alternatives, and be wary of focusing too narrowly on specific functional attributes at the expense of the larger (and different) role they may play in a cultural system.

The latter point is also made in a classic example from Marxist thought that underlines the distinctions between technology and capital (McGuire 1992:95). Because capital represents value accumulated through wage labor, a tractor owned by a farmer is capital if a farmer hires a hand to drive it, but it is not capital if the farmer drives the tractor himself. In each case the tractor serves the same function, yet the relations of production are different. A historical archaeologist excavating tractor parts could make inferences about the selective advantages of a tractor over a horse and plow on the basis of efficiency or risk, but would be sorely tested to say much about wage labor and capital on the basis of an examination of the attributes of tractors alone.

This is precisely why technological studies must consider context simultaneously with function. Elements of technology surviving in the archaeological record may embody observable and measurable attributes related to selective constraints on design, function, and even basic elements of work organization. The social construction of technology, however, can only be explicated by a contextual approach that views technology as central to the reproduction of social relations, and thereby embedded within symbolic, ritual, economic, and political practices (Muller 1997; Sassaman 1994a). To be fair, some archaeologists writing under the selectionist and adaptationist paradigms have discussed the importance of history and context (e.g., Dunnell 1980; O'Brien and Holland 1992), arguing that "laws of contingency" rather than cross-cultural generalizations should be invoked in evolutionary explanations. O'Brien and Holland (1992:44) also deny that most adaptationist studies in archaeology have fallen into the reductionist trap critiqued by Gould and Lewontin (1979).

With regard to history, both adaptationist and evolutionary perspectives have sharp epistemological differences with the approach now advocated by many anthropologists. Ecological and selectionist schools typically subsume history within an objective, scientific paradigm in which history serves to flesh out the empirical details of processes underlain by general mechanisms (i.e., natural selection, adaptation). This is clearly at odds with a more interpretive approach that sees history as anti-generalizing and privileging a perspective based on specific cultural frameworks. Although one may question whether these two perceptions of history are totally inimical (Trigger 1989), within the realm of lithic TO studies the role of history traditionally lies within the evolutionary province. At any rate, the issue of historical explanation is rarely brought forth explicitly in TO studies.

The same critique can be raised with regard to functional reductionism. It is the rare TO analysis that attempts to bring stone tools and their remains back into the realm of social relations. Indeed, given the oft-cited lack of concern with cultural theory espoused by many selectionists, it is questionable whether they would even find that my notion of context (the organization of labor) conforms with their notion of context (ecology? design constraints?).

A MINI–CASE STUDY: STONE SCRAPERS AND THE FUR TRADE IN SOUTHEASTERN NORTH AMERICA

To clarify how a historically framed TO approach based on social as well as ecological considerations might work, I use an example of stone tools from the protohistoric and Colonial eras of the Mississippi Valley and southeastern United States, ca. A.D. 1500 to 1750. My example re-

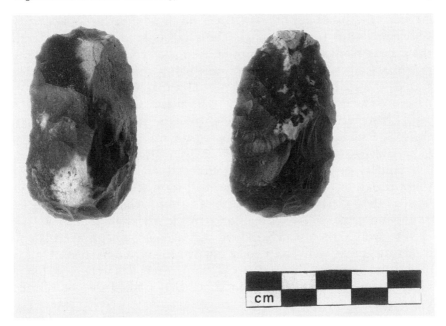

Figure 4.1. Snub-nose scraper.

lies and expands upon research carried out by Jay Johnson (1997) and is not meant as a critique of his pioneering research in lithic technology.

During the period of interest, there was a general replacement of Native American technologies and tools with Euro-American ones. It should be emphasized that this replacement was not uniform, nor necessarily rapid; indigenous practices and world views led to widespread variability in the processes of incorporation and accommodation of Euro-American material culture (e.g., Bradley 1987; Hamell 1983; Miller and Hamell 1986). Nevertheless, native lithic technologies appear to have been hit particularly hard and early by the import of metal tools, although there are some intriguing exceptions. One of these is the so-called Oliver complex of stone tools that occurs in the Lower Valley during the 1600s and 1700s (Brain 1988). A key diagnostic of the Oliver complex is the thumbnail or snub-nose scraper (Figure 4.1); other tools include pipe drills, triangular points, and triangular knives.

The formal attributes of the scrapers are particularly noteworthy. Despite the well-documented reliance on expedient tools in late prehistoric North America, the thumbnail scrapers represent carefully worked, unifacial tools with great regularity in their manufacture. Johnson (1997) has provided the most thorough description of this artifact type based on his work at a number of eighteenth-century Chickasaw sites in Mississippi. The scrapers tend to be made from thick flake blanks. The platform of the flake typically represents the proximal end, which presumably was hafted. The dorsal side of the scraper is usually heavily retouched, and it frequently has a longitudinal ridge along the same side. The ventral face of the flake scraper is often characterized by distal recurve, giving a "hooked" appearance to the tool. Fine secondary retouching on the unifacial scrapers appears to have facilitated hafting. The scrapers were also heavily resharpened.

Brian Hayden's (1990) work with unifacial scrapers in the Northwest Coast region has demonstrated that their form seems to be closely related to their intensity of use within a society, which in turn may be a function of the relative importance of the materials that they were used to work. His research showed that scrapers among hunting and gathering groups were likely to be highly generalized in shape. On the other hand, he found that specialized, formal scrapers were more likely to occur under resource-rich conditions that favored the use of hide garments as display items. The care and intensity of work involved in the preparation of high-quality hide clothing among Northwest Coast groups favored scrapers (nearly identical to Southeastern specimens) that could be readily resharpened. Likewise, in modern Ethiopia, specialists in cowhide processing relied on formal unifacial scrapers with similar attributes (Gallagher 1977). Finally, it should be emphasized that similar scraper types occur in other periods and regions in eastern North America. They are commonly found in Paleoindian assemblages of the terminal Pleistocene era (e.g., Shott 1993a; Walthall and Holley 1997) and also have been reported for the Green River Archaic in Kentucky (Pope 1997; Webb 1974).

It is no small coincidence that widely disparate societies strongly dependent upon hide working derived very similar solutions to the design and manufacture of formal, unifacial scrapers. These tools share important traits widely documented in TO studies: they can be easily resharpened, are often hafted, and are frequently curated. All of these characteristics comfortably conform with notions of efficiency and risk management that underlie many selectionist models.

Returning to the eastern North American case, there is a geographic spread of unifacial scrapers that seems to be related to both tool design and much larger historical forces. Snub-nosed scrapers appear in the late prehistoric era in the Upper Mississippi Valley among Oneota and Plains-related complexes, where they likely were an important component of the bison-processing toolkit (Harvey 1979). However, their prevalence downriver appears to have been a later phenomenon predicated by a new and important historical force: the arrival of Europeans in North America. Following the European entrada, the Oliver complex becomes important in Lower Valley assemblages, and similar tools appear on Quapaw, Armorel, Chickasaw, and other post-Contact sites in certain areas of the South (e.g., Brain 1988; Ford 1961; Johnson 1997).

Alternative uses for the endscrapers should not be overlooked. A high-power functional analysis was conducted on two specimens interred as part of "flintknapper" kits at the sixteenth-century King site in northwestern Georgia (Cobb and Pope 1998). This study revealed that the endscrapers appear to have been worked on wood, not a surprising conclusion if the flintknappers were manufacturing arrow shafts or bows in addition to stone tools. The obvious lesson here is that even morphologically identical tool types did not always have the same function, nor can we rule out the possible multifunctional nature of even the same tool.

Nevertheless, it is widely held that the upsurge in the use of snub-nosed scrapers in southeastern North America appears to have been closely tied to the development of the fur trade (especially deer) with Europeans (Brain 1988; Johnson 1997; Morse and Morse 1983:274). The increased frequency of this tool and related types on sites in the Lower Valley is a direct result of the mercantile economies driving European nations to vie with one another for resources in the Americas, Africa, Oceania, and Asia. Thus, the historical conditions that favored the initial reliance on formal scrapers late in prehistory—primarily for hide processing for domestic consumption—appear to have been quite different from those that spurred the diffusion of the scrapers to the point that they have become a marker for protohistoric and historic Native American sites over a fairly large area.

The posited relationship between the formal, unifacial scrapers and the emerging fur trade in the Southeast is not original on my part. It does emphasize, nonetheless, the diversity of social and cultural causes that may lead to similar manifestations in the archaeological record. Paleoindian bands, Oneota bison hunters, Ethiopian caste specialists, Northwest Coast manufacturers of status garments, and Southeastern Indians tied into an emerging world economy all developed similar technological responses in their toolkits. In other words, very different labor relations governed the daily use of comparable tool types that occur in a variety of cultural settings. It could be argued, for instance, that the labor of Northwest Coast garment producers was appropriated by elites, but through a very subtle means of manipulation that is typical of small-scale societies. In contrast, given the mobility, communality, and very small size of Paleoindian groups, it is difficult to envision similar social processes structuring scraper technology in the late Pleistocene.

In the case of the protohistoric Southeast, the form of labor appropriation associated with the mercantile era involved a much more secular attempt to exploit native resources by pulling them into a burgeoning world economy, although Euro-American impact on labor relations was more indirect than direct. Native Americans may have still "owned" the means of production, so to speak, by their access to forests and hunting grounds that had not yet been appropriated by European powers, but the organization of indigenous labor was undergoing fundamental changes as a result of participation in trade with Euro-Americans. As Hickerson (1973:39) describes it,

> the developed fur trade, although somewhat different in particulars from region to region because of local conditions, enmeshed the Indians into a vast exploitative network. The Indians had become a kind of vast forest proletariat whose production was raw fur and whose wages were drawn in goods which served only to support them through the trapping season.

The penetration of mercantile relations into indigenous economies becomes especially apparent when we examine more closely the actual organization of the fur trade in the historic Southeast—in other words, when we consider the lived experiences of peoples as opposed to the more structural realm of world economies.

Although the mechanics of processing hides were fairly routinized, various groups in the Southeast took different approaches toward organizing the hunt and accommodating hide processing within the yearly cycle. The Choctaw, for example, frequently traveled in small family parties for lengthy winter forays to hunt deer (Braund 1993:67–68), while the Cherokee appear to have developed literal cottage industries within their villages to take advantage of their heavy trade with the English at Charleston.

Despite the logistical diversity documented for harvesting deer and their hides, one common thread was that women were usually assigned the task of preparing deer hides for trade. Furthermore, the increased labor demands represented by the time-consuming process of preparing hides were often a source of tension and acrimony between men and women—particularly since women were heavily saddled with other major chores as well, ranging from harvesting crops to rearing children. Among the Choctaw, women were usually burdened with pack duties for the winter hunt, on top of their tasks of butchering the deer and preparing the hides (Braund 1993:67–68). Furthermore, the tradition of hunting in the territory of male clans segregated Choctaw women from the assistance of matrilineal kin, chipping away at the socioeconomic relations that previously structured women's labor. The heavy involvement of the Cherokee in the fur trade and the development of village-based industries by the mid–eighteenth century likewise led to high demands on women's productive time (Hatley 1989).

An obvious archaeological implication of the ascendancy of women's labor in the fur trade is that formal unifacial scrapers and other tools attributed to hide preparation represent tools primarily used by women. It is a disservice to both lithic TO studies and gender research to leave the matter there, however. The equation of tools with female activities does not necessarily provide a theoretically gendered perspective on the past (Conkey and Gero 1991; Dobres 1995). Instead, we must view the lithic toolkit as one element critical to the reproduction of relations of inequality along lines of gender, which, in turn, were fostered by the articulation of indigenous economies with mercantile systems. Similar to the long-term reliance on women's labor for preparing bison hides in the Plains (Klein 1993), it is likely that Southeastern native women prepared most of the deer hides before and after European contact. The key difference between the two eras is not merely a matter of the volume of hides processed, but the fact that women began to produce commodities under a new form of labor relations that also involved the widespread adoption of a new, formal tool for hide preparation. Lithic technology had become one spoke in a larger wheel that served to alienate producers, particularly women, from the products of their labor.

This perspective raises some other potentially interesting issues about technology and labor relations in the Southeast. For example, Johnson (1997) observes that certain Southeastern ethnic regions exhibit very little reliance on snub-nose scrapers or other known stone counterparts, despite the recorded importance of these regions in the fur trade and the central role of women in hide preparation. Cherokee, Creek, and Choctaw areas are notable in this regard. Were new raw materials and tool forms for hide working in these areas dictated by reduced access to traditional lithic sources? The disruption of traditional Cherokee supply lines for salt and ensuing shortages in the eighteenth century (Hatley 1989:231) demonstrate that we cannot assume historical Native American groups maintained ready access to even the most basic resources. Alternatively, new opportunities to obtain European raw materials may have led to novel replacements of customary hideworking technologies traditionally based on lithic industries. There are examples, for instance, of glass being used in lieu of stone for some tools, such as arrow points (Lawson 1967 [1709]:63).

Another topic of interest is the changing involvement of men and women in particular technological traditions. If we follow traditional assumptions that men usually made formal stone tools in the South- . east, is it possible that women were drawn into activities of lithic procurement and manufacture by using endscrapers at the same time that men's involvement in lithic production was declining as a result of the replacement of indigenous tools with European goods? If so, did new tensions over access to technology emerge, leading to conflicts and shifts in power that were quite different from relations to technology prior to European exploration and colonization? We have already seen in the previous chapter how women were likely the primary consumers of stone hoes. If we continue with the assumption that these were made by men at distant locations, it becomes acutely apparent that TO studies must not only incorporate the various interest groups or classes engaged with a technology, but also must assume a regional or panregional scope as well.

I would suggest that the kinds of questions raised here potentially lead to a deeper appreciation of the roles that the organization of lithic technology may have played in the fur trade of the Southeast, although I admittedly do not attempt to address them. My point is this: the incorporation of unifacial scrapers, drills, and knives into the hideworking assemblage may have been a function of the efficiency of such tools for the processing of large numbers of hides; but leaving the matter there—as frequently occurs in TO studies—demotes technology to a fetish that disguises or ignores the underlying relations that manipulate technology to social ends.

THE ORGANIZATION OF TECHNOLOGY AT LATE PREHISTORIC QUARRIES IN THE MIDCONTINENT

The challenge, of course, is to move such considerations further back in time, when we do not necessarily have the interpretive advantages of historical documents. At this point I have reviewed what is known about the exchange and consumption of hoes during the Mississippian period (chapter 3), variables that are critical for placing production in a larger context. Before moving on to some of the hard data on the regional organization of stone procurement and hoe manufacture in the following chapters, it is useful to consider approaches to quarry studies—particularly during the Mississippian period—in order to lay additional groundwork for articulating stone tools with labor.

By the beginning of the Mississippian period, Native Americans already had been exploiting lithic resources for at least nine to 10 thousand years. As population continued to grow after the Pleistocene peopling of America, there was a steady expansion in the amount and variety of raw materials extracted from the streams, clays, and rock outcrops of eastern North America. Beginning with the more selective strategies of the Paleoindians, Native Americans gradually explored the technological characteristics of an extremely broad range of stone, particularly siliceous materials. Because of the recurrent quarrying of areas recognized to be sources of high-quality knapping materials, there are very few source areas that were exploited during a single archaeological time period. Mississippian lithic procurement is usually the final layer in a mélange of debris that may represent anywhere from several hundred to several thousand years of stoneworking.

It is important to make a technological distinction between quarrying and mining. Mining implies an intensive form of extraction that often involves vertical and horizontal shafts and sophisticated techniques for withstanding collapse (although modern strip mining literally removes layers from the earth's surface). Quarrying employs rudimentary extractive technologies to pry raw materials from parent materials or to excavate shallowly in the earth's mantle. It is not always easy to distinguish between the two techniques, with the main Mill Creek quarries being a case in point. As described in the next chapter, Phillips's (1900) trench found evidence for vertical quasi-shafts that are impressive by North American standards, but they do not seem to represent a true mining technology. Moreover, the extraction techniques were very basic, relying upon crude chert spades. Mining in the traditional sense does not seem to have been carried out in prehistoric eastern North America.

Archaeologists have examined quarrying by a very wide range of societies in North America. In the United States, the Smithsonian's W. H. Holmes is usually credited with being the first professional archaeologist to conduct systematic studies of lithic quarries and their related workshop sites (Johnson 1981; Meltzer and Dunnell 1992:xxxii; Torrence 1986:164). He produced a number of seminal studies at the turn of the century that not only explored the technology of lithic procurement and stone tool manufacture, but also examined the role of quarries in the overall settlement system (e.g., Holmes 1890, 1891, 1894, 1919). Since Holmes's time, interest in quarries and workshops has been sporadic in North America, with an upsurge beginning in the 1970s. The renewed interest in lithic source-area studies coincided with the emergence of TO studies and the desire to develop some forms of broad generalizations that would allow analysts to relate recurrent patterns of technology with certain settlement behaviors. Indeed, source-area studies were naturally enveloped within the corpus of work that was concerned with lithic technology and mobility (e.g., Gramly 1984; Ives 1984; Singer and Ericson 1977; Stoltman et al. 1984).

A common tenet of source-area studies is that for small-scale societies with a high degree of mobility, lithic procurement tends to be relatively unstructured and ancillary to other (often subsistence-related) activities. A group may exploit lithic sources as part of the seasonal round, particularly if the sources are near seasonably predictable food resources—a pattern that Binford (1979) has termed "embedded." This type of exploitation also raises the possibility that other groups will also have access to the same lithic sources, and that any one group will use a number of different sources, leading to a wide representation of lithic types in an assemblage. Such a pattern is often evident at Paleoindian sites in eastern North America (e.g., Koldehoff 1983; Tankersley 1995; but cf. Seeman 1994).

One frequent technological response to high mobility is that stone tools will be completed or nearly completed near source areas in order to reduce the size and weight of a tool before it is transported (Ericson 1984:6). Quarries and nearby workshops used by highly mobile groups thus will be characterized by much of the lithic reduction sequence (e.g., Stoltman et al. 1984). Conversely, as groups move away from source areas, debitage on outlier sites (such as camps) will consist mainly of resharpening and rejuvenation flakes.

Paleoindian groups probably represent an extreme in mobility, and later groups followed a much-reduced round that had a different impact on lithic exploitation and technology. Many Late Archaic groups in the Eastern Woodlands appear to have pursued a restricted territorial mobility, characterized by substantial base camps and small procurement sites within a limited area. They may have preferred nonlocal, high-quality materials for their bifaces, but they also used locally available sources of poor-quality lithic material for flake tools (Andrefsky 1994; Cobb and Webb 1994; Johnson 1986).

In some instances, groups relied almost entirely on local, poor-quality materials for a wide spectrum of tools simply because they had little else available. In stone-poor portions of the Central and Lower Mississippi valleys various types of chert gravels (e.g., Mounds, Lafayette) were commonly used, while in other regions tools were made of middling-quality materials such as felsite. In the Piedmont region of southeastern North America, Middle Archaic groups exhibit a strong dependence on quartz, a stone with unpredictable flaking qualities that is highly prone to shattering. Anderson and Joseph (1988:149) observe that increasing sedentism among Middle Archaic peoples may have promoted the reliance on quartz, but the stone also may have been valued for its white or translucent appearance.

As societies become more sedentary and develop sophisticated systems of production and exchange, their patterns of lithic procurement and production technology may undergo fundamental changes. One interesting feature of these more complex systems is the increased distance between lithic sources and manufacturing areas allowed by the enhanced logistical capability to transport raw materials in large amounts. Highly mobile groups may move raw material away from a quarry before it is developed into a tool, but intensive lithic reduction as manifested in workshops tends to occur at or near the sources. At the other extreme, where predictable long-distance exchange of lithic material exists, urban workshops may be hundreds of miles removed from source areas.

Ericson (1984:7) has argued that several dimensions of raw material procurement and tool production systematically increased as societies became larger and more complex. These dimensions include the structure, size, volume, and efficiency of stone tool manufacture. Groups also may exert territorial control over desirable source areas. We have already seen in this chapter how the great center of Teotihuacan in central Mexico extended its control over the exploitation of obsidian sources in central Mexico (Spence 1981, 1984) and possibly as far away as the Guatemala highlands (Parsons and Price 1971). Where sedentary societies produced large numbers of tools for export, an economy of scale often led to the standardization of procurement and tool manufacturing strategies, as seen with the obsidian blade workshops.

Caution must be urged when equating standardization with specialization, however. Once again, we must question whether similar technological manifestations necessarily reflect similar forms of the organization of production and the mobilization of surplus. Lamellar blade industries occur in several separate and unrelated historical instances in the Americas (Parry 1994). Yet while the end product appears standardized and similar between these cases, the mechanics of production differed widely, and the social contexts of the manufacture and use may have varied even more widely. The manufacture of blades by Paleoindians may have been motivated by efficiency, primarily to prolong the use-life of high-quality chert cores that were not readily obtained because access to source areas was unpredictable. Obsidian blade workers in Mexico also were motivated by efficiency, but for very different reasons. Their access to raw material was much more secure, and they produced blades to extract as many tools as possible from a single core to meet a high consumer demand.

Like other research related to lithic technology, quarry studies seldom confront the social context of labor or related theoretical goals (Torrence 1986:165). Those studies that do take on such issues tend to deal with complex polities. For example, Robin Torrence's (1986) thorough study of the Bronze Age procurement of obsidian and the production, exchange, and consumption of obsidian tools in the Aegean world came up with several interesting conclusions. Primarily, she found that, although the key obsidian quarries at Melos were highly localized spatially, no effort was made to monopolize this valuable resource despite the evidence for centralized control over other sectors of Aegean economies. Furthermore, production was not highly structured and was apparently undertaken by autonomous specialists.

One of the more holistic approaches to a lithic technological system to emerge in recent years is found in Richard Bradley and Mark Edmonds's (1993) study of the Neolithic axe trade in Britain. By combining a diachronic perspective with a sensitivity to changing political, social, and symbolic contexts of the Neolithic era, Bradley and Edmonds were able to chart important variation in the procurement of lithic raw material, and the subsequent production, exchange, and consumption of axes. Their effort demonstrated that it was even possible to postulate that the meaning attached to stone axes may have varied from one region to another, on the basis of variation in the treatment and deposition of the implements. Bradley and Edmonds strongly advocate a historically based frame of reference for lithic studies, one that is cautious in making inferences about systematic relationships between production and exchange, and that decouples a priori assumptions between political, economic, and symbolic realms of behavior.

As we have seen with other lithic TO research, as the number of quarry and workshop studies continues to mount, it becomes apparent that it is difficult to develop neat expectations about the correspondence between raw material procurement, tool manufacture, and other variables, such as mobility or social complexity. We can rely on broad generalizations to serve as a baseline for our research, but these must be flexible and open to modification by case studies. These studies in turn must be situated within a historical context that embraces agency, contingency, labor, and power.

CONCLUSION

Tools and technology are instruments of labor. From a Darwinian perspective, protohistoric unifacial scrapers and related tools in the Southeast were not designed to manipulate women's labor in the fur trade, they were designed to work hides and other materials efficiently. But these tools did become important instruments of newly emerging alliances and tributary labor relations that became the hallmark of the mercantile world system. As we move further back in time, we still must consider the social contexts of tool production, use, and consumption, even if the relations governing those processes are more difficult to discern. Likewise, the lithic source areas that provided the raw material for prehistoric technologies played a larger role in the reproduction of patterns of settlement, mobility, and social inequality.

These conclusions do not lead us away from a concern with elements of design, form, and function that are so basic to lithic technology studies. As in the case of the spandrels of St. Mark's, however, they do require us to step back and consider these variables in a cultural context, and to seek a dialectical unification of technology and labor.

5 Life in the Mississippian Uplands

The primary Mill Creek chert sources are concentrated in a small area in the southwestern corner of Illinois (Figure 5.1). This area—hereafter referred to as the "Mill Creek locale"—is of particular interest in terms of settlement because it represents what is usually considered a Mississippian hinterland, characterized by rolling hills, deeply dissected ridges, and narrow drainages. In contrast, the largest and best-known Mississippian towns typically are located in rich and expansive bottomland settings. These centers have served as the primary basis for defining the ecological parameters of the Mississippian phenomenon, which include settlement on natural levees that (1) are highly suitable for horticulture (especially maize) and (2) provide access to a wide variety of aquatic-related resources from backwater swamps, oxbow lakes, and sloughs (Smith 1978b).

Upland Mississippian sites have not gone unrecognized in the past, but they are usually small and few in number compared with their large-drainage cousins. Many of the interior sites have been presumed to be limited-use stations related to hunting and other specialized activities (Kowalewski and Hatch 1991:6). The number of documented upland Mississippian sites has greatly increased over recent years, largely as a result of mandated cultural resource management studies that have led archaeologists to survey areas formerly viewed as having a low potential for late prehistoric settlement. In many instances, the upland areas have been found to contain sizable settlements that were occupied year-round. These discoveries are providing archaeologists with an ever-greater appreciation of the diversity within the Mississippian lifeway, a testament to its great flexibility. Ceramic styles and other evidence from the hinterland sites also indicate that they were in contact with the polities along the rivers, although in most cases it is not clear whether the uplands were incorporated into floodplain-based chiefdoms or were autonomous settlements. While the links be-

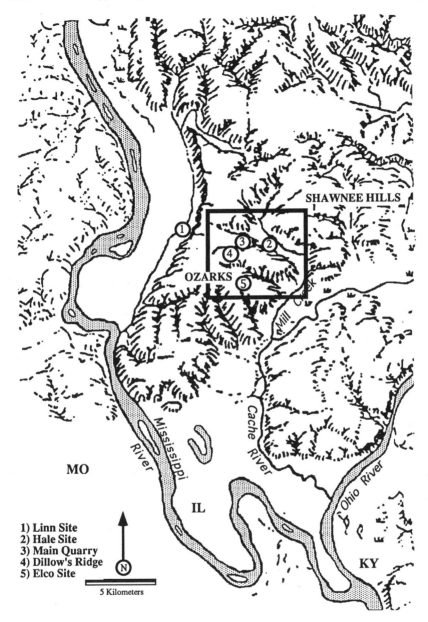

Figure 5.1. Location of Mill Creek region and major sites in the locale.

tween hinterland and floodplain communities in various regions are problematic, it now appears that our notions of Mississippian may have to be revised and expanded to embrace the ecological, political, and economic diversity represented by the upland settlements.

In this chapter, I provide a general background of the environment and history of research in the Mill Creek locale. As a prelude, however, I discuss Mississippian settlement in adjoining regions. There are two major purposes for doing so. First, following the rationale of the above discussion, and the more obvious evidence of hoe exchange, there is good reason to believe that Mill Creek groups were interacting with the larger polities in the nearby floodplains. Second, we know much more about late prehistoric life along the Ohio and Mississippi rivers that circumscribe southern Illinois; until more data are forthcoming from the uplands, the better-documented Mississippian traditions are important for extrapolating about chronology, exchange connections, and basic typological issues for the poorly understood southern Illinois hills.

LATE PREHISTORIC SETTLEMENT IN SOUTHERN ILLINOIS AND ADJOINING AREAS

Although southern Illinois is characterized by a very hilly terrain, its western, southern, and eastern boundaries are defined by two of the major waterways in North America—the Mississippi and Ohio rivers. These drainages witnessed the development of very impressive Mississippian sites and settlement systems (Figure 5.2). A great number of the sites were investigated by the Bureau of (American) Ethnology's Division of Mound Explorations in the late 1800s and have been known for over a century (Thomas 1894). Many have since been destroyed or greatly damaged by historic farming, leveling, and other activities.

MISSISSIPPIAN SETTLEMENT IN THE LOWER OHIO VALLEY

One of the best-documented Mississippian regions in the Southeast is the Black Bottom of southeastern Illinois (Figure 5.2). The Black Bottom is an extremely rich and extensive bottomland on the north side of the Ohio River, across from the modern city of Paducah, Kentucky. It covers an area measuring about 16 kilometers east to west and 10 kilometers north to south. The Black Bottom supported a sizable Mississippian population within a site-size hierarchy comprising one large mound center, the Kincaid site, and over one hundred smaller villages, hamlets, and farmsteads—although the number of sites occupied at any one time is unknown (Muller 1978). Kincaid itself is an impressive multimound site located on a chute of the Ohio River. It contained at least 19 mounds (the tallest over 9 m high) spread out over an area of about 50 to 70 hectares, encircled by a palisade. Despite the size of the Kincaid site, and the numerous Mississippian sites in the larger Black Bottom, Jon Muller (1978, 1986) estimates that at any one point no more than 1,400 to 1,500 people occupied the entire region, with per-

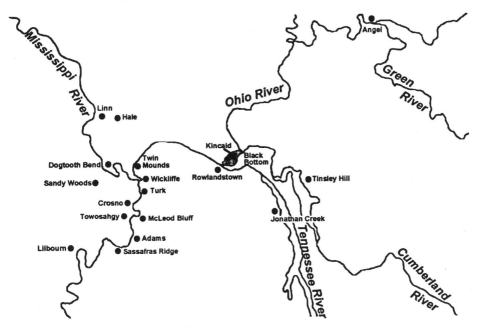

Figure 5.2. Major Mississippian sites in the Lower Ohio and Mississippi Confluence regions.

haps four to five hundred living at Kincaid. He further believes that there is no compelling evidence for a highly centralized political system based at the site of Kincaid.

Additional mound sites and smaller settlements are found across the river on the Kentucky side and continuing northward along the Ohio River (Muller 1986). The Angel site in southwestern Indiana and Kincaid have often been considered "sister" sites because of their parallels, although the Angel site is somewhat smaller (37–47 ha) (Black 1967; Muller 1978, 1986). They have similar site configurations, including a large, semicircular palisaded area directly adjoining a drainage. Both towns are characterized by clusters of houses and mounds, separated by large open areas. The sites are also located in similar environmental and geographical settings. Some have argued that Angel and Kincaid may have comprised a larger polity along the Lower Ohio, but at present there is no strong evidence to either support or refute this idea (Muller 1986:179–80). An alternative scenario sees Angel and Kincaid as sizable contemporaries, with their spheres of influence abutting one another somewhere along the Ohio River (Black 1967:546).

To the southwest of the Black Bottom, the Ohio River floodplain narrows considerably on both sides of the river and the number of Mississippian sites abruptly declines (Muller 1986). The floodplain broadens again on both sides as it approaches the mouth of the Ohio River, providing tracts of expansive bottomlands rich in Mississippian settlements. The last major mound site along the Ohio River drainage proper is the Twin Mounds site (Kreisa 1991). Although smaller than Kincaid and Angel, and with a different spatial layout, Twin Mounds does seem to follow a recurrent pattern for Ohio River centers in that it was constructed opposite the mouth of a major tributary (the Cache River). Likewise, Kincaid and Angel are across from the mouths of the Tennessee and Green rivers, respectively. There are also major Mississippian sites in the lower portions of the Tennessee and Cumberland rivers, which are tributary to the Lower Ohio River. Although these are often treated as a separate tradition in our archaeological taxonomies, there is little question that they interacted with the Lower Ohio Valley communities (Butler 1991; Clay 1997).

A number of the sites in the Lower Ohio Valley and adjoining regions have fortifications. Many of the palisade lines, however, do not appear to have been continuously maintained (Lewis 1996:137; Muller 1986:198–99). This suggests that warfare was a fluctuating concern, rather than a persistent menace.

Mississippian Settlement in the Confluence Region

The Ohio-Mississippi Confluence is part of the larger Central Mississippi River Valley, one of the most densely populated areas of the Southeast in Mississippian times, if the number and size of sites is a reliable indicator. There is little question that a key reason for the major Mississippian presence was ecological. In addition to the rich environs presented by the meeting of two major rivers, the region to the west of the Confluence is a vast floodplain known as the Cairo Lowlands. In comparison, the eastern side of the Mississippi River does contain rich bottomlands, but they are constricted by bluffs running from Illinois south to Tennessee.

The Central Mississippi Valley is particularly well known for the numerous mound centers in northeast Arkansas and southeast Missouri. Parkin, Nodena, Pecan Point, Lilbourn, Beckwith's Fort, Crosno, Matthews, and numerous other sites have yielded an astonishing wealth of burials and museum-quality pots that have spurred over a century of systematic looting. Not surprisingly, archaeological interest in these sites also has a lengthy history, and our understanding of the late prehistory of the Central Mississippi River Valley has been dominated by the archaeology of the western side of the river (Chapman 1980; Morse and Morse 1983; O'Brien and Wood 1998). Many of the towns in northeast Arkansas and southeast Missouri were fortified with encircling moats and palisades. In contrast to Lower Ohio centers such as Kincaid and Angel, which are large but seem to have substantial empty internal areas, the mound centers in Arkansas and Missouri are much more compact (Clay 1976). Many had structures dispersed throughout the entire enclosed portion of the community, with the plaza representing the only major open area (e.g., see illustrations in Chapman 1980:194–99). The frequent threat of warfare is reflected by the pervasive presence of fortifications and is particularly well exemplified by the Powers phase sites on the western edge of the Western Lowland, which were extensively burned and abandoned in the mid–fourteenth century A.D. (Price 1978).

The "western-centric" understanding of the Confluence portion of the Central Mississippi Valley has been compensated for to some extent in recent years, particularly by long-term programs that have been carried out in western Kentucky (Kreisa 1991; Lewis 1986, 1990, 1991; Wesler 1985, 1991, 1997). This research has made important contributions to the prehistoric chronology of the Confluence region, improved artifact typologies, expanded our knowledge about intrasite organization at mound centers, and clarified relationships with the Mississippian traditions across the Mississippi River in southeast Missouri and northeast Arkansas. Similar to the Cairo Lowlands, key centers in western Kentucky such as Wickliffe, Turk, and Adams were compact, fortified villages. Many of the Kentucky mound centers, however, appear on the bluff edges overlooking the Mississippi River floodplain.

Ironically, Lewis (1991:293) argues for close interaction between Mississippian groups of the Black Bottom and those in western Kentucky, on the basis of strong similarities in the artifact record, particularly ceramics. If true, this perhaps should serve as a warning about demarcating regions too tightly on the basis of large-scale phenomena such as geography and site configuration. The not-too-surprising reality is that communities in western Kentucky were likely in regular contact with contemporaries in both the Cairo Lowlands and the Lower Ohio Valley.

MISSISSIPPIAN SETTLEMENT IN EXTREME SOUTHWESTERN ILLINOIS

Recent research in the southwestern tip of Illinois also has contributed to a perspective that encompasses both sides of the Mississippi River (Cobb 1991; Knight and Butler 1995; Milner 1993; Stephens 1995, 1996). Southwestern Illinois is home to several important Mississippian mound centers that are located in the Mississippi River floodplain west and southwest of the Mill Creek locale. The best known of these is the Linn site, located about 10 kilometers due west of the Mill Creek chert quarries (Figure 5.3). This town had six or seven mounds and was surrounded by a rectangular embankment that presumably supported

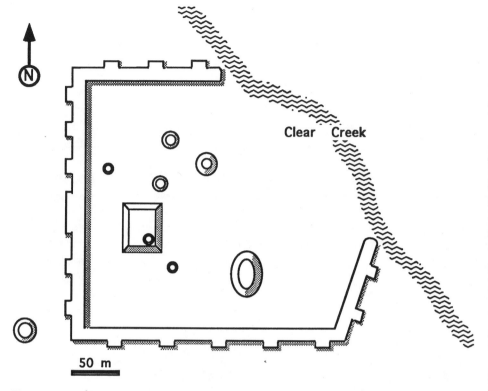

Figure 5.3. Schematic map of the Linn site.

a wooden palisade (Cobb 1991; Merwin 1935; Perrine 1873; Thomas 1894). The area inside the embankment was a little greater than 11 hectares. A widening of the embankment at regular 33-meter intervals is suggestive of bastions, a common feature of Mississippian stockades. Early investigators also reported the presence of numerous "hut rings" within the embankment (Merwin 1935; Thomas 1894). The historical descriptions indicate that the Linn site configuration looked very much like Mississippian centers in the western Confluence region, that is, it was a compact, fortified settlement crowded with residential structures.

The Ware site is a small mound center located about 16 kilometers north of the Linn site. It originally may have had four mounds (Perrine 1873), the tallest two each about 4 meters high (Milner 1993), although only one is clearly visible today. George Milner's (1993) summary of early site excavation records and excavators' letters reveals that burials were present on the site and that an array of intriguing artifacts has been recovered over the years. T. M. Perrine (1874), for example, recovered a large fluorspar figurine that weighed 40 pounds (18 k) by his estimate (see Martin et al. 1947:fig. 92). No modern excavations have been carried out at the Ware site, and very little is known about the intrasite configuration.

Dogtooth Bend is located 22 kilometers south of the Linn site, and it appears to be the southernmost known mound center in the Mississippi River floodplain of Illinois. A compilation of available evidence indicates that it may have had five mounds in its original state, but only two are visible today (Stephens 1996). The largest is a platform mound about 5 meters high. The mounds, a possible plaza, and known residential areas cover an area of about 28 hectares. Like other mound centers in southwestern Illinois, very few professional investigations have been made at Dogtooth Bend, and our knowledge of site configuration and material culture is very spotty. The recent construction of a drainage ditch truncated two wall-trench structures in a residential area of the site, leading to the only excavations at Dogtooth Bend done by modern standards (Stephens 1996).

There are references to several small mound sites in the Mississippi River floodplain of southwestern Illinois (Milner 1993; Thomas 1894), although the exact locations are unknown in many cases. Following the usual Mississippian pattern, smaller hamlets and farmsteads also dot the landscape. Despite the richness of the bottomlands west of the Mill Creek locale, it is uncertain whether a substantial Mississippian population could be supported at any one time. Large tracts of the floodplain were regularly inundated before modern water-control measures, and in some respects Mississippian settlements on elevated landforms from Linn north to Ware were almost like islands for certain parts of the year (Milner 1993).

It must be emphasized that systematic survey in the Mississippi floodplain south of the Kaskaskia River has been limited (Knight and Butler 1995; Stephens 1995), and our overall understanding of Mississippian settlement in the area is extremely poor. On the basis of present evidence, it might be speculated that the Ware, Linn, and Dogtooth Bend sites were the centers of separate Mississippian polities with hinterland regions of unknown size. Ceramics and other diagnostic artifacts from these sites suggest affinities with Mississippian towns in western Kentucky and southeastern Missouri. Milner (1990, 1993) has argued that Cahokia and the American Bottom region constitute a distinct ceramic tradition from that of southwestern Illinois, and that a break between the two traditions can be identified north of the Ware site. Although it is difficult to guess what the stylistic segregation means in cultural or political terms, generally speaking it suggests that southwestern Illinois maintained closer ties with Mississippian traditions to the south, especially those of the Confluence region.

Finally, it should be noted that some sizable drainages, notably the Big Muddy and Cache rivers, do cut through the hills of southwestern Illinois. There is evidence for Mississippian habitations along both of these rivers including a mound center (the Bremer site) on the Cache River. Formal investigations at late prehistoric sites along these waterways have been scarce, however, and we know little about the culture histories of the interior drainages (e.g., Canouts et al. 1984; Denny 1972).

MISSISSIPPIAN PERIOD CHRONOLOGY AND DYNAMICS IN THE LOWER OHIO AND CENTRAL MISSISSIPPI RIVER VALLEYS

The picture provided by research within the Lower Ohio and Confluence regions is one of bustling Mississippian towns, scattered villages farming the rich floodplains, widespread interaction, and intermittent warfare. Nevertheless, that picture is still a static one. A dynamic conception of Mississippian settlement is still hindered by the small number of radiocarbon dates, compounded by the overlap inherent in the standard deviations of the dates. Yet there has been some notable progress in breaking down the monolithic time period of Mississippian, which spans some five hundred years, so that we now have a number of phases that provide some diachronic control over shifts in the political economy of the Lower Ohio and Confluence regions. Until sustained research can clarify Mississippian settlement in the interior, the chronology from adjoining regions must be used to provide a general temporal framework that encompasses southern Illinois.

Before considering the history of Mississippian developments, it is useful to consider briefly what we know about events immediately preceding the Mississippian period. From the long-term perspective, settlement in southern Illinois dates to the Paleoindian groups of the terminal Pleistocene. Native American groups continued to live in the uplands of southern Illinois for the next 8,000 years. Their interaction with surrounding traditions appears to have waxed and waned greatly over time: during some periods groups in southern Illinois appear to have vigorously participated in dynamic trends over a broad area; at other times the region appears isolated.

Beginning around A.D. 800 and lasting until about A.D. 1000, many of the key Mississippian elements appear throughout a number of localities in southeastern North America. These traits include an increasing reliance on maize, new storage technologies, a great upsurge in earthwork construction, and the apparent development of social hierarchies (Griffin 1985; Smith 1986; Steponaitis 1986). Many North American archaeologists refer to this period of time as the Emergent Mississippian period. There have been a number of major typological and interpretive issues raised by the Emergent Mississippian concept (Cobb and Garrow 1996; O'Brien 1991; Smith 1990), but it continues to serve as a useful device for thinking about a dynamic time when many Native American groups were undergoing major social, political, and economic changes.

In southwestern Illinois the Emergent Mississippian period is referred to as the Dillinger phase (Hargrave et al. 1991; Maxwell 1951; Webb 1992). A few Dillinger sites have been excavated, and a number have been identified through surveys. The Dillinger phase incorporates many of the early stages of the trends that we associate with the Mississippian period: a strong movement toward occupation of floodplains, an increasing dependence on maize, and diversification of ceramic vessel morphology. No Dillinger phase components have yet been identified in the Mill Creek locale proper, although the Linn site has yielded diagnostic Dillinger ceramics, as well as a pit with a radiocarbon date of A.D. 1000 ± 150 (Fowler and Hall 1978:562).

One of the best-known Dillinger settlements, the Petitt site, is located in the Mississippi River floodplain about 21 kilometers southwest of the Mill Creek locale (Webb 1992). The Petitt site is located on a Pleistocene bench on the east bank of the Mississippi River. Stripping of the site revealed a large number of pit features and post molds. The Petitt site may have been inhabited by a small residential group, with occasional visits by other groups for fishing or other purposes. Importantly, the site yielded an abundant amount of Mill Creek chert debitage and broken hoe preforms (Parry 1992). The evidence for hoe manufacturing during the Emergent Mississippian period coincides with the earliest documented movement of hoes into the American Bottom on a significant scale. The Petitt site data hint at the idea that, at least during the Emergent Mississippian period, hoe manufacturing was widespread and access to the Mill Creek chert source areas may have been fairly unrestricted.

Not surprisingly, the five hundred years following the Emergent Mississippian period witnessed many changes in localities throughout the Southeast. Mound centers rose and fell; entire regions were occupied, then abandoned—and in some cases reoccupied; and exchange systems were continually reworked. The most refined Mississippian chronology has been achieved in the American Bottom, where scores of radiocarbon dates have allowed researchers to produce a series of well-documented phases on the order of one to two hundred years. The lack

of chronological resolution in many other Mississippian regions traditionally has forced researchers to rely on broader spans of time, usually
referred to as Early, Middle, and Late Mississippian.

The most recent formulation of the Lower Ohio Valley chronology
has been offered by Brian Butler (1991). He proposes four Mississippian
phases after a terminal Late Woodland Douglas phase dating to A.D.
850–1000 (Table 5.1). Prior to these refinements, the working model for
the political economy of the region was that Kincaid was the center of
an extensive polity that subsumed the scattered single-mound sites and
other, smaller settlements along the Ohio River in southern Illinois
and western Kentucky (Butler 1977; Kreisa 1988). Under this scenario,
both the site of Kincaid and its hinterland grew for several centuries
after the Douglas phase, reaching a peak sometime in the thirteenth
century A.D. Then this system disintegrated over a period of one to
two centuries.

A recent synthesis of radiocarbon dates for the region now suggests
an alternative model (Clay 1997). Many of the small mound centers
apparently postdate the zenith of Kincaid. It thus appears that as Kincaid fragmented, populations may have dispersed and coalesced around
smaller nodal communities up and down the valley. Instead of viewing
Mississippian development in the Lower Ohio Valley as a rise and fall
phenomenon, it may be more appropriate to see it as transforming into
another form of political and economic entity—one characterized by
less pronounced social hierarchy. At the same time, there does appear
to have been a gradual loss of population in the latter part of the Mississippian sequence—at least within the floodplains.

Attempts to systematize the chronology for the Confluence region
have met with less success. The problem is that, despite the lengthy
history of investigations in the region, there has been little sustained
work in any one locale or subregion except for western Kentucky, for
which R. Barry Lewis (1990, 1996) has offered a preliminary sequence
of 200-year phases for the late prehistoric era (Table 5.1). The Confluence region also has been subject to very little large-scale systematic
survey, which has hindered our knowledge about settlement systems.
What evidence we do have indicates that a large number of impressive
mound centers occur throughout the Mississippian period up until the
time of European contact, although no single site is known to be occupied for that entire length of time. On the basis of size alone, there
does not seem to have been a paramount center in the Confluence region analogous to Cahokia in the American Bottom or Kincaid in the
Lower Ohio Valley. Instead, there may have been a number of polities
roughly comparable in size engaged in constant competition at any one

Table 5.1 Phases for the Lower Ohio Valley and Confluence Region

LOWER OHIO VALLEY		CONFLUENCE REGION	
Phase Name	Years A.D.	Phase Name	Years A.D.
Caborn-Welborn	1450-1600	Jackson	1500-1700
Tinsley Hill	1300-1450	Medley	1300-1500
Angelly	1200-1300	Dorena	1100-1300
Jonathan Creek	1000-1100	James Bayou	900-1100
Douglas	850-1000	Hoecake	700-900

time, and fluctuating in power through time. This scenario is purely hypothetical, however.

The Lower Ohio and Confluence regions are roughly comparable in that they witnessed the initial Mississippian developments around A.D. 900 to 1100. At that time, settlement hierarchies began to emerge, mound construction began, and material traits such as wall-trench houses and shell-tempered pottery appeared. These trends became consolidated over the next centuries as more mound centers were erected and population increased. Sometime around A.D. 1300 the dynamic trends defining the Mississippian period appeared to lose steam in both regions, as some major mound centers shrank, others were abandoned, and overall population levels declined (as measured by the number of sites). What happens after this is a matter of considerable debate.

The most widely held belief is that there was a dramatic population decrease over a very large area of the Central Mississippi and Lower Ohio River valleys sometime during the 1400s. Best known as the "Vacant Quarter Hypothesis" (Williams 1990), this belief is based on the idea that a great reduction in the number of archaeological sites points to either a large-scale abandonment of the area or a drastic demographic decline. Lewis (1990) has challenged this hypothesis for the Confluence region, and maintains that late Mississippian settlements continued at least until the De Soto entrada in the mid-1500s. He does believe population levels greatly fell soon after that time, primarily as a result of diseases introduced by Europeans. There is no question that some restricted populations in the Vacant Quarter with Mississippian characteristics were in direct or indirect contact with Europeans, notably along the Pemiscot Bayou in southeast Missouri (O'Brien 1994) and the Caborn-Welborn complex upstream of the Black Bottom in the Lower Ohio Valley (Green and Munson 1978). Otherwise, if Lewis is correct about the possibility of late sites in other localities, they are difficult to discern. Factors potentially contributing to the low visibility of these sites include the scarcity of diagnostic artifact types and the high susceptibility of late components to destruction by historic farming because they represent the uppermost and most exposed stratum on the landscape.

Despite the controversy over the final portions of the late prehistoric sequence, one can safely say that a "vigorous"—yet volatile— expression of Mississippian existed from about A.D. 1000 to the early 1400s in the important Mississippian regions adjoining southern Illinois. Further, it can be assumed that events in the Mill Creek locale were impacted to some degree by processes unfolding in the neighboring Lower Ohio and Confluence regions. The nature of these processes and their ramifications on the interior await future study by archaeologists.

ENVIRONMENTAL SETTING OF THE MILL CREEK LOCALE

In southwestern Illinois the fertile bottomlands along the Mississippi River range between 5 and 10 kilometers wide, ending where they are brought up short by a formidable line of limestone and loess bluffs. These bluffs mark the beginning of a steep to rolling topography that spans the southern part of the state—a region that offers a stark contrast to the stereotypical Illinois prairies that occupy the upper three-quarters of the state. The uplands are traditionally referred to as the Shawnee Hills, but in fact the region constitutes two distinct geological entities: the Ozark Plateau and the Shawnee Hills.

The Ozark and Shawnee physiographic divisions constitute the most geologically complex region in Illinois (Weller 1940:10). They are characterized by numerous north-and-south trending faults and folds and igneous intrusions. The Ozark division is an extension of the Salem Plateau of the Ozark dome (Horberg 1950) and in Illinois represents the final eastward extension of the Ozark uplift of Missouri and Arkansas. The Illinois Ozarks constitute a fairly small area of the southern Illinois hills and are restricted to the far western edge. This rugged terrain is characterized by narrow ridge tops and steep and rocky valley walls. The underlying bedrock of the Illinois Ozarks is Devonian, which includes chert-rich limestones.

The remainder of the larger hilly region in southern Illinois belongs to the Shawnee division, which encompasses extreme geological variation. The Shawnees consist of a series of cuestas of Pennsylvanian age to the north and Mississippian age to the south. To the immediate east of the Ozarks in the Mill Creek locale, the Lesser Shawnee Hills are underlain by Mississippian limestones and sandstones (Harris et al.

1977; Horberg 1950). Although the Lesser Shawnees (125–200 m asl) are lower than the Ozarks (230–260 m asl), both divisions are heavily dissected with steep relief. The precise division between the Shawnees and the Ozarks is unclear, but it seems to follow a north-south break traced by a modern highway, Illinois Route 127.

While the Ozarks and Lesser Shawnees represent different geological entities, there are also many parallels between them. The hills in both regions are capped by a mantle of loess, and they share similar topographies, vegetation, and fauna. The scarcity of detailed environmental data on the era prior to Euro-American impact hinders very precise comparisons, however. It is estimated that prior to heavy lumbering in the nineteenth and twentieth centuries, about 95 percent of the hills was forested (Schwegman 1975; Telford 1926). Today substantial tracts are wooded again, in large part because of the creation of the Shawnee National Forest during the 1930s, which has conserved many areas and led to reforestation of others. This region of southern Illinois falls within the Western Mesophytic Forest region, where, prior to lumbering, uplands were dominated by various types of oak and hickory, and sheltered slopes held a variety of species of beech, sugar maple, tulip tree, wild black cherry, ash, elm, mulberry, and hickory (Braun 1967; Rosson 1973). Indeed, the hills comprise a very rich vegetational mosaic, and Neal Lopinot (1984) has defined six distinct microenvironments on the basis of physiographic factors: (1) stream bottom and border, (2) floodplain, (3) mesophytic ravine and lower talus, (4) mesic upland, (5) escarpment-edge, and (6) xeric upland.

Several permanent and intermittent streams run through the research region. Mill Creek is the largest local drainage. Most streams in the area are tributary to the Cache River about 8 kilometers to the southeast, which empties into the Ohio River. Many areas within the Cache River bottomlands were characterized by extensive swamps that have been drained in the past century. In contrast, drainages immediately within the Mill Creek locale do not present the expansive bottomlands associated with larger rivers. Yet the small streams still provide stretches of well-drained soils that originate from the surrounding loess mantle of the uplands and are well suited to agriculture. Likewise, many of the ridge tops have large patches of loess soils that are moderately fertile, but subject to erosion.

With their rugged terrain, narrow stream valleys, and scattered lakes and swamps, the Shawnee and Ozark hills present a vivid contrast with the nearby floodplains of the Mississippi and Ohio rivers. Nevertheless, the hills provided the potential for carrying on a Mississippian lifeway based on horticulture, particularly because they were so rich in mast and other forest resources that traditionally supplemented Native American diets. Furthermore, the Shawnees and Ozarks offered something that often was missing in the large floodplain environs—an abundance of stone, one of the key raw materials for manufacturing tools among Native American populations.

There are at least seven chert-bearing formations in southern Illinois that were exploited in prehistoric times (Koldehoff 1985; May 1984). Some of the chert types saw only a very localized use, whereas others were important raw materials in exchange networks. As noted in the third chapter, Mill Creek chert is associated with the Ullin limestone formation, which is in the Carboniferous Mississippian sequence (Devera et al. 1994). Carboniferous rock is no longer present in the Ozarks, but nodules of Mill Creek chert remain suspended within a clay matrix on the hills, the residuum of the parent Ullin limestone. Mill Creek chert can also be found in the beds of local streams. The attraction of this chert to Mississippian populations led to the development of a complex quarry and workshop system over a large area of the Ozarks and Shawnees, and the remains of this system were still visible to the first Euro-American settlers in the locale in the 1800s.

PREVIOUS INVESTIGATIONS IN THE RESEARCH AREA

The main Mill Creek chert quarry, or "Indian Diggings," and a nearby mound site (the Hale site) were apparently well known by the mid–nineteenth century. The Bureau of (American) Ethnology's Division of Mound Explorations excavated at the Hale site in the 1880s (Thomas 1894). This small Mississippian mound site sits on a natural prominence overlooking the confluence of Mill Creek and Cooper Creek (Figure 5.4). It was reported as having a small platform mound about 2 meters high (which still stands today) and a small mortuary mound described as 20 meters long, 13 meters wide, and 1.3 meters high. Excavations in the burial mound yielded more than 40 stone box graves, most with relatively common burial goods such as utilitarian vessels and shell beads (Cobb 1989; Thomas 1894). Cyrus Thomas also described the site as having a thick midden with abundant amounts of Mill Creek chert debitage, indicating that it was a workshop as well as a living area. The top of the prominence containing the mounds covers an area of about 1.5 hectares, but at the turn of the century activity areas were visible extending into the surrounding floodplain, which would at least double the site area (Phillips 1900).

The main Mill Creek chert quarries are about 1.5 kilometers northwest of the Hale site. W. A. Phillips of the Field Museum of Natural History was the first professional archaeologist to investigate the quarries in a systematic fashion (Phillips 1899, 1900). He reported that the

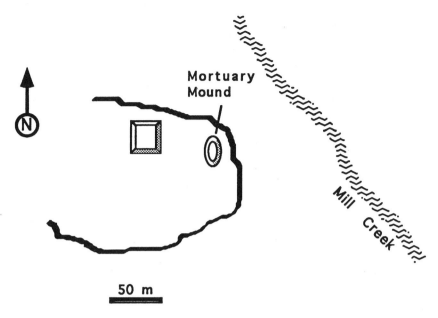

Figure 5.4. Schematic map of the Hale site.

Indian Diggings contained hundreds of quarry pits spread out over 14 to 17 acres (6–7 ha) and covered the tops and slopes of two adjacent ridges. Even at the time of his work, some logging had been carried out on and around his quarries, and his description provides the best picture we have of the site prior to an additional century of intermittent logging:

> Bowl-shaped depressions, twelve to forty feet in diameter, are closely crowded together over the top and down both sides of the hill. Few exceed four feet in depth, but accumulations of leaves hide the surface. While the exploration was in progress, a fire which burned over the area of the smaller group did much to reveal surface appearances. Although scattered refuse is fairly abundant, it is in great measure imbedded in the soil. Along the west slope, at the head of a steep side-valley in the hill, the pits are elongated into indistinct trenches.

Phillips excavated a trench that bisected five of the pits, revealing them to range from 2 to 6 meters deep and to be more than 3 meters wide at the ground surface. His trench profile diagrams show that quarrying consisted of the excavation of quasi-shafts to extract chert nodules from the surrounding clay (Figure 5.5).

The technology involved in the excavation of the pits seems to have

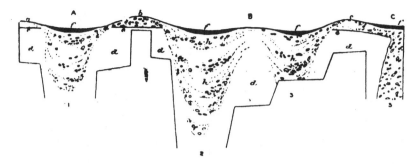

Figure 5.5. Phillips's cross section of quarry pits. (Reproduced by permission of the American Anthropological Association from *American Anthropologist* 21(1): 43, January 1900. Not for further reproduction.)

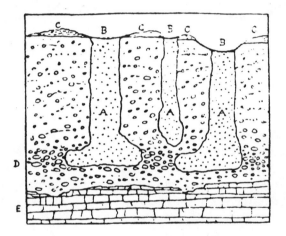

Figure 5.6. Holmes's rendering of Phillips's cross section.

been fairly simple. Phillips (1900) describes excavating tools as being crudely fashioned from Mill Creek chert nodules. It is unclear whether any type of support system, such as timber buttresses, would have been necessary to prevent the walls from collapse. William Holmes's (1919) later description of Phillips's work shows the pits as having slight lateral extensions at the base that are not evident in Phillips's renderings (Figure 5.6). It is uncertain whether Holmes was providing a more accurate picture from the original field notes or was in error. In either case, there is no evidence for the presence of deep horizontal shafts, which would have demonstrated yet another level of technological sophistication equivalent to intensive mining.

Phillips also described a dense litter of broken nodules as well as early-stage tool rejects and failures throughout the quarry area. The abundance of primary reduction debris suggested to him that quarriers were immediately testing their chert samples after removal from the ground. Further, his reconnaissance of the larger region and observations on lithic technology led him to believe that the finishing stages of biface manufacture were carried out in workshops away from the quarry area (Phillips 1900:46). These ideas on the spatial staging of tool manufacture were echoed by Holmes in his remarks on the Hale site.

> There are but slight traces on the quarry-shop sites of the getting out of the smaller blades, but on the Hale place in the valley this work appears to have been a leading feature. Here also all other classes of implements were trimmed and specialized, and heavy beds of chips and other wastage of implement making, including the chipping of implements, are found. (Holmes 1919:192–93)

Phillips's work also identified another, smaller quarry about 3 kilometers to the north of the large quarry, containing 40 pits spread over an area of about 1.25 hectares. This discovery raised the possibility that the extraction of Mill Creek chert occurred over a larger area than previously suspected.

The best evidence for actual Mississippian habitation in the Mill Creek locale was the Hale site with its dense midden and burials. In addition to his work at the quarries, Phillips (1900) excavated at one of the workshops, which also yielded evidence for occupation in the form of charcoal and ceramics; he referred to this category of site as a "lodge." Further confirmation of Mississippian habitation stems from the reports of stone box graves throughout the area (Thomas 1894). However, the lack of systematic excavations at other potential living sites and the absence of large-scale surveys made it difficult to make informed statements about the scale of quarrying or the nature of Mississippian adaptations to the uplands.

Some passing commentary on the Mill Creek locale was made by other researchers early in the twentieth century (Hudelson 1938; Snyder 1910), but no further formal investigations took place until the 1970s. In 1975, a graduate student from Southern Illinois University-Carbondale excavated at the Hale site. Unfortunately, his results were never published, but other archaeologists have reported that he uncovered additional burials (May 1984; Winters 1981). The first modern, intensive survey in the area occurred in a tract of Forest Service property about 2 kilometers south of the Hale site (Lopinot and Butler 1981).

This work found a few lithic workshops that processed Mill Creek chert and another local chert known as Elco. The sites appeared to be Archaic and unrelated to the Mississippian hoe workshops.

In the 1970s and 1980s students and staff associated with the Center for Archaeological Investigations and the department of anthropology at SIU-Carbondale began the systematic exploration of prehistoric chert procurement in the southern Illinois region. Over the years, this work has led to a broad understanding of archaeologically important geological chert outcrops, the distribution of prehistoric quarries and workshops, and changing patterns in chert use through time (Billings 1984; Koldehoff 1985; Lopinot and Butler 1981; May 1984). In the course of this long-term research, investigators documented several Mill Creek chert hoe workshops and another quarry, the Mondino site, which is located about 5 kilometers south of the large quarry (Cobb 1988). It was during this time that my reanalysis of collections from the Linn site demonstrated substantial amounts of debitage from the manufacture of Mill Creek chert hoes (Cobb 1988, 1991), as noted in chapter 3. Although this mound center in the Mississippi River floodplain is not in the Mill Creek locale proper, it is only about 10 kilometers to the west. There are no known quarries in the bluffs and hills immediately to the east of the Linn site, suggesting that Mill Creek chert was procured from the known quarries, either by trade or by forays into the hills.

By the end of the 1980s, archaeologists still lacked an in-depth understanding of the nature of Mill Creek chert exploitation and Mississippian occupation of the surrounding area, but there was at least a strong basis for believing that chert procurement and hoe manufacture were much more extensive than previously known. The main quarry was by far the largest known chert source, but additional ones had been identified, and continuing low-intensity reconnaissance in the region affirmed the widespread presence of workshops. The dense midden and mortuary remains reported for the Hale site, as well as mortuary remains elsewhere, also pointed to the possibility of long-term Mississippian occupation in the hills. It is with this state of knowledge that work in the Mill Creek locale was initiated on a larger and more systematic scale in the 1990s, providing much of the data for the following chapters in this book.

LATE PREHISTORIC LIFE IN THE SOUTHEASTERN UPLANDS

At this point, it is useful to expand the discussion once again and briefly consider the nature of Mississippian settlement in upland regions from a broader perspective. There is ample evidence that Mississippian groups throughout the Southeast strongly exploited a wide spectrum of environmental zones. Upland subsistence resources in particular have long been considered an important supplement to the Mississippian lifeway. Although higher-elevation zones did not always provide ideal farming soils, they were known to be an important source of wild plants and animals. Mississippian sites in these areas often consist of short-term occupations that are usually interpreted as hunting camps or other specialized extractive loci. In southern Illinois, Mississippian components in rockshelters typically contain hoes, ceramics, and processing tools, suggesting that short-term field camps were also a part of the Mississippian settlement system (Winters 1981:27).

In recent years a number of archaeological projects have revealed that there is extreme variation in Mississippian use of upland habitats. While many uplands in the Southeast do seem to have a predominance of short-lived camps, other areas show significant populations in environmental settings not usually considered well suited to Mississippian adaptations. Kowalewski and Hatch (1991) have found that Lamar (Late Mississippian) groups in sixteenth-century Georgia were settling in substantial numbers among small, dispersed settlements in the upper reaches of the Oconee drainage. Likewise, Mississippian and/or Caddoan groups penetrated the Ozarks of northwest Arkansas (Raab 1982). Even the Appalachians are known to have Mississippian settlements, including small mound centers (Dickens 1978).

Closer to the Mill Creek locale, a significant Mississippian occupation has been documented in the uplands east of Cahokia and the American Bottom (Koldehoff 1989; Woods and Holley 1991). It consisted of dispersed small sites and nucleated villages along a number of drainages. The chronology of the upland sites indicates that population levels were unstable, with cycling patterns of demographic upsurge and near abandonment. The population oscillations have been tied to political and ecological events in the nearby American Bottom region, with population movement between floodplain and upland regions reflecting periods of environmental degradation and fluctuations in power in the Cahokia polity.

It must be emphasized that in the above examples Mississippian groups were not living in highly isolated, "hardscrabble" locations; they gravitated toward those environs that still offered an opportunity for carrying out maize horticulture. In some instances these settings may be the floodplains of small drainages, in others they are ridge tops or bluff edges. In fact, it is possible that upland locations did contain some opportunity for soil renewal for agriculture in the form of colluvial processes. Although not offering the rich replenishment of bottomlands, erosion and downward soil movement in some areas may have been sufficient to make upland agriculture at least viable on a sustained basis (Kowalewski and Hatch 1991).

Future comparative research on upland Mississippian groups is sorely needed to address their ecological and social diversity. As it stands now, we tend to use the terms *upland* and *interior* to refer to late prehistoric settlements away from large drainages, yet those locations encompass a wide variety of settings. For example, some of the western Kentucky centers in the Confluence region sit on the bluff crest overlooking the Mississippi River floodplain, which technically could be considered an upland zone in terms of local topography, but it is one with relatively easy access to rich bottomlands. The same can be said for some of the upland sites fringing the American Bottom. This is a far different setting from that of the Hale site, which is located on a floodplain, but a narrow one that is located in the midst of the Ozark and Shawnee hills. In addition to topography, variation in upland Mississippian settlement may have been dictated by warfare, the distribution of valued natural resources, demographic fluctuations, and political instability.

Because of the relative paucity of research on the late prehistoric era of southwestern Illinois, it is difficult to model the types of relationships that Mississippian occupations in the interior hills may have had with contemporary settlements in the nearby floodplains, such as the Linn and Ware sites. Were the upland inhabitants seasonal visitors from the lowlands, full-time residents who enjoyed relative autonomy, or peripheral players in larger polities centered on the mound centers? Despite this ambiguity, it is becoming apparent that much more was occurring in the southern Illinois hills during the Mississippian period than was previously suspected, and all of the preceding alternatives may have been true for different times and places.

For example, Jon Muller's (1984; Muller and Renken 1989) work in the eastern Shawnees has documented a substantial Mississippian effort to extract salt from the Great Salt Springs in the southeastern part of the state along the Saline River. He argues that Mississippian groups occupied the springs on a seasonal basis, over a period of several hundred years. In contrast, the presence of a nucleated Mississippian village at Millstone Bluff in the central part of the state suggests that not all upland settlement was necessarily related to the extraction of important resources, nor was it always seasonal (Butler and Cobb 1996, 2001). There are no known valued Mississippian raw materials around Millstone Bluff as there are with the Great Salt Springs and the Mill Creek locale. Nevertheless, recent excavations at the site strongly indicate that it was continuously occupied for several centuries. Clearly, more work in upland regions is called for in order to clarify the nature of Mississippian movement and adaptation to the Ozark and Shawnee hills.

The lesson here is that, although the chert resources of the Mill Creek locale may have been a primary draw for Mississippian populations, the presence of sites in the region does not necessarily represent a settlement deviation that would have required an extraordinary adaptive effort. There is substantial evidence from throughout the Southeast to show that Mississippian communities were quite adept at settling into environs far removed from the archetypical bottomlands. The challenge for archaeologists is to address the various reasons for those settlement decisions.

6 The Regional Structure of Hoe Production

Archaeologists have a love/hate relationship with lithic source areas. Because stone was such an important raw material for prehistoric toolmaking, we know that lithic quarries, mines, and workshops constitute an excellent vantage point from which to approach the organization of lithic technology. Yet quarries and workshops present our worst nightmares in terms of sampling, dating, and taphonomic processes. The sheer number of lithic artifacts at these sites can be overwhelming, and stratigraphy is usually either absent or highly complex. Worse, these sites often lack nonlithic artifact categories and features to provide supplemental lines of evidence for interpreting and dating site activities. Despite these hurdles, archaeologists have made great headway toward explicating the social and technological parameters that structure diversity in quarry-workshop systems.

In the Central Mississippi River Valley there were several notable lithic sources that were particularly favored by Mississippian groups (see Figure 3.5). Kaolin chert from southwestern Illinois was used for Mississippian hoes as well as fancy implements such as maces and spatulate celts. The Kaolin quarries, about 20 kilometers north of the Mill Creek locale, consist of about 40 pits on the slopes of Iron Mountain. A number of workshops are also found on and around this landform (Billings 1984; May 1984). Because this source was heavily used during at least two periods (Middle Woodland and Mississippian), chronological segregation of Kaolin chert workshop assemblages has proven very difficult. The Crescent quarries in eastern Missouri were also important to Mississippian groups, particularly those in Cahokia and the American Bottom (Ives 1975, 1984). Mississippian communities used Burlington chert from these quarries for a wide variety of tools, including microdrills, flake tools, and the occasional hoe (Koldehoff 1987; Winters 1981). Like the Kaolin quarries, the Crescent quarries were used well before the Mississippian period, as reflected by adjoining workshops yielding diagnostic artifacts from Paleoindian times onward (Ives 1984).

In comparison with the Kaolin and Crescent cherts, Mill Creek chert stands out not only because of its importance to the hoe trade, but also because the parent quarries seem to represent one of the few sources in the Southeast that were exploited primarily during the late prehistoric period. This circumstance seems to be due largely to lesser demand for Mill Creek chert in earlier periods. In southern Illinois, projectile points, adzes, and other tool types were occasionally made from Mill Creek chert before the Mississippian period, but other raw materials seem to have been preferred. Further, larger bifaces made from Mill Creek chert do occur as early as the Late Archaic and Early/Middle Woodland periods (Koldehoff 1992; Koldehoff and Wagner 1998). However, collections of bifaces from the Mill Creek chert quarries are exclusively Mississippian when identifiable to type (Cobb 1988). Presumably, Mill Creek chert nodules were obtained from streams or erosional gullies in earlier periods (Lopinot and Butler 1981; May 1984) or perhaps from small quarries that have not been detected in the heavily forested terrain. Nonetheless, wholesale excavation for the chert corresponds with the upsurge in demand later in time, and all of the known quarries appear to represent primarily Mississippian activities.

The Dover quarries also merit attention here, although they are not in the Central Mississippi River Valley. I have pointed out previously (chapter 3) that hoes made from Dover chert were the one serious competitor to Mill Creek chert hoes. The major Dover chert quarries and workshops are located in western Tennessee. Similar to Mill Creek chert, Dover chert was used in earlier periods, but the significant workshops appear to be Mississippian in age (Gramly 1992).

Despite the well-documented Mississippian use of quarries in the Central Mississippi Valley, a key feature of lithic exploitation during this period was an increased reliance on locally available lithic materials that were often of very poor quality. These typically could be collected as surface gravel or stream residuum. In the American Bottom, Mississippian groups made heavy use of local cherts that are often characterized by numerous fracture planes and flaws. These cherts were typically exploited for their potential for flake tools that could be rapidly produced from bipolar core and freehand amorphous core technologies (Koldehoff 1987). When it came to more specialized tools, such as hoes or microdrills, American Bottom Mississippians relied heavily on imported cherts that were more suitable for specific tasks. Likewise, sites in the Confluence region reflect a heavy use of the locally available Mounds gravel, which was effective for the manufacture of flake tools and small arrow points. Yet Mississippian communities also imported Mill Creek, Kaolin, Dover, and Burlington cherts in substantial amounts, in either raw form or as finished tools, depending on the raw material in question (Carr and Koldehoff 1994; Edging 1990; Stephens 1996).

The heavy use of local raw materials (often of middling quality) by Mississippian groups for the manufacture of small tools is directly related to a major reliance on an expedient technology, a concept that implies that tools were made when needed with little work input and often were discarded after use. These implements typically assume the form of simple flakes detached from bipolar and amorphous cores. The most common late prehistoric bifacial tools are small, triangular projectile points that, like flake tools, could be easily manufactured and maintained. The bow and arrow became widespread in the Southeast sometime in the first millennium A.D. (Blitz 1988; Nassaney and Pyle 1999; Shott 1993b; cf. Bradbury 1997; Odell 1988), supplanting the spear thrower or atlatl, and it rapidly became the weapon of choice for hunting and warfare. In many instances, the small stone arrow points represent a bifacial technology that in itself was expedient, consisting of minor retouch along the edges of an appropriately shaped waste flake. On the other hand, there are many examples of finely made triangular points (notably the large cache with the Mound 72 burial at Cahokia), emphasizing that the line between formal (or curated) and expedient technologies can be very blurry depending upon raw material availability, tool types, and social context, among other variables (Bamforth 1986; Custer 1987; Johnson 1986; Odell 1996; Sassaman 1992).

Finely crafted bifaces, when they do occur during the Mississippian period, seem to be targeted at more specific functions than are bifaces in earlier periods. They often are represented by the fancy types, such as maces and spatulate celts, which presumably had primarily social or ceremonial uses. Even though the potential ability to craft fine bifaces may have been widespread among Mississippian groups, it is questionable how many people actually attained such skills. Certainly, the widespread occurrence of flintknapper burials in North America, as indicated by clusters of interred knapping tools, suggests that most societies held a few individuals who possessed superior skills in stone tool manufacture (Cobb and Pope 1998; Seeman 1984). If we can use the rise to prominence of expedient technologies as an indirect measure of the general decline in the relative number of people honing their knapping skills, then probably only a limited segment of the Mississippian population had developed the skills to manufacture fine bifacial implements on a routine basis—although the potential to do so was not inherently curbed (Koldehoff 1990; Koldehoff and Carr 2001).

From this perspective, Mill Creek chert hoes truly stand out as an unusual commitment to bifacial technology. They represent the most common type of finely made stone tools in the late prehistoric Central Mississippi Valley, although they may not be the most distinguished examples of the flintknapper's craft in prehistoric North America from the eyes of the contemporary archaeologist. Furthermore, the hoes are the result of a commitment to biface manufacture that was highly localized; in other words, certain communities restricted to southwestern Illinois took the time and effort to engage in biface manufacture on a scale unequaled elsewhere in the Southeast during the Mississippian period, with the possible exception of the Dover chert areas in Tennessee. This suggests that hoe production departed from the usual patterns of stone tool making practiced in most Mississippian communities; the question, then, is whether the organization of hoe technology involved a substantial difference in the organization of labor as well.

Until the past decade, our knowledge about production in the Mill Creek locale was limited to general statements derived from the previous century of research: the chert was available in large nodules, but could be obtained in substantial amounts only by excavating into the clay mantles of hills. These prehistoric excavations led to the creation of one very large quarry (the "Indian Diggings") and an unknown number of small quarries. In turn, a number of workshops were dispersed throughout the region, where hoes were apparently completed. They then were exchanged in finished form to consumers over a very wide area.

In 1992, researchers from Binghamton University in New York and Southern Illinois University at Carbondale initiated a multiyear project to carry out survey and excavation in the Mill Creek locale. In this chapter I summarize the results of the survey and data collection from hoe workshops in the Mill Creek locale and examine how this information can be used to argue for the presence of part-time specialization in hoe manufacture.

As I pointed out in chapter 4, it is very difficult to draw clear inferences from patterns of lithic technology alone to issues of political and economic organization. However, those patterns can be used to make general warranting arguments, which then may be buttressed or refuted by independent lines of evidence. There are two general expectations that have guided the lithic analyses that follow. First, a higher degree of centralized control over procurement or production would lead to more structured hoe manufacture, which, in turn, may be manifested in the segregation of hoe technology across the locale.

A second expectation was that a major emphasis on making significant quantities of surplus hoes for exchange would be realized by a large number of workshops that yielded substantial amounts of lithic by-products. In both lines of questioning, complementary forms of evidence were simultaneously considered. For example, the spatial clustering or lack of clustering of sites around sources may be indicative of attempts at control, whereas mortuary patterns also constitute a common avenue for addressing issues of power. In sum, the process of arriving at conclusions about the organization of production (as well as exchange and consumption) was predicated by the idea of searching for converging lines of evidence.

ARCHAEOLOGICAL SURVEY IN THE MILL CREEK LOCALE

Despite the many references over the years to the numerous workshops (typically, sites with concentrations of Mill Creek chert) in the Mill Creek locale (e.g., Hudelson 1938; Phillips 1900; Snyder 1910), no collections from these sites had been analyzed in modern times. In the 1980s I carried out technological studies on limited lithic collections from four workshops and three quarry sites in the Mill Creek locale (Cobb 1988, 1989). Not satisfied with the narrow window into the regional organization of production provided by this small sample, I returned to the area in 1992 to undertake systematic survey and controlled testing of quarries and workshops around the Mill Creek chert source areas.

Given the nearly century-long lapse of sustained investigations in the Mill Creek locale, the commencement of research in the area in the 1990s began from the ground up. Our research questions included (1) What was the spatial distribution of quarries and workshops? (2) How was the organization of production of large bifaces structured regionally? (3) What was the range of lithic manufacturing activities and tool use carried out at quarries and workshops? (4) Could evidence for domestic activities be found on workshops, and what did that say about the articulation of the domestic and hoe production economies?

Our methodology was conceived as a two-stage process. First, we planned to carry out a pedestrian survey over a portion of the research region. Second, we hoped to conduct excavations at one or more workshops discovered through survey, especially sites that yielded evidence for structures, features, and other signs of habitation. Although the identification of quarries was seen as a cornerstone of the research, extensive work on the quarries was avoided because of the logistical difficulties posed by even relatively small-scale testing of such sites. In any event, we were unable to obtain permission to collect or excavate from quarries other than the largest one, and only limited surface collections were allowed there.

Survey Methodology

The survey phase of the research was carried out over an eight-week period during the summer of 1992. The original plan was to conduct reconnaissance over a representative sample of an arbitrarily defined universe that presumably would cover the entire area of Mill Creek chert hoe production. This universe described a locale about 5 to 6 kilometers in diameter based on the previous history of research.

The sampling objective was immediately thwarted by the history of land ownership and landowners' attitudes in the research area. Sizable tracts belong to the Shawnee National Forest, from which permission had been granted for survey. However, much of the sample universe is in private hands, and most landowners hold relatively small plots of land compared with the large tracts held by individuals in the Mississippi River and Ohio River bottomlands. Whereas landowners in the latter areas may hold several hundreds of acres or more, in the Mill Creek locale farms are typically on the order of a few acres to a few dozen acres. Thus, one must approach several times more landowners in the Mill Creek locale in order to cover the same amount of land. Furthermore, for varying reasons, some landowners refused to grant permission to survey their property. Fear of being sued in case of an accident to a crew member was the most cited reason for denying land access. In my experience, this seems to be an increasing concern among landowners in eastern North America, and it does not bode well for future archaeological research on private lands, particularly research dependent upon random, probabilistic survey designs.

Because of the logistical difficulties entailed in developing a non-biased survey sampling scheme, the decision was made to focus on surveying as much land as possible along the three drainages nearest the "core" of the Mill Creek locale as defined by the main quarry and the Hale site. Within these drainages, the survey areas were dictated by the main criterion of gaining permission to enter private property. The three drainages, You-Be Hollow, Cooper Creek, and Mill Creek, run roughly from west to east through the research area (Figure 6.1). We also surveyed portions of the uplands overlooking the creeks, in addition to the floodplains of the drainages. An area of about 445 hectares (1,100 acres) was covered in 1992 following this method. This total also included limited survey that was carried out in dispersed locations around the primary area to gain a better sense of the general extent of the distribution of quarries and workshops.

Although extractive areas referred to as quarries are readily identifi-

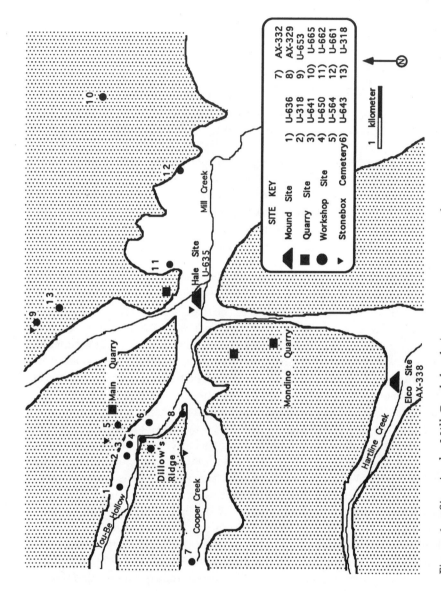

Figure 6.1. Sites in the Mill Creek locale (note: survey coverage does not encompass entire depicted area).

able by depressions and dense amounts of lithic working debris, the definition and identification of a workshop can be more ambiguous. Odell (1996:55) views a workshop as a location characterized by "an abundance of debitage and paucity of finished tools," but he warns that the use of a site or locale for other purposes may obscure this function. Further, what does "an abundance of debitage" really mean? In practice, lithic analysts have tended to view the idea of a workshop in a relative sense; what constitutes an abundance of debitage on an Eastern Woodlands site would be viewed as merely a moderate density on a Mesoamerican or Near Eastern obsidian workshop. For the Mill Creek locale, hoe workshops were defined by three criteria: (1) an abundance of debitage relative to most Mississippian sites, (2) a predominance of Mill Creek chert, and (3) direct evidence of hoe manufacture in the form of large bifaces and very large thinning flakes. Even so, there is a possibility that some workshops overlaid earlier occupations. We occasionally recovered diagnostic artifacts from earlier time periods from a few of the workshops, although they were rare. This study makes the assumption that most of the debitage on the workshops dates to the Mississippian period, although uncontrolled error could be introduced by the mixing of earlier components that we did not recognize.

Many of the sites that we take to be workshops may in fact have had Mississippian residences as well. It will be remembered that at the turn of the century William Phillips (1900) documented the co-occurrence of domestic debris and hoe manufacturing debitage on some of the sites in the region, and he excavated in one of these so-called lodge sites (see chapter 5). There is no reason why a habitation and workshop should not coincide. Given the small amount of subsurface investigations carried out at the sites in the survey (usually through limited shovel testing), it is unclear how many of the sites may in fact have had structures and other domestic features. On the other hand, there are no known Mississippian sites in the locale—with the possible exception of some of the cemeteries—that lack workshops.

A total of 55 sites were documented during the survey phase of the research. These ranged in age from Archaic through Mississippian periods and also included a few twentieth-century homesteads. Of those sites directly related to Mill Creek chert hoe manufacture, 14 new workshops (Table 6.1) and two new quarries were identified (Figure 6.1).

One of the quarries was relatively large and situated on a ridge slope about 3 kilometers southwest of the Hale site (Figure 6.2). Pits on this site were scattered over an area of at least 10,000 square meters. A small quarry was also found about 400 meters north of the Hale site on a knoll known locally as "flint ridge." Only a few pits were visible on the ridge in a small, wooded area, but an adjoining pasture also was

Table 6.1. Hoe Workshops and Their Characteristics

Illinois Site No.	Site Area (m2)	Topography	Soil Type	Soil Character and Suitability for Row Crops	Collection Method	Debitage Count	Density per square m
U-564	7,200	base of ridge	Alford silt loam	well drained; good	shovel test	910	50
U-636	12,000	low knoll in floodplain	Alford silt loam	well drained; good	surface	1872	8
			Alford silty clay loam	well drained; poor			
U-641	3,600	creek floodplain	Wakeland silt loam	somewhat poorly drained; very good	excavation	1180	236
U-643	44,800	creek floodplain	Wakeland silt loam	somewhat poorly drained; very good	surface	1874	37
U-650	9,600	base of ridge/floodplain	Wakeland silt loam	somewhat poorly drained; very good	shovel test	1012	20
U-661	16,000	low knoll in floodplain	Wakeland silt loam	somewhat poorly drained; very good	surface	2016	112
U-662	26,000	low knoll in floodplain	Alford silt loam	well drained; good	surface	448	37
			Alford silty clay loam	well drained; poor			
U-665	14,400	high ridgetop	Alford silt loam	well drained; good	surface	668	9
AX-329	6,000	low knoll in floodplain	Stookey silt loam	somewhat poorly drained; very good	surface	334	7
			Wakeland silt loam	somewhat poorly drained; very good			
AX-332	35,200	creek floodplain	Elsah silt loam	well drained; fair	surface	177	2
			Hosmer silt loam	well drained; poor			
AX-338	126,000	creek floodplain	Wakeland silt loam	somewhat poorly drained; very good	surface	8065	74
U-635	5,000	ridgetop	Goss-Alford complex	well drained; good	Dillow's Ridge, excavations		
			Alford silt loam	well drained; good			
U-318*	16,800	terrace	Alford silty clay loam	well drained; poor	Hale site, probable area at least 3 ha		
U-653*	unknown	top of low ridge	Alford silty clay loam	well drained; poor			
AX-28*	unknown	low knoll in floodplain	Wakeland silt loam	somewhat poorly drained; very good			
			Alford silt loam	well drained; good			
U-77	unknown	top of low ridge	Hosmer silt loam	well drained; poor	documented in earlier survey		

*site visits, but unable to make collections.

Figure 6.2. Surface of quarry.

heavily scattered with Mill Creek chert debitage. It is possible that the pasture may originally have been part of the quarry proper, but plowing destroyed all traces of pits. This raises the issue of whether some of the sites we take to be workshops are actually heavily plowed quarries. Here we must rely on the observations of archaeologists earlier in the nineteenth and twentieth centuries, who in their frequent visits to the area mention only one other quarry in addition to the Indian Diggings (Phillips 1900). It is thus assumed that most of the sites identified as workshops were not primary areas of chert extraction.

With one exception (U-635), the physical character of the workshops differs markedly from those documented at certain lithic tool production centers like Colha, Belize, where there are deep accumulations of debitage (Shafer and Hester 1983). However, debitage density was much higher than the typical lithic scatters in eastern North America, with workshop collections averaging from a handful to hundreds of flakes per square meter of surface area (Table 6.1). For a site such as AX-332, where the density per square meter was very low (n = 2), one may question the validity of the appellation *workshop*. In this case, the presence of large, bifacial thinning flakes and occasional roughed-out hoes led us to designate it a workshop. Nevertheless, the variability evident within this category of site is suggestive of very complex organizational behaviors that comparative surface collections can only hint at.

The density of debitage and tool fragments across individual work-shops was quite uneven, possibly reflecting zones of more intensive flintknapping in high-density areas, and habitations or other activity areas in low-density areas (with plowing and topography possibly play-ing a role in surface distributions as well). As will be discussed in the following section, different artifact collection strategies also played a role in the variation in density between workshops. Artifact-bearing soils on workshops (with U-635 the exception) were inevitably shal-low and restricted to the plowzone—usually 30 centimeters or less in depth. Through the years, the churning effect of plowing has destroyed the stratigraphic integrity of these sites, although it is quite conceiv-able that feature remnants still survive below the plowzone.

Overall, the results of the survey showed that sites related to Mill Creek hoe manufacture were concentrated in an area measuring at least 15 square kilometers, with a sprinkling of sites outside of this zone. Not surprisingly, there is a cluster of workshops along You-Be Hollow near the main quarry. Importantly, a previously undocumented mound site with a hoe workshop (the Elco site) was located about 8 kilometers south of the Hale site. Although the site does not appear in any site records, I should point out that William Phillips shows a mound in this approximate location on one of his maps (Phillips 1900:40), and our discovery is more likely a rediscovery. The Elco site has a single mound about 3 meters high. It is now conical in shape, but the current landowner noted that it had been greatly modified by plowing. It is unknown whether the mound was originally conical or a platform, but its association with Mill Creek chert debitage and bro-ken hoes strongly suggests a Mississippian origin. Unfortunately, de-spite intensive searching, no ceramics were recovered from the surface of the site.

Likewise, ceramics were extremely scarce throughout the entire sur-veyed area. Only a handful of small fragments of shell-tempered ce-ramics was recovered from the entire sample of workshops. The poor survival rate of Mississippian shell-tempered ceramics in the culti-vated fields of southern and central Illinois has been remarked upon by several researchers (e.g., Harn 1978:243; Koldehoff 1989:46). How-ever, the fragments we found are at least suggestive of the presence of residential activities at a few of the workshops.

Workshops were located in different topographic settings, but were mainly found on low knolls or terraces in the floodplains of the local creeks (Table 6.1). In some cases, they were located on low to medium ridges. The size of the workshops varied greatly. The largest (excluding the Elco mound site), U-643, covered 44,800 square meters. It is likely

no accident that this large workshop was located in the floodplain below the ridge system where the main quarry is located. The distribution of waste flakes at the Elco site covered an area of about 126,000
square meters. At the other end of the scale, the smallest workshop was
3,600 square meters.

A review of 30 Mississippian sites in the uplands east of the American Bottom found that all of them were within 100 meters of Wakeland
soils (Woods 1987:283). This moderately well-drained and fertile type
of silt loam represents one of the best agricultural soils in that region, although it occurs only in scattered patches. Likewise, soils on
and around the hoe workshops in the Mill Creek locale typically were
those most favorable for maize agriculture—particularly the Wakeland
and Alford series. Although ceramics and other "domestic" debris are
sparse at these sites, their location on elevated landforms with arable,
productive soils reflects the typical pattern for Mississippian residential sites.

Our more restricted survey in localities farther away from the main
quarry and the Hale site indicated a substantial drop-off in the number
of workshops. For example, an extensive survey along Lingle Creek,
less than a mile north from the main quarry, failed to locate any workshops. Along You-Be Hollow, workshops disappear altogether about 1.5
kilometers west of the main quarry. Outlier workshops may cluster
around other quarries or streams rich in Mill Creek chert residuum,
possibly reflecting a patchy distribution of sites around suitable source
areas rather than a gradual fall-off from the main quarry. For example,
there is an isolated Mississippian farmstead and workshop near Dutch
Creek, about 13 kilometers north of the main quarry. Residents of this
site were apparently obtaining their chert from the creek bed, which
is rich in Mill Creek and other cherts.

George Milner (1986) has estimated a Mississippian population density range for the American Bottom (47.9 km^2) during the Stirling phase
(A.D. 1050–1150) of 14 to 46 persons per square kilometer. The two
numbers represent conservative and liberal estimates, respectively,
based on house structure longevity, with an average between the two
of 30 persons per square kilometer. For the Black Bottom, Muller
(1978:288) derived an estimate of about 21 persons per square kilometer, easily within the range set by Milner. If one takes the average of
their two figures (25.5 persons/km^2) and multiplies it by the area of
greatest concentration of Mill Creek chert quarries and workshops (15
km^2), a population estimate of 383 for the Mill Creek locale is reached.
Assuming that about 20 to 40 percent of the estimated inhabitants
were involved in manufacturing hoes, then between 77 and 153 flint-

knappers may have lived in the area at any one time—not really a significant number in light of some of the more grandiose projections about specialized production in the locale. Although population estimates based on archaeological data are notoriously unreliable, it is difficult to imagine more than a few hundred people at any one time lived in the locale.

It must be kept in mind that Milner's and Muller's estimates were for two extremely fertile bottomlands. It is likely that the population density in the Mill Creek locale was lower, on the basis of the limited agricultural productivity of the upland landscape. There are workshops, and presumably habitations, outside of the 15-square-kilometer zone used for my estimates, which would raise the potential number of flintknappers (e.g., the Dutch Creek farmstead). At the same time, it is unlikely that all of the workshops were contemporaneous. In short, while the significance of a movement of Mississippian populations to this upland setting should not be underemphasized, neither should the numbers of people living in the uplands be overplayed. The Mill Creek locale, as defined by the distribution of quarries and workshops, does not appear to have encompassed the amount and quality of arable land needed to have supported a very large population of flintknappers and their families. The small number of known sites with substantial habitation debris (the Hale and Dillow's Ridge sites) further supports this contention. Nevertheless, the presence of these sites, combined with the reports of stone box grave cemeteries in the region (Figure 6.1), indicates that people were living in the area, even if in relatively small numbers.

Underlying the estimates on population limits in the locale is the assumption that habitations are somewhat typical Mississippian year-round residences. The evidence presented in the following chapter for Dillow's Ridge suggests that this is true for at least some sites. The Hale site likely falls in this category as well. However, on the basis of our present level of information, it cannot be ruled out that some groups may have lived in the area on a part-time basis only. It is possible to imagine a scenario in which, for instance, early in the Mississippian period groups of flintknappers may have traveled to the source areas on a seasonal basis. Or, archaeologists who propose more complex models of political economy might argue for flintknappers working at and around the quarries, but supported by food distributed to them by elites outside of the locale; such groups would leave workshops but little in the way of the domestic remains we tend to associate with living areas. Although I consider the latter alternative to be particularly unlikely, the point should be made that further analyses rely on my assumption of year-round habitations.

LITHIC ACTIVITIES AT THE HOE WORKSHOPS

Collections were made from 12 of the 14 identified workshops. Artifact recovery from the quarries and workshops followed several widely used North American methods, predicated by surface visibility and land-use practices. Where land was forested or in pasture, artifacts were recovered using shovel test probes at 5-meter intervals. Shovel tests averaged about 30 to 40 centimeters in diameter and were excavated to subsoil, which could vary greatly from one location to another but usually was no more than 30 to 40 centimeters deep. Artifacts were recovered from shovel probe soils using screens with one-quarter-inch mesh.

One small (50 × 50 cm) unit was excavated at one site (U-641). The site was in a forested area, and an intermittent drainage had bisected an area of dense debitage at least 30 to 40 centimeters below ground surface. A formal excavation square represented the most expedient method of systematically evaluating the landform adjoining the stream.

In cultivated fields, artifacts were collected in one of two ways. If crops had not yet come up, a series of circular "dog-leash" units were collected. These were demarcated by laying a nail on a given coordinate on a site, then attaching a 3.37-meter-long string to the nail. Crew members would surface collect all artifacts within a radius around the nail defined by the length of the string. Where crops had grown to a sufficient size so as to interfere with the dog-leash method, rectangular collection units were placed along the crop rows. These were 2 meters long and 50 centimeters wide. Again, all surface artifacts were collected from these units. At first, an attempt was made to place surface collection units randomly. However, when it became evident that surface distributions of debitage were highly patchy, the decision was made to place collection units judgmentally in high-density areas so as to ensure a substantial debitage sample for analysis. It would have been possible to lay out a larger number of random units to ensure a representative debitage sample based on density, but I opted for a more expedient sample in order to devote more time to increasing the regional coverage of the site survey.

In addition to working with the surface collection units, the crew walked open fields and selectively collected diagnostic artifacts and bifaces. It should be pointed out that the numbers of bifaces on workshops is now greatly reduced from the substantial numbers reported by archaeologists earlier in the century. Local landowners have remarked that several decades ago the density of bifaces on some workshops was actually a hindrance to plowing; thus, through the years they have systematically removed hoe fragments and dumped them elsewhere. I have images of a lost "elephant's graveyard" piled high with broken hoes somewhere in the Mill Creek locale, but have yet to encounter it.

It is apparent that the different collection methods—some screened, some surface collected—and judgmental placement of both collection units and survey tracts disallow inferential statistical techniques for making quantitative estimates on the number of sites in the Mill Creek locale, or the abundance of debitage on a given site. For these reasons, results of the analyses carried out in the remainder of the chapter should be viewed as descriptive statements or preliminary models about lithic technology.

The past 20 to 25 years have seen a steady growth in the study of bifacial technological traditions, with great strides made in our understanding of fracture mechanics and the physical changes manifested in bifacial cores and waste flakes as a tool progresses through the manufacturing stages (e.g., Andrefsky 1998; Burton 1980; Magne 1989; Magne and Pokotylo 1981; Mauldin and Amick 1989; Newcomer 1971; Patterson 1990; Shott 1994; Stahle and Dunn 1982). Although there is much agreement on the general characteristics of biface reduction, there is much less unity on how best to reconstruct that process using the broken bifaces and debitage that make up the lithic record. In the remainder of the chapter, I attempt to demonstrate how certain tenets of reduction analysis and other lithic methodologies can be used to reconstruct the nature of tool production and use at hoe workshops.

A GENERALIZED HOE PRODUCTION SEQUENCE

As a prelude to the analysis, it is instructive to consider the general types of debitage created in the manufacture of a hoe. Preforms and blanks from quarry sites provide a good sense of the general stages of hoe manufacture (Figure 6.3). As pointed out, many of these artifacts have been removed from workshop sites and insufficient sample sizes survive to perform rigorous, comparative biface analyses. Waste flakes abound, however. Insights from debitage collections are used here to present a linear, normative model of hoe manufacture (Figure 6.4), with the understanding that discrete production stages are an artifice of our analysis rather than a technological reality. Different flake types are created at all points of manufacture, although certain attributes tend to predominate at various stages as a result of changes in flake removal strategies, for example, a shift from hard-hammer to soft-hammer percussors.

I have noted in earlier chapters how the lenticular shape of Mill Creek nodules provides a ready-made preform or blank for a hoe. For this reason, workshops yield a relatively small proportion of the angu-

Figure 6.3. Successive stages of manufacture for hoes of the flared variety.

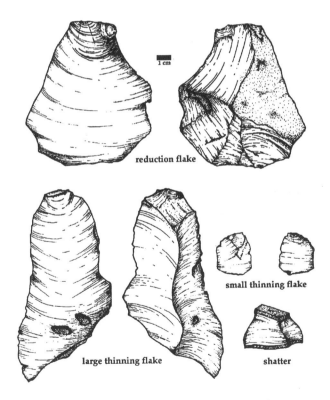

reduction flake

large thinning flake

small thinning flake

shatter

Figure 6.4. Flake types from hoe manufacture. (Drawn by Eric Drake.)

lar fragments usually associated with the early reduction of chert in either cobble or tabular form. Although Mill Creek chert quarries do contain a substantial amount of large, irregular pieces of chert, these appear to be mainly fragments from testing chert nodules.

The first step in hoe manufacture consisted of trimming irregularities (e.g., protrusions) from a lenticular piece of Mill Creek chert. This process was the one most likely to create the angular fragments that have a large amount of cortex. Next, some initial shaping was carried out to achieve a symmetrical biface shape. This stage is usually associated with sizable reduction flakes exhibiting pronounced bulbs of force, single-facet platforms approximately perpendicular to the flake surface, and varying amounts of cortex on the dorsal surface of the flake.

It is the next stage that is most singular in large biface production. Hoe workshops are characterized by extremely large bifacial thinning flakes. These flakes can be over 12 centimeters long and 6 centimeters wide and can weigh upward of 125 grams. In terms of discrete traits, the bifacial flakes appear like those in other traditions: they have a diffuse bulb of force and exhibit a multifaceted platform that is angled acutely to the surface of the flake. Because relatively little preparation of raw chert was necessary before moving to the detachment of large thinning flakes, they often exhibit cortical material, a trait not typically associated with bifacial flakes. In effect, middle stages of reduction and bifacial thinning constitute the same step in the production of hoes from Mill Creek chert. The platform lip of the large, bifacial flakes typically displays heavy grinding. In the Central Mississippi Valley, unusually large bifacial thinning flakes are diagnostic of hoe manufacture, and also have been documented at Kaolin chert workshops at Iron Mountain (Billings 1984), where hoes were manufactured on a smaller scale (Winters 1981).

Completion of the hoe involved a shift to the removal of progressively smaller bifacial thinning flakes in order to hone the edge of the implement and finalize its shape. Pressure flaking was not customarily used to sharpen the edges of the tool. Overall, due in large part to the close correlation in morphology between natural chert nodules and finished tools, the bifacial reduction of hoes appears to have been a somewhat abbreviated process compared with that of many other bifacial traditions.

There appears to have been a strong reliance on soft-hammer percussion throughout the production sequence. Two deer antler billets were recovered at Dillow's Ridge, tools that are rarely recovered because they do not preserve well. Hammerstones were extremely rare to absent in our workshop collections, and several seasons of excavations at Dillow's Ridge likewise found very few cobbles or durable, spherical stones that could be categorized as hammers. However, chert hammers have been recovered from the Mondino quarry (Brad Koldehoff, personal communication, 1999), and crude, spherical bifaces recovered from Dillow's Ridge (described in the following chapter) may also have served as hammerstones. It is possible that early-stage trimming of nodules relied heavily on rock hammers, with subsequent stages of hoe manufacture carried out primarily with soft-hammer billets made from antler and possibly hardwood.

BIFACE TRAJECTORIES

The biface trajectory analysis was directed toward describing and explaining variability (or lack thereof) in hoe manufacturing sequences between workshops. Two issues of central concern were (1) whether hoes appear to have been completed at one or more workshops and (2) whether there was a high degree of similarity in production between workshops. The study first considers general types of debitage present at the workshops, then compares them on the basis of an experimental data set created by Errett Callahan in the manufacture of two hoes. Finally, the biface trajectory study uses hoe collections from the Smithsonian Institution to evaluate whether there were significant differences in the staging of production between the main quarry and the Hale site.

Debitage Analysis I. The first portion of the analysis segregated the debitage from each workshop into four categories. These included the reduction and thinning flakes described above, as well as angular fragments and shatter. These categories are more explicitly defined as follows:

• Shatter: irregular pieces of chert that do not display classic flake attributes such as a platform. They often represent early stages of nodule reduction, or may be the by-products of flake production.

• Reduction flakes: waste flakes characterized by platforms approximately perpendicular to the body of the flake. Platforms tend to have one or two facets. Bulbs of force are pronounced, and dorsal scars are few to moderate in number. For hoes made from Mill Creek chert, reduction flakes typically have varying amounts of cortex. Reduction flakes are often associated with early to middle stages of biface manufacture, but may occur in later stages.

• Thinning flakes: flakes typical of advanced biface preparation, sometimes referred to as "flakes of bifacial retouch." Platforms are at an acute angle to the body of the flake, are multifaceted, and exhibit grinding. Dorsal scars are common. Although cortex tends to be absent, small amounts are not uncommon on thinning flakes from hoes.

In fact, larger thinning flakes may have 25 percent or so of the dorsal surface covered by cortex.

• Broken flakes: flakes that lack a platform and are not readily assigned to either reduction or thinning categories. Broken flakes often constitute a sizable proportion of biface technology (e.g., Mauldin and Amick 1989:84), but they may also develop as a result of post-depositional processes. Thus, the second portion of the debitage analysis focuses on intact flakes only.

Lithic studies have not found an easy compromise between the notion that biface manufacture may represent a staged process, based on shifts in reduction techniques and tools in the production sequence (e.g., Callahan 1979; Newcomer 1971), versus the idea that stone tool production is a continuum that is not easily segregated into stages (e.g., Sullivan and Rozen 1985). In some respects, this issue is a resuscitation of the Ford/Spaulding debate with respect to the "reality" of the analytical categories used by the lithic researcher. There is little question that qualitative changes occur in the creation of a biface, as tools and techniques shift to a more controlled removal of flakes. However, the process is not as discrete as it may sound, and a flintknapper's methods may occasionally move back and forth so that dissimilar flakes (e.g., reduction versus thinning flakes) may occur in the same stage even though one technique may predominate. Further, different knapping tools may produce the same flake type. A skilled knapper can remove small, bifacial flakes with a hammerstone, or large reduction flakes with a billet. As a consequence, the concept of stages rarely plays out as cleanly as one would hope, and the resulting flake assemblage assumes the characteristics of a continuum.

In practice, this means that the lithic analyst, depending on his or her viewpoint, can never be completely certain one hundred percent of the time whether a given flake is from an early stage, middle stage, or late stage; or exactly from where in the continuum it derives. In other words, we are dealing with probabilities rather than certainties (Teltser 1991). Although some seem to see this as a serious shortcoming (e.g., Shott 1994:77), I see it as a matter of the ontological ambiguity typical of archaeological types that can be systematically addressed, if not completely overcome. In particular, I believe, as Andrefsky (1998:126) advocates, that it is possible to model debitage assemblages from a population perspective, in which an individual flake analysis is used to create a general technological profile. Although there may be instances of incorrect flake classification, the overall pattern is still sensitive to technological characteristics.

Figure 6.5 displays the results of the debitage analysis of 11 of the 12 workshops (lithics from Dillow's Ridge are discussed in the follow-

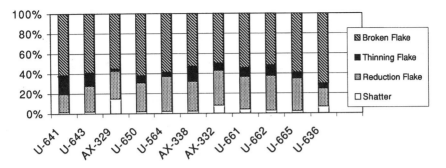

Figure 6.5. Workshop debitage categories.

ing chapter), relying on a technological profile comprised of shatter, reduction flakes, thinning flakes, and broken flakes (Table 6.2). An attempt was made to collect all flakes from each site's collection units to reduce the bias of collection strategy on the debitage patterns. Although there is variation in the percentage of flakes of the same type among sites, there are some regularities evident. Broken flakes are the most commonly represented debitage type. Reduction flakes are the second most commonly occurring debitage type on all of the sites. Thinning flakes and shatter are the least common types, although their proportions relative to each other are not constant across all of the sites. At AX-329, for example, shatter (15 percent) greatly outnumbers thinning flakes (1–2 percent), which constitute a small percentage of the lithic assemblage. This may be one case in which a workshop clearly demonstrates an emphasis on early-stage reduction. The opposite pattern is seen at U-641, where thinning flakes (19 percent) comprise a substantial portion of the debitage, but shatter represents only about 1 percent.

One inference arising from these results is that chert nodules were often carried to workshops with little advance preparation. The high proportions of reduction flakes on all of the sites, as well as the high proportions of shatter on many of the sites, suggest that substantial trimming and preparation of chert nodules took place at the workshops. Despite the intensive clearing of large bifaces from workshops by farmers, we did recover a number of roughed out hoes from several of the sites, confirming that some early-stage reduction was occurring away from the quarries.

As a rule of thumb, experimental biface trajectories contain a higher number of small, late-stage flakes and broken flakes than early-stage reduction flakes (Andrefsky 1998:115; Magne 1989:16; Patterson 1990). This trend is evidenced at the workshops by the high proportions of

Table 6.2 Counts and Percentages of Debitage Categories at Workshops

	U-564		U-636		U-641		U-643		U-650		U-661		U-662		U-665		AX-329		AX-332		AX-338	
	no.	%	no.	%	no.	%	no.	%	no.	%	no.	%	no.	%	no.	%	no.	%	no.	%	no.	%
Shatter	18	2	120	6	16	1	34	2	18	2	81	4	12	2	14	2	49	15	14	8	175	2
Reduction flake	319	35	337	18	212	18	482	26	291	29	657	33	156	35	219	33	96	29	62	35	2395	30
Thinning flake	40	4	96	5	228	19	255	14	77	7	184	9	48	11	41	6	5	1	13	7	1245	15
Broken Flake	533	59	1319	71	724	62	1103	58	626	62	1094	54	232	52	394	59	184	55	88	50	4250	53
Total	910	100	1872	100	1180	100	1874	100	1012	100	2016	100	448	100	668	100	334	100	177	100	8065	100

broken flakes, but the proportion of bifacial thinning flakes across workshops tends to be outnumbered by that of reduction flakes. The small percentages of thinning flakes may be a function of the abbreviated nature of biface production from lenticular nodules. Recovery bias may also play a role in the smaller number of thinning flakes, since surface pickup techniques are more likely to miss smaller artifacts.

There also is no clear trend in spatial patterning of debitage on workshops based on their relative distance from known quarries. Site U-641, which lies in the shadow of the main quarry, had one of the highest proportions of thinning flakes (19 percent) relative to reduction flakes (18 percent). Site U-564 is located about the same distance from the main quarry, but had a much greater proportion of reduction flakes (35 percent) than thinning flakes (4 percent). Both U-636 (5 percent) and AX-329 (1-2 percent) had a relatively small amount of thinning flakes, despite being farther from the main quarry than U-641 and U-564. Overall, there is no clear segregation across space with distance from the source as posited by William Phillips (1900:46) and William Holmes (1919:192–93), with early-stage reduction carried out at the main quarry and finishing conducted at the Hale site and other workshops. It is possible that the large, angular shatter from testing nodules that is prevalent at the main quarry skewed their perspective on the degree of separation between technological stages, an understandable error based on surface observations.

Debitage Analysis II. The second portion of the debitage analysis compared reduction and thinning flake assemblages from the workshops with a replica set of hoe debitage created by Errett Callahan. I also used amount of cortex as a proxy for approximate position in the reduction sequence. There is some debate over how useful cortex is in this regard (cf. Bradbury and Carr 1995; J. Johnson 1989; Mauldin and Amick 1989; Odell 1989; Shott 1994; Sullivan and Rozen 1985; Tomka 1989), but the replica set suggested that it was pertinent to biface reduction with Mill Creek chert.

Callahan segregated the debitage into four general categories based on methods of flake removal (Table 6.3). His first stage consisted of hammerstone percussion and was composed entirely of flakes that would fit the reduction flake definition that I have used. His second stage involved heavy billet percussion, which he also denoted as "bifacial contouring." This was dominated by reduction flakes, but with much less cortex, on the average, than seen in the first stage. The last two stages, secondary finishing and finishing, resulted in debitage created by billet percussion and pressure flaking. These flakes had all been combined into a single bag; they will be referred to as stage 3 debitage here.

Table 6.3 Hoe Replica Debitage

Stage 1: hammerstone percussion

Flake type	Cortex %	No.
Reduction	25–100	22
Reduction	0–25	28

Stage 2: heavy billet percussion

Flake type	Cortex %	No.
Reduction	25–100	28
Reduction	0-25	60
Thinning	25-75	1
Thinning	0-25	10

Stages 3 & 4: billet & tine

Flake type	Cortex %	No.
Reduction	0–25	21
Thinning	25-75	5
Thinning	0–25	104

Not surprisingly, there was overlap between the technological stages in terms of the flake categories I have employed. Thinning flakes, for instance, were created in the second stage, whereas reduction flakes were still by-products of the final two stages. From a population perspective, however, there are clear trends evident. Using the attribute of flake type (reduction versus thinning) with the attribute of cortex on the dorsal surface of the flake, there is a movement toward less cortex and greater representation of thinning flakes from earlier to later portions of hoe manufacture. With these data, I have created a three-flake typology to guide the analysis: (1) reduction flake I, that is, reduction flakes with 25 percent or more of the dorsal surface covered by cortex; (2) reduction flake II, reduction flakes with less than one-quarter of the dorsal surface covered by cortex; and (3) thinning flakes (Table 6.4).

In Figure 6.6, the relative frequencies of the three flake types from the hoe replica are represented as a cumulative frequency graph, as are similar flake categories from the workshops. Note that I am not making a one-to-one correspondence between flake types and reduction stages. This figure merely demonstrates the relative proportions of flake types evident when all of the reduction sequence is represented from a population perspective. Based on Callahan's hoe replica, the

Table 6.4 Replica and Workshop Flake Frequencies

	replica		U-564		U-636		U-643		U-650		U-661		U-662		U-665		AX-329		AX-332		AX-338	
	no.	%	no.	%	no.	%	no.	%	no.	%	no.	%	no.	%	no.	%	no.	%	no.	%	no.	%
Reduction I	50	0.179	50	0.139	88	0.203	168	0.222	24	0.238	60	0.071	49	0.240	90	0.346	90	0.891	19	0.253	775	0.213
Reduction II	109	0.391	269	0.749	249	0.575	333	0.440	72	0.713	597	0.710	107	0.525	129	0.496	6	0.059	43	0.573	1620	0.445
Thinning	120	0.430	40	0.111	96	0.222	255	0.337	5	0.050	184	0.219	48	0.235	41	0.158	5	0.050	13	0.173	1245	0.342
Total	279	1.000	359	1.000	433	1.000	756	1.000	101	1.000	841	1.000	204	1.000	260	1.000	101	1.000	75	1.000	3640	1.000

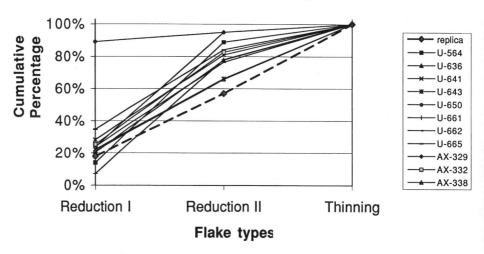

Figure 6.6. Workshop debitage cumulative graphs.

relative proportions of the three flake types create a relatively straight line.

When the workshop flakes were transformed into cumulative graphs, a moderate degree of variability was evident between sites. One site (AX-329) departs most strongly from the general trend, with a high proportion (89 percent) of reduction I flakes. While this might be indicative of an emphasis on early-stage reduction at the site, AX-329 also has the smallest sample size (n = 329), which could also be problematic. It did, however, also have a high proportion of shatter, as pointed out in the analysis in the previous section. Another strong pattern is the smaller proportions of thinning flakes recovered from the workshops relative to the replica data, and corresponding high proportions of reduction II flakes. Reduction I flakes typically occurred in higher proportions than in the experimental set, with three exceptions, U-661 (7 percent), U-564 (14 percent), and U-641 (14 percent).

The proportion of thinning flakes could potentially be attributed to at least two factors. First, the Callahan replica set did not contain, in my opinion, the very large thinning flakes typical of large biface traditions in southern Illinois. He may have compensated by producing a larger number of small thinning flakes than did prehistoric flintknappers to achieve a final product. Alternatively, final touching up of bifaces may have occurred at one or more transit sites (e.g., the Hale site) before they were exchanged out of the locale. The latter possibility is intriguing in that it would suggest some degree of higher-order control over the structure of biface production, although the accuracy of replica sets for comparative purposes is, unfortunately, always open to question. Thus, this latter possibility must remain as such based on the lithic data, although I will have more to say on it based upon other lines of evidence.

It should be pointed out, nonetheless, that the variability between the workshop data sets could be used to argue against any degree of centralized control over hoe production. In other words, there may have been substantial autonomy or lack of coordination in manufacturing from one locus to another, such that rough nodules may have been reduced to complete hoes at one location, whereas at another workshop hoes may have arrived partially completed from a quarry, then were completed at the workshop. Or, through time, multiple strategies may be represented at any one workshop. The impact of different sampling strategies on the range of variability is always a concern, of course. If the small sample sizes for some of the workshops (e.g., AX-329) are truly reflective of small amounts of hoe manufacturing debitage, it raises the possibility that some of the sites designated as workshops may have instead been small residential occupations that were producing largely for domestic consumption.

Comparison of Bifaces. Production trajectories may also be compared by using bifaces. Although many of the workshops have been stripped of hoes, workers in the 1800s collected samples of large bifaces from both the main quarry and Hale sites, which are now curated at the Smithsonian Institution. These samples, although judgmental, can be used to make quantitative, descriptive comparisons between the two sites. They are particularly useful since significant debitage collections were not available from either site.

I restricted the analysis to bifaces that were mainly whole and were recognizable as hoe preforms (incomplete bifaces). Because of the lenticular shape of the nodules, hoes appear to have assumed shape rapidly in the reduction sequence, so that even very early-stage bifaces are recognizable as hoes (see Figure 6.3). The sample size included 65 preforms from the quarry and 14 from the Hale site. Many appear to have not been completed as a result of reduction flaws such as extensive hinging or various kinds of fractures. I first categorized the preforms into stages of manufacture generally following Callahan's (1979) criteria (Table 6.5): stage 1 bifaces were crudely worked though generally symmetrical, thick, and with an undulating edge created by prepared platforms. Stage 2 bifaces were further completed than stage 1 specimens, as witnessed by a more symmetrical shape, a thinner cross section, and evidence for some degree of advanced thinning of the tool edge. Stage 3 bifaces were complete to near-complete tools, with a thin cross section and advanced thinning along the tool margins. A chi-square test of these data, comparing relative proportions of stage types

Table 6.5 Chi-Square Analysis
of Biface Stages

Contingency Table

Biface Stage	Hale Site	Main Quarry
1	7	26
2	4	10
3	3	29

Chi-square	d.f.	Probability
3.04	2	0.22

by site, indicated that there was no significant difference between the quarry and Hale sites at a 0.05 level of probability (p = 0.22).

A t-test was also used with the bifacial data in order to evaluate the chi-square results from another perspective, using continuous rather than nominal measurements. To convert hoe preform morphology into a continuous scale, a variation of Jay Johnson's (1981) thinning index was used. In his study, Johnson divided the weight of the artifact by its plan view area, arriving at an index expressed as grams per square centimeter. Generally speaking, high index values within a lithic tradition are associated with early-stage production, whereas low values indicate late-stage production. One advantage of the thinning index is that it is not dependent upon qualitative classification of biface stages.

Johnson arrived at his plan view value by a complex and labor-intensive process using polar grid coordinates derived from photocopy outlines of individual bifaces. For my study, I used a shortcut approach and calculated the same value by measuring the length and width of the biface along approximate midpoints to obtain a plan area in square centimeters. The weight of the biface was then divided by this number to obtain a value of grams per square centimeter. The descriptive statistics for the thinning index distributions are reported in Table 6.6. A two-tailed t-test of these data was not significant at the 0.05 level of probability (p = 0.08). The t-test suggests that there is no statistical difference in staging between the quarry and Hale sites, on the basis of their respective average thinning index values.

Both the chi-square and t-test statistics suggest that biface reduction strategies at the quarry and Hale sites were similar, although the selective nature of the sample makes this a descriptive conclusion rather than an inferential one. Nevertheless, in a regional perspective, these results do not support a strict segregation of biface technology

Table 6.6 T-Test of Thinning Index

Descriptive Statistics	Main Quarry	Hale Site
Mean	156.65	247.21
Maximum	347.00	433.00
Minimum	41.00	92.00
S.D.	71.01	105.04
N	65.00	14.00

t value	d.f.	Probability
1.89	13	0.08

across space, in contradiction to the observations of Phillips (1900) and Holmes (1919). The results further indicate that producers at the various loci may have had equal access to source areas and were autonomously manufacturing hoes, a conclusion somewhat supported by the debitage from the workshops. It is also noteworthy that the Smithsonian collection contains complete or nearly complete bifaces from the main quarry. These specimens indicate that flintknappers—at least occasionally—were finishing hoes within the confines of the primary source area.

PRODUCTION ESTIMATES

Various lithic studies have attempted to derive estimates for the number of tool types produced over a given span of time, based upon quantities of recovered debitage (e.g., Mallory 1986; Sassaman 1994b; Singer and Ericson 1977). Such estimates are fraught with problems and should be taken as gross measures at best. A primary difficulty is that no single tool type is usually manufactured at any one location. Thus, one may be estimating numbers of dart points produced at a workshop, when in reality endscrapers, knives, adzes, and other tools may have been produced as well. Chronological control poses another problem. Not only is it difficult to assess when a site was occupied and deserted, but also the intensity of tool production may have varied through time. Production estimates tend to average across these difficulties. Despite these and other problems, production estimates may be of some value if they are used in a very relative sense to monitor very general spatial and diachronic patterns—and if one does not grow too attached to the numbers.

Michael Gramly (1992) has excavated several Dover chert hoe workshops in Tennessee, providing the only lithic data that are comparable to those from Mill Creek chert workshops. He estimated that producers were making more than 3,200 hoes and other large tools a year per workshop. His figures led him to conclude that flintknappers were working a substantial part of the day making stone tools, and that they could be viewed as full-time specialists. Muller (1997:337–40) has taken these estimates to task on several counts. Foremost, Gramly proposed a one-year life span for the workshops, which is highly problematic because workshops and quarries are notoriously difficult to date. Muller also pointed out that Gramly made several mathematical errors in his calculations; when revised, the stone tool estimates fell by about 90 percent. On the basis of the new numbers, it could be argued that stone tool production, even of hoes that presumably were exported, could have easily fit into the yearly round of "domestic" activities.

For this study, I have derived estimates for Mill Creek chert hoe production based on excavation collections from site U-636, one of the moderate-sized workshops. The purpose of this particular analysis is to provide a general cautionary note about hoe production estimates when conservative parameters are used. My calculation rests upon time and debitage estimates from the manufacture of two experimental hoes by Errett Callahan (Cobb 1988). The average time of manufacture was 2.17 hours, with 263 waste flakes created in the reduction of a nodule to a finished tool. Although it is very likely that other tools were made at the workshops, I will assume that hoes were the primary product with the knowledge that this assumption will inflate the hoe numbers somewhat.

A key obstacle to estimating the number of hoes produced per workshop using surface collections is that they represent only a two-dimensional transverse of debitage. Without controlling for depth of deposits, these data would lead to underestimates of hoe production. In order to incorporate a volumetric component into the estimates, 10 1 × 1-meter units were excavated at site U-636. The units were placed at 5-meter intervals running down a low ridge that constituted the central part of the site based upon our observations of surface artifact density. Like the other workshops, U-636 had been plowed at one time. Culture-bearing deposits were relatively shallow at the site, on the order of 20 to 30 centimeters. The 10 units yielded a total of 4,738 flakes with a one-quarter-inch screening method, for an average of approximately 474 flakes per 1 × 1-meter unit.

Put another way, one could extrapolate that every square meter of surface area on a workshop on the average contains about 474 flakes from surface to sterile deposits. Using the site area estimates from

Table 6.7 Estimates of Hoe Production for U-636

Estimated Flakes*	Estimated Hoes**	Estimated Hours***
5685600	21618.25	46911.60

Years	Total Hoes	Hoes/day
2	10809	29.6
20	1081	3.0
200	108	0.3

*site area (12,000 square m) x 473.8 flakes
** estimated flakes/263
***estimated hoes x 2.17

Table 6.1, it is then possible to use this base figure to estimate the total number of flakes at the workshop on the basis of volume, rather than just surface area. Table 6.7 presents a summary of the estimates.

At this point I should emphasize that I have not forgotten my own warnings. Yet, forgetting for a moment lack of chronological control, and intrasite variability in debitage density, it is still instructive to examine the numbers. I find it very unlikely that workshops were used for a single year, or for even a few years. This skepticism has been fueled in part by our excavations at Dillow's Ridge, which show at least a 200-year occupation span for that site. The numbers in Table 6.7 use 2-, 20-, and 200-year site duration estimates as a way of showing extremes of production at either end of the spectrum, as well as a middle-range value. For a 20-year period, the number of hoes per day is only three, and, looking at the calculations for a 200-year workshop span, production estimates are very small indeed (0.3 hoes/day). On the other hand, if one wishes to push for a short span for workshops, then fairly impressive numbers of hoes per year for U-636 (over 10,000) can perhaps be used to support a scenario of fairly intensive production.

Given that these numbers do rest upon a shaky foundation, it is not useful to push for too much additional interpretation from them. Stretching these numbers to other workshops is a tenuous enterprise as well, given likely variation in occupation spans and intensity of production. Two points seem clear, however. First, if a location is used repeatedly for the manufacture of stone tools, an impressive amount of waste flakes will accumulate no matter what kind of specialization is occurring. This will become markedly clear in the descriptions of the Dillow's Ridge site. Second, despite the numbers of flakes estimated to be lying beneath the ground at the Mill Creek chert workshops, it seems reasonable to argue—much as Muller (1997) has for the Dover chert workshops—that the actual number of hoes produced per person need not have been inordinately high. The latter point becomes especially important with regard to the alternative explanation that, given the modest estimated population for the region, quantities of hoes produced per flintknapper must have been high. Although I would argue the evidence points the other way, to be on firmer ground with these kinds of numbers we not only need more secure data on formation processes and the number and contemporaneity of sites, but we also require detailed studies of consumption rates of hoes at the various consumer regions—information that we unfortunately do not have at this time.

The only longitudinal perspective on hoe production is provided by the Petitt site, located about 20 kilometers southwest of the Mill Creek locale on the east bank of the Mississippi River in Illinois. Despite its distance from the known quarry areas, this Emergent Mississippian occupation described in the previous chapter yielded the range of early- and late-stage Mill Creek chert debitage typical of hoe production (Parry 1992). However, the amount of debris is suggestive of low-intensity production and the site does not contain workshop areas in the more restricted sense used here. The amount of hoes available for export after immediate consumption would have been very small, even compared with the conservative estimates I use for the Mill Creek chert workshops.

The Petitt site data, in conjunction with the hoe workshop data, are useful for forwarding several working hypotheses about hoe production. First, access to the Mill Creek chert source areas does not seem to have been highly restricted prior to the Mississippian period, if groups along the Mississippi River could obtain nodules. Second, while the onset of significant production of large, Mill Creek chert hoes can be traced to the Emergent Mississippian period (also reflected by hoe resharpening flakes at contemporary sites in the American Bottom, chapter 3), the appearance of large-scale quarrying and associated workshops may date specifically to the Mississippian period. The latter point is supported by the lack of Emergent Mississippian sherds from any of our survey sites, despite the fact that the grog-tempered ceramics of that era have a much better survival rate in the ground than do shell-tempered wares. Here it is worth noting that recent analyses of a sample of lithics from Wickliffe Mounds, only about 30 kilometers south of the source areas, indicate that Mill Creek chert hoe production debitage is absent from all Mississippian components, although recycling debris is commonplace (Koldehoff and Carr 2001). Thus, the florescence of quarrying and the development of substantial workshops appear to occur early in the Mississippian period, and this development may signal the closure of access to the source areas to Mississippian groups outside of the uplands.

ANCILLARY ACTIVITIES

That the Mill Creek workshops were not loci of highly specialized, intensive hoe manufacture is supported by other lines of evidence. It will be remembered that William Phillips (1900) found evidence that at least some of these sites were habitations as well. Despite the apparent poor preservation of shell-tempered ceramics in the local soils, a few of the sites did contain pottery. It thus appears that at least some of the workshops discovered in our survey were likely residential sites.

The presence of activities unrelated to hoe manufacture is reflected by the variety of other tools found on the workshops. Formal bifacial tools were extremely rare on the workshops, and it is possible that the long history of amateur surface collecting in the region has depleted the number of arrowheads and other bifaces. Given that these sites are primarily Mississippian, however, it can be expected that expedient tools would still represent the primary tool category.

Table 6.8 clearly demonstrates the variety of flake tools found at all of the workshops. Utilized flakes (n = 1,387) are the most numerous tools and represent about 62 percent of the total. This category includes flakes that exhibit intentional retouch or else the kind of "nibbled" margin that results from briefly sawing or scraping with a flake edge. Flakes were also commonly used as scrapers at all of the sites (n = 362), comprising a little over 16 percent of all of the tools. These flakes exhibit the steeply beveled edge associated with hide working and similar activities. Notches (or spokeshaves), another common type, have a pronounced concavity along one or more of the flake edges. These are often assumed to have been used for shaving arrow shafts and other cylindrical objects. Gravers, used for scoring or perforating, were identified at all of the workshops except one, although they were less abundant than notches. Denticulates, presumably used for sawing, occurred at most of the sites, although in substantially smaller num-

Table 6.8. Workshop Tools

Tool Type	U-564	U-636	U-641	U-643	U-650	U-661	U-662	U-665	AX-329	AX-332	AX-338	Total	Percent.
Utilized Flake	5	9	21	13	13	32	9	1		2	200	305	26
Arrow Point							1					1	<1
Point Preform						1	1					2	<1
Biface				4			4					8	1
Pick				1								1	<1
Adze						1	1		1			3	<1
Scraper	3	22	4	54	11	21	15	23	3	4	202	362	31
Denticulate	1	1	1	3	3	3	2	3		1	33	51	4
Graver	4	8		7	4	13	8	15	1	8	71	139	12
Notch	1	17	1	17	11	8	5	16		3	101	180	15
Multipurpose		11		18	3	15	2	5		3	57	114	10
Total	14	68	27	117	45	94	48	63	5	21	664	1166	100

bers than the other flake tool types. Multifunctional flakes were also somewhat common. These exhibit two or more patterns of use, such as a notch on one margin and a steeply beveled edge on another.

The flake tools were classified by general morphology and overt signs of use rather than microwear, and it is likely that a functional analysis of debitage under magnification would have elevated the count even higher. It should be emphasized that the precise functions associated with these categories are open to question in the absence of detailed microscopic analyses. The important point for this study, however, is not the exact activities represented by the presumed functions of the tools and their relative proportions. Instead, it is that all of the workshops display evidence for a range of activities taking place in addition to the production of hoes and other large tools for export. It is quite likely that hides, wood, and other materials were transformed at these loci into items of everyday use.

It has been observed elsewhere that quarry and workshop sites may demonstrate signs of manufacturing activity beyond the production of stone tools, the logic being that groups may have taken advantage of a ready abundance of raw material and stone tools to carry out tasks not so easily accomplished at living sites where stone might be in short supply (Gramly 1984). Although this rationale does make sense for mobile hunter-gatherers, a more likely explanation for sedentary groups is that the mixture of workshop debris and items not being produced for export reflects the juxtaposition of flintknapping and living areas (see, for example, Shafer 1985).

REGIONAL CONSIDERATIONS

At this point it is useful to step back and consider what the lithic evidence from the workshops may say about the regional organization of production. Perhaps most important from a perspective that privileges the notion of labor, there is not strong evidence for an intensity of manufacturing that would warrant arguments supporting highly specialized hoe production. From what we know about Mississippian domestic economies, it appears that the manufacture of hoes in all likelihood could have been accommodated within the daily round of activities. Second, there appears to have been a wide range of activities in addition to flint working carried out within the confines of what we refer to as "workshops." It is quite likely that some—if not all—of these sites were the loci of seasonal or year-round habitations where hide working, tool rejuvenation, food preparation, and other domestic activities took place. Finally, there does not seem to be a strong degree of regional structure to hoe production, as was once thought. Hoes seem to have been completed throughout the Mill Creek locale, and raw material was available from a number of sources despite the impressive size of the main quarry. Moreover, although the mound "centers" of Hale and Elco have lithic workshops, the small size of these communities speaks more to their status as firsts among equals. There is no clearly differentiated site-size hierarchy of the sort we associate with Mississippian polities in the larger floodplains.

There is little question that the development of the large biface technology, the work invested in quarrying, and the number of bifaces produced over the course of several centuries are impressive achievements. Nevertheless, the complexity of the organization of labor required to maintain the entire system does not appear to have exceeded that associated with most other typical Mississippian settlement systems. Indeed, despite the likelihood of some degree of part-time specialization, the evidence for centralization (here defined as supralocal political authority) is in fact quite weak. The wide spatial distribution of workshops and quarries suggests a very extensive system with groups conducting chert extraction and hoe manufacture autonomously.

Of course, the lack of a spatial manifestation of centralization does not have to correspond with the absence of political centralization; centralized control over spatially extensive resources is feasible for more powerful polities. However, political centralization also is not apparent from the mortuary evidence, in which one would presumably see signs of clear social differentiation if one or more individuals had the power to monopolize chert sources and the production of hoes.

The largest known cemetery in the region was the stone box grave mound at the Hale site. In 1882 the mound was apparently excavated in its entirety by the Smithsonian, yielding more than 30 burials. As one of the workers reported, "we dug that mound on Mr. Hale's land all to pieces" (Thing 1882). Despite the lack of modern methodology, the contents of the graves were reported in some detail by nineteenth-century standards (Thomas 1894). The burial goods are fairly mundane by Mississippian standards (Table 6.9). They consist of Mississippian plainware vessels, bone pins, ornaments of turtle carapace, and other, presumably locally made, goods (Figure 6.7). Nonlocal materials included traces of copper and some galena. Some additional graves were located and excavated at the Hale site in the 1970s by a graduate student, and copper earspools and galena, among other items, were reportedly recovered (May 1984; Winters 1981). One of the current Hale site landowners is in possession of a fluorspar bead necklace from this work. Galena is available in southeastern Missouri (Walthall 1981) and fluorspar is found in southeastern Illinois, and these materials speak to regional trade, but certainly not any privileged access to nonlocal,

Table 6.9 Mortuary Goods from the Hale Site

Grave	General Age	Burial Goods	Other
1	unknown	unknown	contents missing
2	not given	*Unio* shells, turtle shell, pottery frags.	
3	unknown	unknown	contents missing
4	not given	2 bifaces, antler, perforated bone	skull supported on deer antler
5	unknown	unknown	contents missing
6	not given	none	
7		few pebbles	
8		few pebbles	
9	infant	lead ore (galena), 8-10 bifaces	
10	infant	2 bifaces	
11	infant	none	
12	adult	small jar	
13	infant	none	
14		2 pieces "fossil" wood	
15	adult	none	
16	adult	none	
17,18,19			no information
20		shell beads, red paint (ochre?)	
21	infant	galena, perforated univalve shells	
22	infant	1 gastropod shell	
23	2 infants	none	
24	not given	shell beads	around waist
25	not given	wooden beads	copper stains
26	not given	bone needle, copper flakes, woven bark matting, wooden bead	copper stains on bark and bead
27	not given	none	
28	not given	none	copper stains by skull (earspools?)
29	not given	effigy pot	
30	not given	drilled bone "plates"	
31	not given	none	
32	child	jar	
33	3 interments	*Unio* shells, yellow "paint", 2 pebbles	

exotic materials, or even unusually large amounts of regionally available materials. The copper is noteworthy because it clearly is not local, but the small amounts recovered are typical for Mississippian cemeteries, even rural ones.

A concerted effort was made by the Smithsonian workers to locate and excavate as many cemeteries as possible in the locale, given the

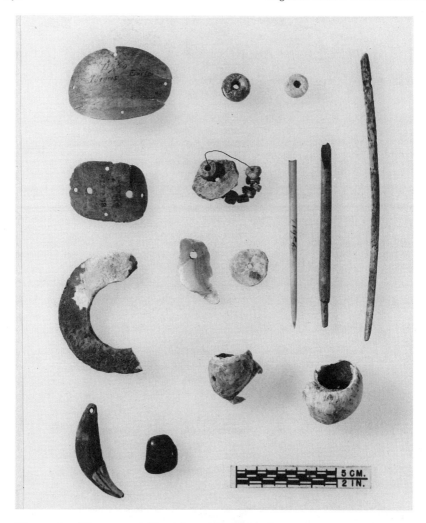

Figure 6.7. Mortuary artifacts from the Hale site.

well-known association of fancy goods with the easily located stone box graves. Three additional stone box cemeteries are described in the reports and archives (Thing 1882; Thomas 1894), and at least two were excavated. The descriptions of the burial goods suggest the presence of a few ceramic vessels and little else. Another stone box cemetery north of Dillow's Ridge has been subject to some pothunting earlier in the century, but no descriptions of the grave goods have been reported.

Overall, two key conclusions from the workshop results are supported by the lack of a clearly defined site-size hierarchy, the distribution of stone box cemeteries, and the contents of the known burials.

First, habitation in the region was likely dispersed, and not limited to one or two sites. Second, the inhabitants were probably small-scale specialists working in the absence of a centralized production system overseen by powerful Mississippian elites.

Yet such conclusions are not entirely satisfactory. The argument being made is that in one sense the Mill Creek biface production system was not exceptional; that it fit within the realm of possibilities of sustained production without centralization that has been documented for other Mississippian regions. To leave the matter there is to deny history, however. It is impossible to believe that there was not considerable diversity in the daily structure of Mississippian labor and lifeways. Categories such as "egalitarian" or "decentralized" and the like obscure what we would really like to know about daily life for flintknappers. It is thus important to scrutinize in more detail the wider range of activities taking place within a settlement/workshop. Such information would allow us to understand more precisely how hoe manufacture may have articulated with other daily activities. Further, it would indicate how the arrangement of daily life and labor within the Mill Creek locale may have differed from that of other Mississippian regions. For these questions we are fortunate that we have detailed excavation data from a superbly preserved village and lithic workshop known as Dillow's Ridge.

7 Hoe Production and the Domestic Economy

Undisturbed sites, while not unheard of, are certainly a rarity in eastern North America. Mechanized cultivation, the development of towns and cities, the growth of highways, and other products of our modern life have wreaked havoc on the archaeological record. Nevertheless, a small number of undisturbed sites do occur throughout the Eastern Woodlands. *Undisturbed* is a relative term, because the natural landscape is not static. Freeze/thaw action, burrowing animals, erosion, and uprooted trees are but a few of the many processes and events that move artifacts and alter cultural features. However, the distorting effect of natural processes on the archaeological record often is overshadowed by human agents. For that reason, North American archaeologists often refer to sites that have suffered minimal impact from cultivation or urbanization as "undisturbed" or "unplowed." The rare opportunity to excavate an undisturbed site provides a sobering insight into what we have lost. For example, excavators at the Lab Woofie site, an unplowed Mississippian habitation in west-central Illinois, estimated that 50 percent of the features were relatively shallow and would have been lost to modern cultivation practices (Prentice and Mehrer 1981:34).

One of the most important finds of our research in the Mill Creek locale—indeed, one of the most important archaeological discoveries in southern Illinois in recent years—was an unplowed site known as Dillow's Ridge. This Mississippian village and hoe workshop is located about 1 kilometer southwest of the main quarry described in previous chapters (see Figure 6.1). Of all the sites identified during our work, Dillow's Ridge is the only one that yielded substantial evidence for living remains—not because it necessarily represents a unique site type in the locale, but because its location on an isolated hilltop spared it from modern cultivation. As a consequence, Dillow's Ridge has provided an excellent glimpse into the everyday life of those peoples involved in the production of Mill Creek chert hoes.

In the following pages I describe the results of three seasons of fieldwork at Dillow's Ridge, from 1993 to 1995. This site is the only one in the Mill Creek locale that has been intensively excavated and documented by modern standards. Although Dillow's Ridge cannot be unquestioningly used as an archetype for all settlements involved in hoe production, our research there can be used to generate a number of important baseline statements about specialization and daily life in the Illinois uplands during the Mississippian period. Refinements and revisions to these ideas hopefully will be generated by additional research in the future.

Dillow's Ridge also provides the opportunity to clarify the articulation between "domestic" activities and the organization of hoe manufacture. In the only comparable study in the region, Jon Muller's (1997; Muller and Renken 1989) work at the Great Salt Springs in southeastern Illinois suggests Mississippian groups lived there only part of the year, supporting his contention that salt production was intermittent and deeply embedded within the domestic economy. The lithic workshop assemblages from the Mill Creek locale in themselves do not provide adequate data for making comparisons with his conclusions, or those of other studies on specialization, because they are primarily surface collections. Dillow's Ridge, on the other hand, contains the intact subsurface deposits to make more accurate estimates of the range and intensity of stone tool production than we could with surface collections, as well as the radiocarbon samples to establish a measure of chronological control. Unusually rich midden deposits have also yielded a diverse corpus of ceramics and organic remains with which to flesh out a picture of everyday life. Finally, Dillow's Ridge provided the possible opportunity to clarify one of the great conundrums in Mississippian political economy: What were regionally specialized producers obtaining in exchange for their goods?

SITE SETTING AND DESCRIPTION

Dillow's Ridge is located on a northeast extension of a large ridge system 1 kilometer southwest of the main quarry and about 2.4 kilometers west of the Hale site. It occupies a small hilltop about 35 meters above the floodplain of an intermittent creek known as You-Be Hollow. The site covers the entire hilltop, extending about 80 meters east-west and 60 meters north-south. The west, north, and east sides of the landform are relatively steep. Moderately sloping finger ridges radiate downward in several directions from Dillow's Ridge, providing relatively accessible approaches. South of the hilltop a narrow saddle leads to the larger ridge system.

The nearest water source to Dillow's Ridge is You-Be Hollow, which runs near the northern and eastern flanks of the hill. According to local landowners, the drainage followed the base of the hill before it was channelized and moved farther north. You-Be Hollow has running water only on a periodic basis, but even in the height of summer usually has standing pools that would have provided a reliable water supply. It is questionable whether You-Be Hollow would ever have been viable for watercraft, but Dillow's Ridge is only 2.5 kilometers west of Mill Creek, which provided easy access south to the Cache and Ohio rivers.

Whereas drainages provided a southerly route to the Ohio River (about 27 km away) for Dillow's Ridge inhabitants, access to the Mississippi River 14 kilometers to the west is hampered by about 5 kilometers of rugged Illinois Ozarks. The hills form a steep drainage divide, and there is no straightforward east-west passage in the locale. Certainly, the linear distance between the Mill Creek locale and the Mississippi River to the west is not that far, but in the context of this study, moving significant numbers of large bifaces through a region of substantial vertical relief may have posed some logistical challenges. The significance of those challenges to prehistoric peoples, however, can easily be overestimated by the sedentary academic.

A distinctive aspect of Dillow's Ridge is the presence of 27 shallow depressions that pockmark the ground surface. These basins represent the eroded remnants of Mississippian semi-subterranean houses. Mississippian houses in the Midwest and Midsouth are usually square to rectangular with the floor excavated to subsoil. Wall support posts were placed in trenches, giving rise to the term "wall-trench" houses. Larger support posts were frequently added in the middle of the structure to uphold the roof. Historic evidence suggests that these houses were of single-gable construction, typically with a thatched roof (Figure 7.1). The exteriors were often covered with daub.

Interior features of Mississippian houses included hearths and a variety of storage and preparation pits. External pit features usually surround structures as well. Historic accounts describe winter and summer houses among some Southeastern communities (Adair 1930 [1775]:404; Bartram 1955 [1791]:55–56; Romans 1962 [1775]:96). Winter houses usually were substantial structures that provided protection against cold and wet weather, and summer houses were often represented by open structures. The *household*, as opposed to the *house*, could also include other outbuildings such as storage structures. In

Figure 7.1. Mississippian structure and farmstead. (From *The Archaeology of Carrier Mills: 10,000 Years in the Saline Valley of Illinois,* by Richard W. Jefferies; illustrated by Thomas W. Gatlin; copyright 1987 by the Board of Trustees, Southern Illinois University.)

the archaeological record, winter houses are often inferred by wattle-and-daub construction with basin and wall trenches, whereas summer houses are presumed to be manifested by single-post structures. Paired houses of this sort have been most obvious at certain Southeastern sites (e.g., Hally 1993a; Polhemus 1990; Sullivan 1995). In the Midwestern archaeological record, this distinct duality has been the exception rather than the rule, and it is possible that Mississippian families tended to live in single structures rather than in multistructure units.

The slumping of abandoned Mississippian house basins usually leaves a circular depression in the ground surface. These "hut rings" were a common feature of Mississippian sites in the nineteenth century before plowing destroyed their traces. The occurrence of intact basins at Dillow's Ridge means that this site has a dual significance for archaeologists. First, it is important because it is a habitation site associated with hoe production. Second, it represents a Mississippian community that has suffered only minor damage from historic land-modification practices. Our research suggests that Dillow's Ridge has never been plowed, and it probably has not been logged for at least a century.

SITE STRUCTURE

The 27 house basins at Dillow's Ridge appear to be randomly distributed across the hilltop, with no signs of a plaza or formal site configuration (Figure 7.2). Excavation trenches within basins revealed that
houses ranged in size from 4 to 5 meters across, typical for Mississippian domestic structures. Most basins had multiple rebuildings, with
up to four structures erected in the same location. The houses are oriented generally north-south, perhaps showing a continuity in construction throughout the site. Concentrations of daub around some of the
structures indicate that clay was regularly used to insulate the walls.
It is interesting that daub is rarely recovered in the American Bottom,
perhaps reflecting variation in building techniques in the lower Midwest. This variation could be attributed to style, the need to protect
the Dillow's Ridge structures in their exposed hilltop setting, or other
factors.

There is a shift in construction techniques in the final occupation
of the site to single-post structures, with the posts supported by chert
nodules (Figure 7.3). The single-post structures display a continuity
with the wall-trench houses in that they were built in the same basins,
are of about the same size, and have the same orientation. Lacking additional evidence, it is difficult to say whether an architectural shift of
this sort is a manifestation of larger social changes. The post structures
do appear to coincide with the late A.D. 1400s, a time of possible dramatic change among the Mississippian societies of the region (discussed below). One possibility is that the final occupation of the community consisted of a small group who opted not to make the
energy investment to excavate the trenches required for more substantial structures.

Systematic augering of the site on a 5-meter grid revealed the presence of at least 15 to 20 buried basins that are not visible as depressions
today (McGimsey 1994). These were backfilled prehistorically. Considering both the extant basins with multiple rebuildings and the additional, buried basins, it is conceivable that a total of 100 to 150 structures were built at Dillow's Ridge during the Mississippian period.
Given the confined space of the hilltop, however, it is difficult to envision more than eight to 10 structures being occupied at any one time,
representing perhaps around a maximum of 50 people. Our excavations
suggest that little of the hilltop escaped remodeling during its occupation, which has made it almost impossible to reconstruct the site plan
for any one point in time.

Most of the structures were destroyed by burning. However, the
floors of all of the houses are remarkably clean of artifacts, suggesting

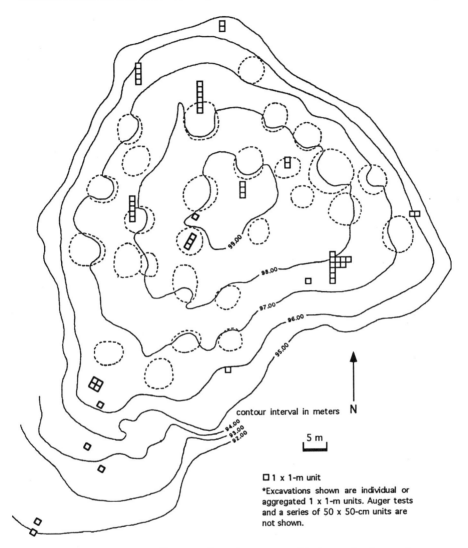

Figure 7.2. Plan view of Dillow's Ridge, showing visible house basins and excavation units.

the structures were intentionally fired as they became dilapidated. Although it is likely that Dillow's Ridge residents were placing the torch to their own homes in a cycle of rebuilding, fear of external threat may still have been a concern. We have located a line of posts on the north side of the site, along the crest of the hill, which possibly represents a single-phase palisade.

Refuse deposits ranging from 0.4 to 1 meter deep ring the margin of the hilltop, just outside the habitation area. It is probably no accident

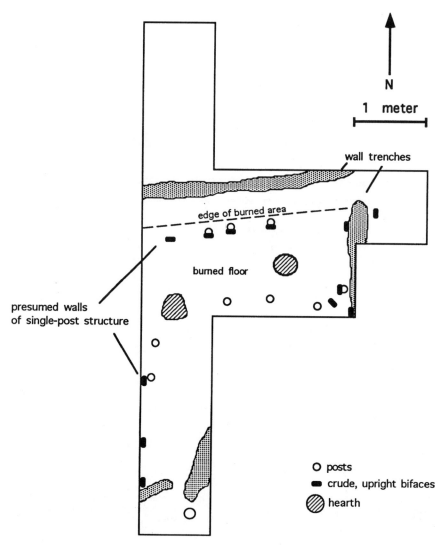

Figure 7.3. Single-post structure inside (post-dating) wall trench structure.

that the deepest midden deposits are located along the southerly edge of the site, downwind from the prevailing winds in the midcontinent. The midden contains a fairly standard range of Mississippian domestic debris (discussed further below), including a large variety of stone tool and ceramic vessel types, and unusually well-preserved floral and faunal remains. The accumulations of Mill Creek chert debitage are especially impressive. In the deeper midden deposits on the south edge of the site there are multiple strata, each at least 10 to 15 centimeters

Figure 7.4. Midden profile.

thick, consisting almost entirely of waste flakes (Figure 7.4). Although not every provenience was analyzed, the "typical" 10-centimeter arbitrary stratum in the midden contained on the order of 3,500 to 7,000 flakes in a 1 × 1-meter unit.

Most Mississippian sites contain a wide variety of pit features, ranging from shallow basins to large, bell-shaped pits that may be a meter wide and over a meter deep. The number of pit features located to date at Dillow's Ridge, however, is low. A total of only eight have been identified, and these typically consist of shallow basins. One interesting feature appears to have been a large roasting pit containing wood, nutshell, and cane charcoal. A huge quantity of associated debitage in the same pit may have been used to retain heat, analogous to a hearth stone. Formal clay-lined, circular hearths have also been found in some of the houses. Overall, however, the functional data potentially available from pit features are largely lacking from Dillow's Ridge. It is unknown whether the scarcity of pits relates to bad luck in our sampling, their destruction by the constant remodeling of the site, their actual rarity, or whether many of the tasks that would require pit features were carried out in the thick midden zone where they would be difficult to identify because of the complex stratigraphy.

A final aspect of the site structure that has yet to be resolved is the

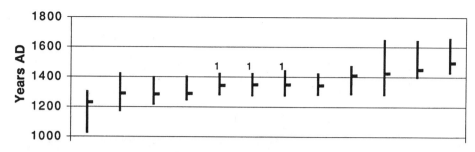

Years AD

¹Multiple intercepts. Middle intercept displayed.

Figure 7.5. Calibrated radiocarbon intervals (95 percent probability) and intercepts from Dillow's Ridge.

possibility of quarrying on the hillside. There are suspicious piles and depressions on the slopes that are suggestive of quarrying, but there are no distinct pits as seen at other quarries in the region. There are a few crudely worked nodules of Mill Creek chert on the ground surface of Dillow's Ridge. If quarrying was not conducted on the hillside, it does appear that chert was being carried from a nearby source area (likely the main quarry) with only minimal shaping.

The one saving grace to the complex site stratigraphy is that Dillow's Ridge represents an occupation restricted to the latter half of the Mississippian period. No diagnostic artifacts preceding the Mississippian period have been recovered in three years of excavations, and that includes Emergent Mississippian materials. Moreover, the 12 radiocarbon dates for the site cluster in the mid-1200s to the late 1400s A.D. (Figure 7.5). As a side note, the latest dates for Dillow's Ridge coincide with the presumed abandonment associated with the "Vacant Quarter." We are left to wonder whether Mississippian groups scattered to the hills, or maintained a presence in the hills, before finally leaving the region.

Muller (1997:189–90) observes that many archaeological and historical estimates of Mississippian structure life range from six to 20 years. It is likely this variation reflects not only different ways of estimating structure longevity, but also the realities of how well different house fabrics survive in different regions. Pauketat (1989), using the average life of ceramic containers, found that even within the confines of the American Bottom house life seemed to range from less than five years to as long as about 10 years. If we take the liberal estimate for the total number of houses at Dillow's Ridge (n = 150) and divide it by the estimated maximum number of contemporaneous structures (n = 10), we arrive at an estimated sequence of 15 generations of houses covering a span of from 90 to 300 years (using 6- and 20-year estimates). The latter figure conforms most closely to our chronometric evidence. These data also support the idea that Dillow's Ridge was continuously occupied throughout the two to three centuries represented by our radiocarbon dates. While we still lack the fine-grained resolution of the site that would allow us to seriate structures and identify specific occupational episodes, it is still possible to make some generalizations for an approximate 250-year slice of time—not too bad by archaeological standards, particularly in eastern North America.

ANALYSES OF CULTURAL MATERIALS

Lithic Assemblage

The lithic assemblage consisted of two major elements: (1) a wide variety of tools that apparently were used by the residents of Dillow's Ridge in their daily activities and (2) broken large bifaces and prodigious amounts of debitage related to the manufacture of hoes and other implements for export. I will discuss the locally used tools before moving on to considerations of hoe manufacture. All artifacts were recovered by one-quarter-inch dry screening.

Locally Used Tools. A wide variety of bifacial (non-hoe) tools are present in the lithic assemblage, reflecting the diverse activities carried out within the confines of Dillow's Ridge (Table 7.1). The most common bifacial tool is the small, triangular point (Figure 7.6). The prevalence of this tool type underscores the importance of hunting in the subsistence economy, although the use of arrows for raiding and defense cannot be discounted. One example each of a celt and a chisel was recovered, as were five adzes, reflecting the working of non-lithic materials, such as wood. Drills were somewhat common, and these too were presumably worked on nonlithic materials. Preforms for these various tool types were found occasionally, pointing to the not-surprising conclusion that flintknappers were manufacturing a wide variety of tools for their domestic consumption, in addition to hoes. One unusual tool type was a large, disc-shaped biface (Figure 7.6), roughly worked and with evidence of battering and use on the edges. These appear to be some form of crude chopping implement, or they may be hammerstones.

Expedient flake tools were much more common than formal tools (although the impact of trampling and other processes in the formation of pseudo-tools must be acknowledged [e.g., McBrearty et al. 1998]). Most exhibit retouch or damage on the tool margins, likely related to a variety of cutting, sawing, and slicing motions. A number of sizable

Table 7.1. Tools from Dillow's Ridge, the Bridges Site, and the Bonnie Creek Site

Dillow's Ridge		Bridges Site		Bonnie Creek	
Blank	19	Proj. Point	16	Biface	65
Hoe Preform	13	Biface	23	Cutting Tool	83
Knife Preform	13	Scraper	30	Scraper	125
Adze Preform	1	Drill	3	Spokeshave	6
Chisel Preform	1	Other Tool	7	Denticulate	6
Other Preform	7	Utilized Flake	126	Graver	3
Hoe	20	Core	3	Drill	4
Ramey Knife	29			Microdrill	1
Other Biface	22			Core	61
Triangular PP	94				
Other PP	33				
Pick	0				
Adze	5				
Celt	1				
Chisel	1				
Drill	14				
Core	20				
Tested Nodule	23				
Utilized Flakes	1114				
Serrated Flakes	92				
Scraper	35				
Knife	7				
Notch	38				
Reamer	7				
Microdrill	1				
Blade-like Flake	1				

flake scrapers were recovered, characterized by steep beveling on the lateral and distal edges of large bifacial thinning and reduction flakes (Figure 7.7). Presumably, these were used for hide working and similar activities. Another common expedient tool type was a linear flake with marked serrations (included under the "denticulate" category) on the long, parallel margins (Figure 7.7). Such edges are commonly created by a sawing motion (Odell 1981), or else are manufactured for that purpose, and the denticulated flakes may have been used on harder materials such as bone, antler, or wood. Spokeshaves, or notches, were another common flake tool. Reamers, or perforators, were occasionally recovered.

The flake tool assemblage is distinguished by the use of very large flakes for tools like the scrapers and denticulates, which usually appear in a smaller form at other Mississippian sites. Ready access to such a

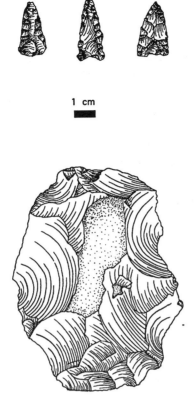

1 cm

Figure 7.6. Arrow points and
chopper/hammerstone. (Drawn
by Brian DelCastello.)

large reservoir of waste flakes likely accounts for this pattern. Very
large flakes of Mill Creek chert have been found in small numbers at
Wickliffe, leading Koldehoff and Carr (2001) to posit that such flakes
may have been occasionally traded alongside hoes, to be transformed
into smaller cutting and scraping tools.

Overall, the Dillow's Ridge lithic assemblage reflects the wide range
of activities carried out with stone tools by the site inhabitants. Most
of the tool types from the site are also found at nearby, contemporary
workshops, and they are also commonly represented at most Mississippian habitations. However, rarely does any one Mississippian site
display the broad array and quantity of stone tools seen in the Dillow's
Ridge assemblage. For comparative purposes, the stone tool assemblages from two other Mississippian sites in southern Illinois have
been included in Table 7.1. These include the Bridges site (Hargrave et

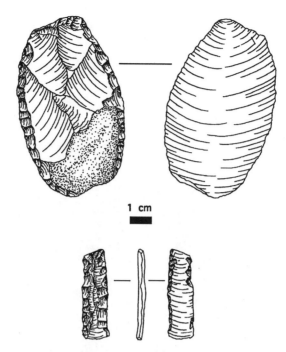

1 cm

Figure 7.7. Scraper (*top*) and serrated flake (*bottom*). (Drawn by Brian DelCastello.)

al. 1983), a village with plaza, and Bonnie Creek (Koldehoff 1986), a small hamlet. Even accounting for discrepancies in tool nomenclature by different analysts, the diversity of the Dillow's Ridge assemblage is apparent.

Relative access to lithic raw materials obviously accounts for the disparities in the respective lithic assemblages. Not only did Dillow's Ridge inhabitants have the luxury of abundant raw materials for making large numbers of tools, but also it is likely that Mississippian groups in other localities relied on nonlithic raw materials to make some of the tool types that may have been made of stone in the Mill Creek locale. Cane, for example, was widely used by historic Native Americans for making cutting and piercing tools.

The occasional appearance of lithic raw materials other than Mill Creek chert at Dillow's Ridge is limited to southern Illinois types, such as Cobden and Kaolin cherts. The sample size of the regional cherts numbers in the hundreds of flakes, which is not insignificant, but it still represents a tiny percentage of the total debitage on the site. Perhaps most interesting is why individuals living in such a chert-rich locale would find the need to acquire nonlocal raw materials. The

answer to this may lie in part with the tools that are often made
from materials other than Mill Creek chert, which are primarily triangular projectile points. It is assumed that the more fine-grained, nonlocal cherts would create a sharper piercing edge than would Mill
Creek chert. The projectile points that are made from Mill Creek chert,
which still constitute most of the sample, are commonly heat-treated,
which lends a finer grain to the usually coarse chert (Dunnell et al.
1994). However, color also may have played a role in the selection or
treatment of cherts for projectile points. Thomas (1997:162–64) has observed that the point sample from Dillow's Ridge is dominated by three
colors considered sacred to Southeastern Indians: red (heat-treated Mill
Creek), deep gray/black (Cobden), and white (Kaolin, some variants of
Mill Creek).

Large Biface Production. Tested chert nodules (n = 23), hoe preforms
(n = 13), and hoes (n = 20; usually broken) are all present at Dillow's
Ridge, indicating that at least some of the chert was arriving in raw
form to be reduced to hoes and other tools (Table 7.1). Lithic workshops
in other technological traditions are often distinguished by large numbers of production failures or incomplete preforms. The somewhat
modest sample from Dillow's Ridge may indicate that the resident
population was quick to recycle production failures into smaller tools
that could be used locally. One example of this is a notched hoe type
that has been reworked into a large perforating tool (Figure 7.8).

Interestingly, 29 Ramey knives and knife fragments and 13 Ramey
knife preforms were also recovered (Figure 7.9), numbers on a par with
the sample of hoes (Table 7.1). Ramey knives continued to be imported into the American Bottom as late as the Sand Prairie phase (e.g.,
Milner et al. 1984:181); apparently these tools—in addition to hoes—
continued to be an important export from the Mill Creek locale late
in the Mississippian sequence. As described in chapter 3, Ramey knives
occur in both ceremonial and domestic contexts, so one cannot clearly
say whether the Dillow's Ridge specimens were intended for a realm
of social consumption that is clearly distinct from hoes. In any event,
the evidence from Dillow's Ridge demonstrates that hoes and Ramey
knives were manufactured side by side and may have been exported in
similar quantities.

Our three seasons of fieldwork failed to recover any signs of the
manufacture of what are presumed to be lithic exotics, namely, spatulate celts and maces. This leads to the question of whether the fancy
chert implements were primarily manufactured in the first half of the
Mississippian sequence (ca. A.D. 1000–1250), before Dillow's Ridge was
occupied. In contrast, Gramly (1992) has recovered "eccentric" preforms from Dover chert workshops. The dates from one of these work-

Figure 7.8. Reworked hoe (*upper right*) and roughed-
out bifaces.

shops, the Revnik site, show it to be contemporary with Dillow's Ridge
(Gramly 1992:120), leading one to speculate whether Dover chert ex-
otics were being produced later into the Mississippian sequence than
Mill Creek chert ones.

The quantity of waste flakes recovered from Dillow's Ridge is quite
impressive for a North American site, even one that was a workshop.
For example, the 1993 excavations that concentrated in the midden on
the south side of the site recovered 30 5-gallon (22 l) buckets of debitage, most of this deriving from six 1 × 1-meter units. While the quantities of chert debris at Dillow's Ridge are very impressive, they are
compatible with a scenario of part-time production. Using data from
a 5-meter-grid systematic auger survey, supplemented by excavation
data, Brian Butler (Butler and Cobb 1996) has estimated that slightly

Figure 7.9. Ramey knife production failures.

more than 86,000 kilograms (95 tons) of debitage lies beneath the site surface. This weight refers only to flake debris and does not include primary forms, rejects, or tool fragments other than retouched flakes.

Using biface replication data from both Gramly (1992) and Cobb (1988), Butler derived 1,000 grams as the average debitage weight resulting from the production of a large Mill Creek biface (figures for hoes and Ramey knives were averaged on the basis of the assumption that knives were also an important export). This debitage weight includes an additional allocation for flakes resulting from rejects, tool failures, and recycling. Averaging these numbers over a 200-year occupation span results in a mean annual output of only 432 large bifaces per year. Using three hours as the average time required for producing

Table 7.2 Debitage Sorted by Screen Mesh Size

Unit	Level	1" Mesh	1/2" Mesh	1/4" Mesh	Total
3	3	387	1888	6216	8491
3	4	395	1929	6325	8649
5	6	673	3177	12689	16539
5	7	438	2118	8520	11076
5	8	385	1761	4727	6873
12	1	382	2284	10132	12798
12	2	380	2535	10004	12919
9B	Feature 16	390	2243	2776	5409
Total		3430	17935	61389	82754

Sample averages (n=4940)

	1" Mesh	1/2" Mesh	1/4" Mesh
Mean Wt. (g)	19.4	2.3	0.45
Lacking Cortex	28%	70%	85%

a large biface (hoe or Ramey knife), a small group of only 10 knappers working modest eight-hour days could account for the entire annual production in about 16 to 17 days.

A mass analysis (see Ahler 1989) of a sample of the 1993 collections from Dillow's Ridge largely confirms the various inferences we have made regarding the staging of biface manufacture and the quantities of tools produced. Mass analysis was developed specifically for quarry and workshop situations in which large amounts of debitage stretch the logistical capabilities of conventional lithic studies. The underlying method of mass analysis is the size sorting of debitage through graduated screens. This approach to lithic analysis is based on the widely substantiated observation that the reduction of lithic materials in biface manufacture leads to progressively smaller (and lighter) flakes (see Henry et al. 1976; Magne and Pokotylo 1981; Patterson 1990). An emphasis on later-stage reduction will produce proportionately larger amounts of small flakes when compared with a typical reduction sequence, whereas an emphasis on early-stage reduction will lead to proportionately larger amounts of sizable debitage fragments.

The mass analysis was based on eight samples (10-cm levels within 1 × 1-m units) within midden contexts that yielded a total of more than 82,000 waste flakes (Table 7.2). The samples were size graded through one-, one-half-, and one-quarter-inch nested screens. For the complete sample presented in Figure 7.10, the trends of flake size and weight follow a pattern typical of complete bifacial reduction assemblages. Small category flakes are present in exponentially higher amounts than

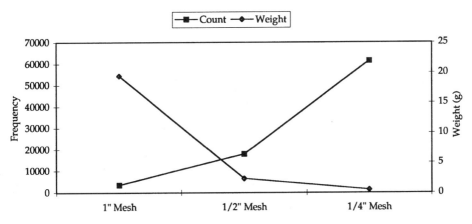

Figure 7.10. Frequency and mean weight of size grade categories.

flakes in the larger categories. Conversely, there is an extremely sharp drop in the size of flakes per size grade as determined by mean weight. Debitage from the one-inch screen is over eight times larger than that from the one-half-inch screen by weight, while debitage from the one-half-inch screen is about five times larger than that from the quarter-inch screen. A measure of the amount of cortex on a subsample of about 6,000 flakes showed that, despite the relatively large size of the debitage recovered from the one-inch screen, a substantial amount of it (28 percent) does not exhibit cortex. Much of that includes the big thinning flakes associated with the manufacture of large bifacial implements. However, the one-inch size grade also contains reduction flakes and angular fragments customarily linked with the trimming and early reduction of chert nodules, consistent with the evidence from the biface assemblage that chert nodules were brought directly from a quarry to the site. As observed previously, some quarrying may have taken place on the slopes below the ridge top, so the nodules may have been moved only a short distance.

When the mass analysis is broken down by provenience, the results are fairly consistent. For all contexts except Feature 16, the number of flakes in progressively smaller categories tends to dramatically increase (Figure 7.11). Feature 16 represents a house basin intruding into the midden fill on the south side of the site. The debitage placed within the basin may represent secondary fill carried from a knapping episode at another location, thus biasing the sample toward larger flakes that would have been more likely to be picked up. Although this interpretation is speculative, it does suggest that mass analysis has the poten-

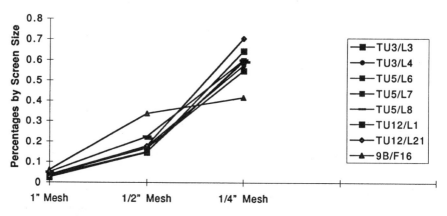

Figure 7.11. Debitage percentages by screen size.

tial to highlight differences among what appear to be homogeneous piles of debris from the same site (Ahler 1989; Healan 1995).

At the other end of the spectrum, several specimens of complete and near-complete hoes were recovered from the site. This evidence, in conjunction with the significant numbers of small flakes (usually lacking cortex), indicates that implements were also finished at Dillow's Ridge. In short, it appears that the entire reduction sequence is present at Dillow's Ridge, ranging from the transporting of raw nodules to the site, to the shaping of them into complete tools.

One difficulty with flake analyses is that the presence of multiple technologies may skew the interpretation of the results (Ahler 1989:113). In the case of Dillow's Ridge, it is somewhat safe to assume that most of the flintknapping was dedicated to various forms of large bifaces. Therefore the by-products of manufacturing arrowheads and the like for local consumption presumably would be so swamped by debris from large bifaces that the skewing effects of multiple technologies would be negligible. Furthermore, most of the domestic tools were of an expedient nature and were likely drawn from debitage piles created by the manufacture of large bifaces.

CERAMIC ASSEMBLAGE

The ceramic assemblage from Dillow's Ridge included only one intact vessel. However, a substantial number of rimsherds were recovered, reflecting a wide range of vessel types, including jars, bowls, plates, and bottles (Table 7.3). Within these categories there was significant variation as well; jars and bowls embody numerous rim and neck shapes, and vessel categories encompass a wide range of sizes. The functional

Table 7.3 Absolute and Relative Frequencies
of Vessel Types from Dillow's Ridge

Vessel Type	No.	%
Jars	85	32.8
Bowls	114	44.0
Miniature bowls	12	4.6
Pans	23	8.9
Plates	4	1.5
Bottles	17	6.6
Bean Pot	1	0.4
Stumpware	3	1.2
Total	259	100.0

diversity of the ceramic assemblage is similar to that seen at other Mississippian sites and further supports the notion that residents of Dillow's Ridge engaged in a wide suite of domestic activities and lived in the area year-round (Thomas 1997).

One of the more unusual functional characteristics of the Dillow's Ridge ceramic assemblage is the low ratio (0.62:1) of jars to bowls (the ratio combines pans with bowls, and excludes miniature bowls). Mississippian sites in the American Bottom consistently have a larger number of jars to bowls, with ratios ranging from over nine to one in the Emergent Mississippian period to about two to one in the later Mississippian phases (Hargrave 1992:217). This pattern does not appear to be limited to the American Bottom, either. At the Chambers site in western Kentucky, for instance, jars comprised 70 percent of the Mississippi Plain assemblage (Pollack and Railey 1987).

With a sample consisting of only one upland late prehistoric site from southwestern Illinois, it is difficult to evaluate the significance of the prevalence of bowl forms at Dillow's Ridge. One obvious possibility is that upland Mississippian groups relied upon a different mix of foods and food preparation techniques than did groups living in bottomland areas. Because either bowls or jars could be used as both processing and serving vessels, using vessel types alone to make this argument is somewhat problematic (Hargrave 1992; Thomas 1997). As discussed below, the floral and faunal remains from Dillow's Ridge show some departures from food assemblages from bottomland sites, but those differences do not seem major. At present, we can merely hypothesize that upland Mississippian groups may have followed a different dietary regime that resulted in a substantially higher use of

Figure 7.12. Incised ceramics.

bowls than found with Mississippian groups elsewhere in the Central Mississippi and Lower Ohio valleys.

The stylistic and typological aspects of the assemblage are similar to those of Mississippian complexes in the Confluence region and the Lower Ohio Valley. On the basis of the 1993 season collections, which contain the largest corpus of ceramics (n = 5,427), 96 percent of the sherds were shell-tempered (n = 5,185), 2 percent were tempered with a mixture of grog and shell (n = 117), and 2 percent were tempered with a mixture of limestone and grit (n = 125). Surface decoration was rare, usually consisting of single or double incised lines, a type in the Confluence region referred to as O'Byam Incised (Figure 7.12). Plates, which tend to occur later in the Mississippian sequence, exhibited various forms of incising, burnishing, or red slipping (Thomas 1997:227). A few small sherds with possible paint were identified, a rare type at sites in the Lower Ohio and Confluence regions, but there is no reason to think these were not locally manufactured.

There is no evidence of trade wares from the American Bottom at Dillow's Ridge, or even any stylistic affinities with American Bottom types. Mill Creek chert artifacts are still common in the last of the American Bottom Mississippian phases, so the late date of Dillow's Ridge alone does not account for the lack of American Bottom influence. Because Mill Creek chert implements continued to flow into the American Bottom during the period of Cahokia's decline and collapse, there apparently was no need for powerful elites in that region to maintain the flow of hoes and Ramey knives. More simple types of exchange apparently sufficed.

FAUNAL ASSEMBLAGE

The faunal assemblage from Dillow's Ridge (Table 7.4) shares many characteristics with Mississippian faunal assemblages elsewhere in the Central Mississippi Valley (e.g., Breitburg 1992; Kelly and Cross 1984; Smith 1975). Mammalian remains (recovered from one-quarter-inch mesh) constitute the bulk of the bone by frequency (73 percent), followed by fish (10 percent), reptiles (8 percent), birds (7 percent), and molluscs (2 percent) (Table 7.5). Only one amphibian bone was recovered. Among the identifiable mammalian remains, white-tailed deer dominate by count (63 percent) (Table 7.6). The representation of other species reflects emphases that one might expect of an upland assemblage. For example, gray and fox squirrel combined comprise 20 percent of the mammalian bone count and also constitute a substantial number of the individuals recovered (combined MNI = 14). The proportions of squirrel are larger than typically encountered at floodplain sites (Smith 1975:113–14, appendixes A–E). Of course, the available meat weight from squirrel is overshadowed by that of many of the other mammalian species. Domestic dog also assumes a prominent percentage of the mammalian bone at Dillow's Ridge, but much of this comes from a single feature, and the MNI is only 2.

Fish were the next most common category by bone count (n = 382) and by MNI (n = 27). This number encompasses a broad variety (n = 15) of fish families and genera. Birds were plentiful as well, making up 7 percent of the bone by weight (n = 249) and 14 percent by MNI (n = 12). Similar to Mississippian sites elsewhere, turkey was the most common bird, and it also constituted a significant portion of the overall assemblage. It is noteworthy that reptile remains, particularly turtle, are relatively abundant in the Dillow's Ridge faunal assemblage. This pattern is also seen at a number of Mississippian sites in western Kentucky (Lewis 1986; Pollack and Railey 1987), in contrast with the American

Table 7.A. Faunal Remains from Dillow's Ridge

Common Name	Taxa	Count	MNI*	Burnt	Cut	Modified
Mammals						
White-tailed deer	Odocoileus virginianus	453	7	179	19	10
Raccoon	Procyon lotor	16	1	5		
Gray fox	Urocyon cinereoargenteus	2	1			
Domestic dog	Canis familiaris	60	2	9		
Small carnivore		1	1			
Rice rat	Oryzomys palustris	1	1			
Chipmunk	Tamias striatus	4	1	1		
Gray squirrel	Sciurus carolinensis	80	8	32		1
Fox squirrel	Sciurus niger	68	6	31	1	1
Squirrel spp.		12		1		
Woodchuck	Marmota monax	6	2	1		
Cottontail rabbit	Sylvilagus floridanus	12	2	4		
Rabbit	Sylvilagus sp.	1				
Opossum	Didelphis marsupialis	8	2	3		
Large mammal		1813		1378	2	8
Mammal fragments		7				
Small mammal		185		80		
Small rodent		9		7		
	Total Mammal	**2738**	**34**	**1731**	**22**	**20**
Birds						
Perching bird	Passerine sp.	1	1			
Turkey	Meleagris gallapavo	22	3	9	1	
Bobwhite quail	Colinus virginianus	5	1	2		
Passenger pigeon	Ectopistes migratorius	1	1	1		
Mallard spp.	Anas sp.	1	1			
Medium-sized duck	Anas sp.	1	1	1		
Blue-winged teal	Anas	2	1			
Teal-sized duck	Anas sp.	5	1	3		
Duck spp.	Anas spp.	2	1	1		
Pied-billed grebe	Podilymbus podiceps	2	1	1		
Bird fragments		207		134		2
	Total Bird	**249**	**12**	**152**	**1**	**2**
Reptiles						
Softshell/snapping turtle sp.	Trionyx/Cheldra	1	1			
Map/painted turtle	Chrysemys/Graptemys spp.	10	1			
Box turtle	Terrapene carolina	109	3	53		9
Turtle fragments		163		126		
Snake sp.		1	1			
	Total Reptile	**284**	**6**	**179**	**0**	**9**
Amphibian						
Frog/toad sp.	Rana/Bufo sp.	1	1			
	Total Amphibian	**1**	**1**	**0**	**0**	**0**
Fish						
Freshwater drum	Aplodinotus grunniens	9	2	1		
Largemouth bass	Micropterus salmoides	1	1			
Bass spp.	Morone spp.	4	2	1		
Yellow bullhead	Ictalurus natalis	6	2	2		
Channel catfish	Ictalurus punctatus	1	1	1		
Catfish spp.	Ictalurus spp.	20	4	7		
River redhorse	Moxostoma cf. carinatum	3	2	1		
Golden redhorse	Moxostoma cf. erythrurum	1	1			
Redhorse spp.	Moxostoma spp.	12	4	1		
Smallmouth buffalo	Ictiobus cf. bubalus	1	1			
Sucker family	Catostomidae	2				
Minnow family	Cyrpinidae	3	3	3		
Shad sp.	Dorsoma sp.?	1	1			
Bowfin	Amia calva	51	2	20		
Gar spp.	Lepisosteus spp.	3	1	1		
Fish fragments		264		115		
	Total Fish	**382**	**27**	**153**	**0**	**0**

Mollusc						
Three-ridge	Amblema plicata	4	2	2		
Mucket	Actinonaias ligamentina	1	1			
Spike	Elliptio dilatata	1	1			
Fluted-shell	Lasmigona costata	1	1			
Black sandshell	Ligumia recta	1	1			
Aquatic snail	Campeloma sp.	1	1	1		
Bivalve fragments		41		13		
Terrestrial snail		37				
	Total Mollusc	87	7	16	0	0
Other						
Miscellaneous		101		8		
	Total Misc.	101	0	8	0	0
	GRAND TOTAL	3842	87	2239	23	31

*minimum number of individuals

Table 7.5. Absolute and Relative Frequencies
of Dillow's Ridge Fauna

Class	No.	%
Total Mammal	2738	73
Birds	249	7
Reptiles	284	8
Amphibian	1	<1
Fish	382	10
Mollusc	87	2
Total	3741	100

Bottom where reptile remains are rare at many sites (Kelly and Cross 1984:231).

Overall, the Dillow's Ridge faunal assemblage reflects a diverse diet, with an emphasis on certain animals such as white-tailed deer and turkey. This pattern is similar to that on Mississippian sites elsewhere in broad outline, but it also departs from a number of bottomland sites by the community's heavier reliance on animals such as squirrel and turtle. Emanuel Breitburg (1996:3) observes that

Perhaps the most interesting aspect of the sample is the presence of aquatic and semiaquatic turtle, bird, and fish taxa. Given the upland nature of the site at the headwaters of Mill Creek, it is surprising that major riverine fishes such as drumfish and suckers were exploited. In one case a smallmouth buffalofish exceeded 13.6 kilograms (30 pounds). Such fish had to be taken from a large stream. Other fish species (yellow bullhead, bass spp., bowfin and shad) were probably taken from small streams or backwater areas. The most obvious point of procurement is the large pools that occur along the

Table 7.6 Absolute and Relative Frequencies of Mammalian Remains
from Dillow's Ridge

Common Name	Taxa	No.	%
White-tailed deer	Odocoileus virginianus	453	62.6
Gray squirrel	Sciurus carolinensis	80	11.0
Fox squirrel	Sciurus niger	68	9.4
Domestic dog	Canis familiaris	60	8.3
Racoon	Procyon lotor	16	2.2
Squirrel spp.		12	1.7
Cottontail rabbit	Sylvilagus floridanus	12	1.7
Opposum	Didelphis marsupialis	8	1.1
Woodchuck	Marmota monax	6	0.8
Chipmunk	Tamias striatus	4	0.6
Gray fox	Urocyon cinereoargenteus	2	0.3
Small carnivore		1	0.1
Rice rat	Oryzomys palustris	1	0.1
Rabbit	Sylvilagus sp.	1	0.1
	Total	724	100.0

Cache River. The river was probably the source of semiaquatic birds
(duck and grebe) also.

Bones were occasionally modified for tool use. One socketed projectile point was made from an antler tip, a trait often associated with
late Mississippian complexes farther south in the Mississippi Valley
(Morse and Morse 1983:273). Antler batons and bone awl fragments
were recovered as well (Breitburg 1996).

The faunal assemblage may give some indications of patterns of landscape use. Cottontail rabbit, woodchuck, and fox squirrel prefer more
open habitats than the riparian swamp rabbit and forest-dwelling gray
squirrel, raccoon, gray fox, and opossum, and the presence/absence or
relative proportions of these species may point to land alteration practices by human beings (Breitburg 1992:299; Welch 1991:101–3). Only
cottontail rabbits were identified in the Dillow's Ridge assemblage,
at least two specimens of woodchuck were present, and fox squirrel
(n = 68) was almost as common as gray squirrel (n = 80). The common
presence of animals associated with open and semiforested areas in
conjunction with forest species suggests that the Dillow's Ridge inhabitants (and other Mill Creek communities) may have been living

in a patchwork of cleared fields and forest resulting from long-term agricultural practices.

FLORAL ASSEMBLAGE

The importance of agriculture to the upland groups is further supported by the floral assemblage from Dillow's Ridge. Table 7.7 depicts the result of floral analyses of nine flotation samples containing a total of 73 liters of soil. Maize is by far the most common of the domesticated plants, occurring in the form of both kernels and cupules. Curcubits are also represented, although in relatively small amounts of fragments compared with maize. North American domesticates and cultigens are widely represented, including chenopod, amaranth, sumpweed, maygrass, and knotweed. Most of the plants are starchy-seed varieties (chenopod, maygrass, and knotweed) that were very important in many Middle Woodland and Late Woodland complexes in the Midwest. Knotweed is prominent among the indigenous cultigens at Woodland sites in west-central Illinois and the American Bottom (Asch and Asch 1985:183; Johannessen 1984) and far outnumbers the other native cultigens at Dillow's Ridge, reflecting its continuing importance in the Mississippian period in southwestern Illinois.

The site soils are represented by the Goss-Alford complex, a typical well-drained series for the hilly Ozarks, consisting of both loess and soil formed from the residuum of the underlying limestone (Miles 1979). That portion of the ridge just to the south of the site is topped by an Alford silt loam, a well-drained and moderately permeable loess (Miles 1979). It is possible that the relatively fertile loesses on the ridge top may have served as horticultural fields for inhabitants of Dillow's Ridge, in addition to the floodplain soils along You-Be Hollow.

Despite the apparent importance of agriculture to the residents of Dillow's Ridge, like most Mississippian groups they utilized a wide variety of wild plant foods. Nuts, particularly hickory, appear to have been very important to the diet. Several kinds of berries, wild grapes, and other plants contributed to the subsistence base too. Although it is difficult to assess the relative importance of wild versus domesticated plants, it is evident that the people at Dillow's Ridge made liberal use of the available upland flora.

OTHER ACTIVITIES

It is axiomatic in archaeology that we deal with but a small proportion of the material culture used in the past, that which is durable enough to withstand decomposition and corrosion. Penelope Drooker (1992) has provided an indirect look at the textiles and clothes used

Table 7.7 Floral Remains from Dillow's Ridge

Common Name	Taxa		Count
	Nuts		
Pecan	Carya illinoensis		2
Hickory	Carya sp.		5313
Black walnut	Juglans sp.		12
Acorn	Quercus sp.		19
Unidentified small nut shell			269
Unidentified thick nut shell			13
		Total	5628
	Maize		
Cupules (whole and frag.)			81
Kernels (whole and frag.)			107
Small fragments			1008
		Total	1196
	Other Plant Remains		
Squash/gourd	cf. cucurbitaceae		4
Squash/gourd	cucurbitaceae		3
Cane or corn stalk	monocot stem		3
Grass rhizome section	Poaceae rhizome section		1
Small fruit fragments			2
		Total	13

(continued on next page)

by Mississippian peoples through her groundbreaking work on fabric-impressed ceramics. Her study (Drooker 1998) of the small sample (n = 23) of impressed sherds from Dillow's Ridge came up with several interesting observations: there appears to have been a diverse set of fabrics used, including styles with twining, knotting, and weft-faced interlacing. She believes many of the fabrics represented would have been suitable for clothing, but the coarse examples could also have been used for bags, nets, or mats. For example, one decorative specimen of alternate-pair-twine fabric with crossed warps is similar to that seen used for decorative bags in the historic era.

Of course, not all was work or food production for the residents of Dillow's Ridge. The Spanish, British, and French accounts of Southeastern communities detail a rich life of laughter, games, ceremony, petty jealousies, and all of the other facets of the human condition that we take for granted, but that are so difficult to access from the archaeological record. Thomas (1997) has documented that a number of these activities are evident in the material culture from Dillow's Ridge. Several ceramic discoidal fragments were recovered, and these were likely

Seeds (Carbonized)

Amaranth (frag.)	Amaranthus/Cycloloma?	1
Chenopodium (frags.)	Chenopodium	12
Chenopodium (whole)	Chenopodium	12
Hawthorn	Crataegus sp. (cf. C. rotundifolia)	2
Persimmon (frags.)	Diospyros virginiana	2
Persimmon (whole)	Diospyros virginiana	1
Sumpweed	Iva annua	2
Sumpweed like	cf. Iva sp.	9
Sweetgum	Liquidambar styraciflua	1
Panicoid grass	Panicoid grass	1
Maygrass	Phalaris caroliniana	6
Bean (frag.)	cf. Phasaeolus sp.	1
Pokeweed	Phytolacca sp.	1
Knotweed (frags.)	Polygonum erectum	110
Knotweed (whole)	Polygonum erectum	107
Knotweed like	cf. Polygonum sp.	2
Purslane	Portulaca sp. (cf. P. oleracea)	1
Sumac	Rhus sp.	2
Blackberry (frags.)	Rubus sp.	2
Blackberry (whole)	Rubus sp.	2
Elderberry	Sambucus canadensis	1
Nightshade	Solanum sp.	2
Wild bean	Strophostyles helvola	4
Muscadine grape	Vitis rotundifolia	1
Grape (frags.)	Vitis sp.	6
Grape (whole)	Vitis sp.	9
Grape like (frags.)	cf. Vitis sp.	7
Grape like (whole)	cf. Vitis sp.	15
Other unidentified	(whole and frags.)	193
	Total	**515**

used in the game of chunkey, in which a discoidal (or chunkey stone) was rolled along the ground and the goal was to shoot arrows or throw spears at the estimated point where it would fall. A ceramic disk and a clay sphere were also found, and these may have been used in games as well.

It is unfortunate that our models of prehistoric political economy cannot do (or have not done) more justice to incorporating goods and activities outside the typical spheres of important utilitarian or status objects. Warren DeBoer's (1993) idea that elites at Cahokia may have structured the chunkey game during part of the Mississippian period is an intriguing move in this direction. Certainly, leisure time is as much a social construction as is the labor we associate with making a living, and the social reproduction of our communities involves notions of how we play, joke, or gamble, as well as how we work (Beaudry et al. 1991:154).

HOUSEHOLD AND COMMUNITY PRODUCTION OF HOES

The various lines of evidence from Dillow's Ridge all support the idea that this was a village continuously occupied during the latter half of the Mississippian sequence, with perhaps eight to 10 families living on the hilltop at any one time. The domestic assemblage is generally comparable with those of other small Mississippian villages in the Lower Ohio and Confluence regions. In these respects, we can make the normative argument that Dillow's Ridge looks like many other late prehistoric settlements in the midcontinent. Yet there is a major exception to this statement, and that is the vast quantities of Mill Creek chert debitage found in the site deposits. From this perspective, Dillow's Ridge is unique among the sample of excavated Mississippian sites in the Southeast and Midwest.

Despite the accumulations of debitage at Dillow's Ridge and other workshops, the number of bifaces produced on an annual basis was probably moderate if these sites were not short-term occupations or activity areas. Indeed, the numbers seem sufficiently low to make it seem likely that production could have been accommodated within a seasonal subsistence cycle, particularly during winter and early spring when planting activities would have been at low ebb. As Thomas (1997) has argued, historic Southeastern Indians probably had sufficient "down time" (or at least the men did), so that it is unlikely that hoe production made major inroads into the time required for subsistence activities. Admittedly, if hoe production did detract from time previously construed as leisure or dedicated to social and ritual activities, the stage may have been set for conflicts in the organization of labor.

On the basis of the results so far presented, it can be argued that hoe production was closely interwoven with the domestic economy: manufacture appears to have been spatially integrated into the living community; per annum output was apparently low and could be carried out by simple, part-time specialization within the household; and year-round residence in the locale indicates that chert procurement and tool production could have easily been integrated into the yearly round of activities. For these reasons, it is probably a conceptual mistake and a misnomer to conceive of there being two economies— one dedicated to local consumption and the other for export (see also Thomas 1997). Nevertheless, this observation does not necessarily imply that household relations of production were well-balanced and harmonious.

Many archaeological studies seem to make the ideological assumption that households fall into a natural divide of either the moral economy or the political economy (see Cheal 1989; also Yanagisako 1979:189). From this perspective, the pre-capitalist household (read "Mississippian" here) is characterized by a moral economy of mutual support and is a natural center of economic life. It is not until the shift to the industrial era that the political economy overtakes the household and the pursuit of self-interest and unequal relations invade the sacredness of the hearth.

In reality, even households in small-scale societies are marked by tensions between self-interest and reciprocity (Sahlins 1972:125), and it is a false dichotomy to tease apart "domestic" from "political" behavior. What we are seeing is merely a different realm of the political economy, one that is played out at the micro-scale rather than the macro-scale. It is true that if production is rationalized at the level of the household or community, then the ties of family and kinship are more likely to curb unreasonable demands on surplus production. Yet it is just as true that it is naive to deny that dissension over the mobilization of surplus and the allocation of labor is absent in household economies. For this reason, there can be a political economy of the household just as there is a political economy of chiefdoms or states. And this political economy is not merely inward-looking; households engage in relations of production, exchange, and consumption with other households within the same community, as well as with households in more distant locations.

Not only is the reality of this divide between moral and political economies questionable, but linking the pre-capitalist household with the moral economy also leads to a homogenized view of household relations, in which households become interchangeable "building blocks" characterized by cooperation and altruistic resource sharing (Hendon 1996:46; Price 1999). There is strong evidence, however, of considerable variation between and within households in small-scale societies (e.g., Kramer 1982; Marshall 1989; Netting 1982), and pooling is not always the norm (e.g., Clark 1989).

Nevertheless, there is a tendency in Mississippian studies to see homesteads or households as elemental building blocks of communities (e.g., Muller 1997:185). As an analytical device, this perspective may be appropriate for examining larger-scale issues of the political economy, but it does tend to obscure potentially important differences that may occur between these units. As Hammel (1984) points out, this is not a matter of right versus wrong in approaches toward households, but, rather, of what one gains or loses by adopting one or the other viewpoint. The use of the household as an elemental unit of analysis is very useful for comparative studies, but it is not historic. On the other hand, an approach that looks at the social construction of households better lends itself to a historical perspective, but it can also make it difficult to conduct comparative research.

Bruce Smith (1995:245), implicitly adopting the latter perspective, remarks in his overview of Mississippian households that

> rather than yielding any clearly and consistently identifiable pattern of household unit integration within Mississippian societies, excavation of a growing number of short-term homestead settlements has underscored both the variety of different frameworks of social cohesion that could have existed and the difficulties inherent in attempting to describe such social networks with any degree of specificity.

While Smith is referring to the variety of ways in which single-family homestead sites may have articulated with one another or with larger polities, I would argue that the same point applies to interhousehold variation within the same community. There is sufficient evidence from Southeastern sites to argue that all Mississippian households were not alike, but we are still uncertain as to the meaning and political-economic importance of this diversity. Major impediments to addressing this issue are the well-recognized difficulties in defining households ethnographically (Bender 1967; Kramer 1982; Wong 1984; Yanagisako 1979) and identifying them archaeologically (Brown 1989; Rogers 1995; Wilk and Rathje 1982).

Once again, the American Bottom provides some of the best data for interhousehold variation at Mississippian sites. Mississippian communities in the American Bottom begin to display a complex internal differentiation by the Lohmann phase (Pauketat 1994). During the subsequent Stirling phase there is also evidence that some households in rural communities may have assumed special ceremonial and civic functions (Emerson 1997; Mehrer and Collins 1995). Similar patterns are seen elsewhere. At the Toqua site in eastern Tennessee, it has been postulated that clusters of elite households stood out by their larger size and possible preferential access to meat and maize (Polhemus 1987). Larissa Thomas's (1997) comparative study of three small upland sites in Illinois (including Dillow's Ridge) suggests that the division of labor by gender may have been a central factor accounting for variation between Mississippian households.

At the same time, it cannot be ignored that archaeologists interested in Mississippian households argue that, in some cases, these units exhibit considerable homogeneity (e.g., Pauketat 1997:9)—although this is a very relative judgment. The problem is in part one of surface appearances versus actual relations: households with the same number of members, the same kinship structure, and the same developmental cycle (and presumably similar material culture) can still organize work very differently (Wilk 1989:25). To be fair, some of the unusual structures or compounds identified as outlier households may have been special-purpose buildings that did not serve domestic purposes (e.g., Pauketat 1994:138). This ambiguity merely reinforces the difficulty of conducting household studies in archaeology. Nevertheless, with the great bulk of ethnographic and historic data pointing to considerable variation between households within the same societies, the homogeneity of the household and its functions in a particular setting cannot be assumed; it must be demonstrated.

That said, there does not seem to be much that is distinctive about any of the structures qua households at the Dillow's Ridge site, although the paucity of pit features, the stratigraphic complexity of overlapping structures, and the lack of completely excavated domiciles may skew our perspective somewhat. Much of the debris that might reflect variation in patterns of consumption (and thus economic differentiation) appears to have been dumped in the communal midden ringing the site. Nevertheless, little of this discarded assemblage is distinctive. All of the structures have about the same size dimensions, including the very late single-post houses, so there do not seem to be any "elite" structures as defined for other Mississippian sites. Thus, the external relations presumably maintained in part by hoe exchange do not appear to have created overt changes in the household political economy, which, in turn, would have set the stage for the pronounced social and economic inequalities, and alienation of labor, that have been argued for some other Mississippian polities (Emerson 1997; Pauketat 1994).

FINAL THOUGHTS: HOES FOR FISH?

The ecological and archaeological evidence indicates that the natural landscape of the Mill Creek locale provided the resources to support a low density of Mississippian peoples. The archaeological survey suggests that the number of habitations was low and their size small, while the Dillow's Ridge floral and faunal assemblages demonstrate that wild and domesticated foods could be gathered and produced in abundance by communities of limited size. While some Mississippian forays into the area may have been transient, certainly not all of them were. For those groups that did remain, it appears unlikely that they needed to trade to support their subsistence economy—at least in good years. This observation, however, does beg the question, What were communities getting for their hoes?

The archaeological record is frustratingly silent on this count. In the previous chapter I discussed the paucity of nonlocal goods in the known cemeteries. A few traces of copper and some galena were the only unambiguous imports from outside of southern Illinois proper. Three seasons of fieldwork at Dillow's Ridge have yielded few items of unequivocal nonlocal origin: a cylindrical fluorspar bead and a small number of chert types. The source areas for these materials are all in the southern Illinois region. These artifacts, combined with the sparse evidence of interregional exchange from the cemeteries, do not demonstrate a capability to acquire goods that is superior to that of most Mississippian farmsteads or villages.

Alternatively, there is the possibility that nondurable goods were actively traded for hoes. Although I believe the Mill Creek communities were self-sufficient in good times, the presence of large riverine fish in the faunal assemblage may reflect active exchange with neighboring groups. Likewise, as Drooker (1992) suggests for Wickliffe and other Mississippian sites, there may have been a thriving trade in the cloth and textile items that we see imprinted on ceramics, ranging from clothing to bags. The list of potentially important exchange goods that are poorly preserved is very large; what unites them is the likelihood that they could have been obtained from nearby groups. This also holds true for the nonlocal cherts present at Dillow's Ridge. Thus, the exchange relations that fostered the production of hoes were likely tied to friends and neighbors in the larger region, rather than faceless consumers living in distant chiefdoms. Finally, while it may be a Western notion to think that hoes did not have the "value" to merit exchange with prestige goods, at the very least we must entertain the notion that Mississippian trade involved different spheres of exchange (sensu Bohannon 1955; Malinowski 1961).

8 Production and Power: Defining Scales

Using traditional nomenclature, the available evidence from the Mill Creek locale suggests the presence of part-time specialists working within a production system that was dispersed yet encompassed a few mound sites. The wide spatial distribution of communities, workshops, and source areas—combined with the lack of any clearly defined social hierarchy—further indicates that centralization of production was absent or very attenuated. Yet the descriptors "specialized" and "centralized" are very general concepts, even when broken down into subcategories, and they do not give much of a sense of the historical relations of production among hoe producers. Nor do such categories provide much assistance in describing the multiplicity of power relations surrounding producers, exchangers, and consumers of hoes.

To best characterize these various sets of relations, I will return to the themes of scale and history that I argued for at the beginning of the book. Specifically, I examine how relations of production and power in the Mill Creek locale were resolved at different scales, from the local to the regional, and how these different fields of relations were poised in a dynamic tension. Further, I consider the social reproduction of labor and power, not as an essentialistic Mississippian phenomenon involving widely shared strategies across the Southeast, but as a historical set of relations within the Mill Creek locale. As I believe the data have shown, this region does not appear to have undergone the sort of transformation that some have argued for Mississippian regions elsewhere, in which elites may have usurped some control over the economy for their own gain (e.g., Emerson 1997; Pauketat 1994; Welch 1991). Yet labor relations in the Mill Creek locale were not necessarily like those in other small-scale Mississippian polities, either, and grasping this sense of variability entails the historically framed understanding of social reproduction that I have argued for. Finally, I propose that an important element of this history involves the formation and maintenance of a community identity; that from an agency-centered or bottom-up perspective, communities in the Mill Creek locale produced and exchanged hoes in part because they were interested in combining local tradition with the wider sphere of symbols and materials that we associate with "Mississippian."

FROM PRODUCER TO CONSUMER: A *CHAÎNE DE TRAVAIL*

As I observed in the first chapter, one difficulty with addressing different scales of political-economic activity is delineating the various levels of interaction. It has been particularly difficult to reconcile binary concepts of agency and structure with the more nuanced layering of practices and beliefs that underlie social organization in all of its complexities. North American archaeologists typically deal with this issue in terms of the interplay between panregional manifestations of traits, on the one hand, and how they are modified at specific sites or localities, on the other (e.g., Nassaney and Sassaman 1995). For my purposes, I will define three levels of social reproduction and potentially different fields of power: the specific communities involved in hoe production (e.g., Dillow's Ridge, the Hale site); the aggregate of hoe-producing communities, which I have referred to as the Mill Creek locale; and the larger Mississippian world of the Lower Ohio and Central Mississippi valleys.

PRODUCTION AND POWER: LOCAL COMMUNITIES

What I would like to suggest first is that the form of specialization evident at specific communities such as Dillow's Ridge was part of the process of immediate social reproduction, which occurred in the absence of sharply defined opposing interests outside of gender relations or the kin system. In contrast to elite-sponsored specialization in which one major outcome is to perpetuate positions of status, specialization in hoe-producing communities was devoted to more communal notions of social reproduction. The mobilization of labor for making hoes involved a form of power to as opposed to power over. Or, to use Wolf's (1990) nomenclature, it appears unlikely that interest groups were able to achieve a level of tactical power over the production of hoes. There are several lines of evidence to support this contention. For one, it is difficult to envision huge amounts of hoes being produced over very short intervals in the Mill Creek locale on the basis of the relative dispersion of workshops and very general estimates of biface production amounts. Also, lithic reduction strategies among sites do not seem to reflect a very strong adherence to any type of structured production of the sort that might be mandated by elites. Further, there is no evidence for elite burials at likely locations such as the Hale site. Finally, there is no hard evidence (e.g., diagnostic ceramic types such as Ramey Incised) whatsoever that elites (or any individuals) from major consumer regions had any direct contact with the Mill Creek locale, much less controlled the source areas.

Those individuals living at the Hale site, Dillow's Ridge, and other workshop communities, and who were specifically engaged in the production of hoes, likely represented some form of interest group. But this interest group was not necessarily defined by the manufacture of implements for trade as is commonly assumed in studies of specialization; rather, it is likely that lithic production was subsumed or assumed by a preexisting interest group. If we can use the mortuary evidence for flintknappers from other sites in eastern North America as an example (Cobb and Pope 1998; Seeman 1984), that group probably consisted of adult males. Moreover, there is no evidence that they were alienated from the means of production. The botanical and faunal remains from Dillow's Ridge suggest that the community consisted of farmers and foragers, reminiscent of other Mississippian groups. Subsistence practices were likely carried out by all families, as is well documented in the ethnohistoric record for the Southeast. Furthermore, access to chert sources does not appear to have been restricted to only select groups within the Mill Creek locale given the widespread distribution of quarries and workshops.

Flintknappers, on the other hand, may have had privileged access to the means of reproduction, if hoes and Ramey knives constituted an important source for acquiring goods from elsewhere. Yet we have no evidence that flintknappers converted this capability into the positions of power and privilege as manifested at the large, well-known Mississippian sites such as Cahokia, Etowah, and Moundville. Consequently, I would argue that the interest groups who took on the production of hoes more closely resemble the "classes" that Saitta (1994) contends were characteristic of communal political economies. In other words, the impetus for the mobilization of surplus likely welled up from within the social or kinship group, rather than at the behest of elites. Yet such pressures were not completely divorced from regional forces.

PRODUCTION, DISTRIBUTION, AND POWER: THE MILL CREEK LOCALE

Tensions within the Mill Creek locale could have been created through attempts by ambitious individuals or select groups to promote control over chert resources and thereby the surplus production of hoes. Within the area, the best evidence so far of attempts to transcend the local order is the Hale site. This strategically located community is near a number of the quarries and enjoys access to the confluence of the two major streams in the area, one of which (Mill Creek) is tributary to the Cache River, a key outlet to the Ohio River. The construction of small platform and mortuary mounds does display an attempt by inhabitants to engage in the trappings of Mississippian ceremonialism. Wolf (1990) has observed that the role of power becomes evident where major organizational changes put signification under challenge. In this context, the construction of symbol-laden mounds (Knight 1986) at the Hale site may have challenged local power structures, but the process may have been more successful at spurring intercommunity tensions, rather than transforming local power relations into an arena of structural power or power over.

The comparative, statistical study of bifaces from the main quarry and Hale sites did not support the notion that occupants of the Hale site were differentially completing hoes roughed out at source areas, which, if true, could have been used to argue for attempts to control the final product in a staged sequence of manufacture. Yet that kind of lithic reduction analysis cannot assess whether hoes completed elsewhere in the locale still had to pass through the Hale site or other "gatekeepers" before moving out into the Mississippian world. Reduction patterns based on debitage from the workshops are more equivocal with respect to the degree of biface completion at the various loci.

Practically speaking, even with the somewhat ambiguous lithic results, the small scale of the Hale earthworks suggests a significant lack of control over labor even within that community, with efforts at monumentality probably impeded by low population levels as well. Furthermore, the sparse funerary inventory at the Hale site indicates an attenuated development of local leadership positions and inability to actively engage in the far-flung Mississippian exchange networks that one might expect with a monopolization of local surplus and initial exchange through a single outlet (Cobb 1989). The manufacture of hoes at the Linn site to the west further attests to the success of some groups peripheral to the source areas in obtaining access to raw materials. It does appear that the Linn and Hale sites both enjoyed a potentially advantageous location with respect to how hoes may have moved out of the Mill Creek locale. Again, however, if Hale site residents somehow manipulated external exchange, they apparently did not gain great material recompense for their efforts.

The "underdevelopment" of social hierarchy in the Mill Creek locale presents a seeming paradox: How did the demand for hoes at a wide scale resolve itself into a continuity of production at the local scale without the intermediary of a centralized authority? The apparent contradiction is heightened by the fact that the continuity of production is on the order of four centuries. Moreover, from the onset of the Mississippian period the large bifaces seem to have been exchanged out of the Mill Creek area in finished form, indicating some sense of pancommunity structure despite the lack of evidence for the strong development of elites and centralized power.

Although one is hesitant in going too far afield in drawing analogies, it is noteworthy that a somewhat similar case has been documented for stone axe production in the New Guinea highlands (Burton 1984, 1989). At the time of contact with Europeans during the first part of the twentieth century, it is estimated that a limited number of groups with access to quarry areas were manufacturing 1,000 axes per year. The axes were instrumental in field clearing for agricultural production, yet had little exchange value compared with prestige items. Importantly, major cooperative ventures in chert procurement and axe production were achieved in the absence of centralization—local communities controlled their own surplus labor.

In this case demand was not felt directly by axe producers through the needs of distant agriculturists from afar, although the axes were widely exchanged to such areas. Instead, Burton argues that two factors drove production: (1) relatively high values for axes in the immediate vicinity outside of the source areas and (2) the production of large, ceremonial axes that were used for bride prices and to forge prestigious exchange relations. The latter were exchanged alongside the utilitarian axes.

A key point in the preceding example is that down-the-line exchange operating at short intervals was able to accommodate and promote a large-scale production of utilitarian items without fostering a major transformation in the relations of production. Groups involved in axe manufacture were actively involved in exchange networks with a number of neighboring groups for underwriting an expanded scale of social reproduction without the intermediary of a strong central authority. The demands on surplus production were more immediate one-to-one relations and alliances with adjacent groups, yet the recognized value of utilitarian and, in particular, exotic bifaces led to sustained, cooperative production ventures in which labor was under the direct control of the producer.

Meillassoux (1978:160), Wolf (1982:91), and others (following Marx 1977:284–85) have argued that one trend evident in groups that move from a foraging to a more agriculturally based economy is that land becomes an instrument of labor rather than the subject of labor. Groups begin to work under a notion that returns on production may be delayed and long-term cooperation may be necessary for certain efforts.

In turn, this process typically leads to a situation in which communities form discrete social units with well-defined membership, some sense of larger structure, and the emergence of leadership positions (but not necessarily powerful elites). Nevertheless, production continues to be rationalized at the local level even at the same time that matrimonial and exchange alliances are extending outward. Such societies may exhibit a general structure that is "at once cellular and segmented and yet able to generate links between different cells and segments" (Wolf 1982:48).

This trend embodies a growing disparity between the scale of production and the scale of social reproduction. In small-scale societies the realms of production and reproduction may not be isomorphic, but they are much more closely correlated (Thomas 1987:408–9). In other words, producers are more likely to develop exchange alliances with other producers who are closely related or who live nearby. Yet when land and resources have become a developed instrument of labor, production may still be segmented locally while local social structures may be maintained through a larger social unit of reproduction (Meillassoux 1978). At this point, emergent leaders may develop a control over external exchange transactions to acquire prestige goods that promote their status, although they still have weak control over production and labor within their own communities (Frankenstein and Rowlands 1978; Friedman 1975; Schneider 1977). This kind of power is difficult to characterize with either a power to or power over designation, particularly since it may involve subtle forms of control closely linked to ritual and ideology (e.g., Keesing 1987; McGuire and Saitta 1996; Pauketat 1994).

Chronological data on changes in the spatial scale of hoe manufacture are currently sparse, but they may manifest similar trends in the historical transformation in the scale of social reproduction. For example, in chapter 6 I noted that the Emergent Mississippian Petitt site on the banks of the Mississippi River—a locale that seems to have been outside of the nuclear area of hoe production during later Mississippian times—contains evidence for the production of Mill Creek hoes (Parry 1992). This may suggest that prior to the onset of the Mississippian period hoe manufacture and primary exchange were more widely dispersed and locally autonomous. Social production and reproduction likely operated at fairly restricted scales, with low hoe production output. Although hoes were moving into the American Bottom during this time frame, the lack of nonlocal objects at the Petitt site suggests that their immediate trading partners were more likely to be neighbors.

Moving into the Mississippian period, production of finished bifaces seems to have contracted closer around the chert sources into a collection of loose-knit, interacting communities for a period of several centuries. Simultaneously, there was a great upsurge in hoe output and exchange, which presumably was a major factor in the establishment of external relations. In return, copper, galena, fluorspar, and other nonlocal materials are found with burials in the Mill Creek community, reflecting a more sustained interaction with outside communities than seen during the Emergent Mississippian period. The scale of effective social reproduction thus seems to have increased to a larger zone beyond the Mill Creek locale, as nonlocal goods became integrated into notions of community identity.

Here it must be admitted that this diachronic model in fact suffers serious shortcomings in terms of what happened within the Mississippian period. The only radiocarbon dates we have are from Dillow's Ridge, but I have tended to speak of the site types as roughly synchronous. In other words, I have treated the mound sites (Linn, Hale, Elco) and Dillow's Ridge as at least overlapping in time and have assumed that at least some of the workshops and quarries were contemporaneous as well. In reality, however, future research in the region may discover other alternatives. One possibility is that access to the quarries was still open in the first part of the Mississippian sequence and workshops from that era are remnants of seasonal hoe production. The locale may not have been occupied full-time until sometime in the 1200s A.D. In this regard, stone box graves, the primary form of interment recorded in the region, are considered to be a relatively late Mississippian phenomenon. It is also possible to envision the mound sites as being sequentially occupied with a regionwide influence around the sources—even if weak—as opposed to contemporary entities with very small spatial domains.

Nevertheless, whatever form of Mississippian settlement history transpired within the Mill Creek locale, it apparently did not involve the development of a strong central authority. While in a technical sense there was a specialization in the production of large bifaces, surplus labor seems to have been mobilized at the community level without involving institutionalized appropriation by elites. This is a far cry from the sort of specialization called to mind by historic accounts of more complex chiefdoms in which elites enjoyed institutionalized access to goods made by specialized producers (e.g., Earle 1987b; Helms 1979).

Some studies have made the interesting point that control over lithic production may be eschewed by elites because they find that workers themselves can more effectively manage the manufacturing process (Pope and Pollock 1995; Shafer and Hester 1983). Lineages or similar groups may organize production, while elites may attempt some degree of control over distribution. The Mill Creek locale appears to depart from this model in that elites apparently played no role whatsoever in the production process or immediate exchange networks, coming into the picture only as hoes moved into more distant polities, where local leaders may have overseen the dissemination of the tools within their respective spheres of influence. In this respect, the traditional prestige-goods model does fail us, because the elites who presumably serve as the driving impetus behind exchange were not present in the Mill Creek locale. Thus we must turn to other alternatives as a driving force behind social reproduction.

EXCHANGE, CONSUMPTION, AND POWER: THE MISSISSIPPIAN WORLD

It has now become conventional to point out that production, exchange, and consumption cannot be divorced; that each represents part of a larger whole that, in itself, is not merely economic. As a point of departure, though, archaeologists frequently focus on just one of these elements. This is perhaps understandable from a methodological viewpoint because, in some instances, a good part of one's career can be devoted to unraveling basic patterns of exchange or consumption for a single artifact type. I have been fortunate in this respect in that a number of outstanding scholars, ranging from William Phillips and William Holmes at the turn of the century to Howard Winters more recently, have provided a wealth of basic data upon which to build this study.

Yet we should never lose sight of the economic or social totality. Even if we focus on production, we should keep in mind that Giddens's (1979) notion of *structuration* probably has some salience to traditional conceptions of the political economy. In other words, production (or exchange, or consumption) may play an important role in determining the political economy, but the political economy in turn structures production. And, because the political economy encompasses the realm of symbols and meaning, as well as the lower levels of Hawkes's (1954) ladder of inference, we must continually explore the wider ramifications of those changes that we document in the technological and economic realms.

In most cases, the final resting place for a hoe appears to have been just as humble as its beginnings—typically within a household context, either in its original form or recycled into another utilitarian tool. If the labor involved in production was predominately male, however, the predominant labor involved in consumption was likely female. If, as Engels (1972) argued, an original form of oppression was along the lines of gender, the hoe may have served as an instrument in the reproduction of gender inequality during the Mississippian era. The contradiction here is that, even if agricultural labor involved domination, the demand for hoes may have been spurred by that very group who constituted the dominated. Chert hoes represented a form of technology that, because of their superiority over other raw materials, potentially alleviated some of the work associated with agricultural tasks. As a consequence, widespread consumption at a small scale may have snowballed into a regional demand that had an impact that was far more than the sum of its parts.

Recognition of that demand appears to have presented an opportunity for strategically located Mississippian elites. The coincidence of distributional caches at mound sites appears to represent instances in which hoes were being held over before ultimate dissemination to hinterlands. The very low profile of hoes in Mississippian art and iconography renders suspect the degree of symbolic power associated with their control. Nevertheless, hoes may have been part of a larger parcel of mundane goods that were plied through Mississippian networks and contributed to the various degrees of authority enjoyed by elites in various regions.

It is important to emphasize here the loose and unstable articulation of various realms of power envisioned in my tripartite, scalar scenario. Elites may have taken advantage of the interregional trade of hoes, but were unable to control source areas or production in southwestern Illinois. Hoe producers may have had differential access to the source areas, but were unable to effect a regional monopoly that would allow them to manipulate the value of the tools. If the same is true for other goods in the world of Mississippian long-distance exchange, it emphasizes why it is so difficult to picture a Mississippian world system that has any strong analogues with modern world system models: the latter require much more strongly articulated relations of power and inequality between cores and peripheries.

SOCIAL REPRODUCTION AND COMMUNITY IDENTITY

Even given the multiplicity of power relations involved in the entire cycle of the hoes, from production to exchange to consumption, the arguments I have made still seem to have a functional cast. To wit, hoes played an important role in agriculture at one level and in perpetuating relations of production and power at another. Yet, I cannot help but think that hoes, and by extension Mississippian exchange in general, involved even deeper relations below the fetish of technology. Even considering the possibility that stone tools may have played a role in the political economy of households fails to peel away all of the layers of meaning attached to their production, exchange, and consumption. As one of my closing thoughts, I would like to entertain the notion that Mississippian exchange and consumption also may have played a role in identity formation; that producing hoes may have been one route for communities in the Mill Creek locale to procure materials and symbols that proclaimed them as part of a larger sphere of interaction and meaning.

Within the framework of reproduction, production for exchange converges with consumption and identity. Producers create goods and services with the expectation that goods and services (or wages) will be returned, whereupon the producer also becomes consumer. Consumption, in turn, is closely linked to strategies of self-definition and self-maintenance (Friedman 1994:148; S. Jones 1996:72). Although processual and post-processual archaeologists alike seem to agree that we must shy away from viewing culture in a normative sense, social reproduction does imply an attempt to maintain a thread of continuity. That is not to say that the thread is invariant through time, but societies do endeavor at some level to replicate commonly held practices and beliefs that are tied to a sense of social identity. Identity is thus not a static outcome; it is an ongoing process. One reason identities are always in a state of flux concerns the power relations that underlie corporate notions of self: societies are continually beset by struggles between factions attempting to control the discourse, practice, and materiality of identity—and these types of struggles constitute a central focus of political-economic studies.

Research on identity and power in anthropology encompasses a long history involving acculturation, transculturation, and ethnicity studies, among other approaches. Many of these works involve notions of multiscalar power relations in that they typically address the assimilation or admixture of cultural traits in fields of uneven power relations: most often when capitalism or mercantilism penetrate areas outside of Europe. While this body of research has shown an increasing sophistication in the treatment of interchange between cultures, until very recently there has not been much call to look further back in time, before the world system as we know it existed (see Dietler 1998; Jones 1997; Wells 1998).

I should emphasize that, if hoes were important to social reproduction, and thereby identity reproduction, for producers in the Mill Creek locale, it is unlikely they were the only means to that end. I do not wish to lapse into "litho-centrism" merely because I find the production of these implements intrinsically interesting. However, social reproduction does involve recreating the realities and experiences of everyday lives and is just as likely to include the production and consumption of utilitarian items as it is so-called prestige goods (Keesing 1987:164). In this regard, hoes were probably just one of a number of items—even in the Mill Creek locale—that constituted the currency of exchange, consumption, and identity formation.

Much of the archaeological literature linking material culture to notions of identity has relied heavily upon style, and in eastern North America the vagaries of preservation have made ceramics particularly important in this area of research (e.g., Braun and Plog 1982; Pauketat and Emerson 1991). Yet technology may also have been intertwined with style in identity formation (e.g., Lemonnier 1992:85–87). In this regard, arrows tipped by Kaolin, Cobden, and regional cherts, rather than Mill Creek chert, may have been just as important and visible markers of community as the motifs and decorations seen on pottery. As Cathy Costin (1998) has pointed out, the idea of using social identity to get at the organization of production is a recent endeavor, but one that seems to show great promise.

Within the Mill Creek locale, the contingent conditions of culture history (the rise of agriculture), and even geology, may have provided an unanticipated opportunity for using hoe exchange for the mundane social reproduction involving objects from everyday life, whereas producers in other Mississippian communities were relying on other objects of daily exchange. Hence, the labor involved with large biface manufacture may have replaced, rather than added to, many of the non-subsistence productive tasks we often associate with Mississippian households and communities. Instead of making shell beads for exchange, for example—a common product of Mississippian households in other regions—communities in the Mill Creek locale may have opted to focus on producing hoes to exchange for beads and other objects deemed essential for adornment, ritual, or other purposes. Even comestibles may have been key to the formation and maintenance of identities. The consumption of large riverine fish at the upland community of Dillow's Ridge may say just as much about "you are what you eat" as it does about ingesting protein; that is, participating in the Mississippian world may have involved eating what other people ate, just as it involved the construction of mounds or the use of widely shared iconography (Emanuel Breitburg, personal communication, 1998). Mark Rees (1997) has suggested that mortuary offerings of fish and a prevalence of fish effigy vessels in the Central Mississippi River Valley are indicative of the use of fish for tribute and as symbols of alliance in that region during the Mississippian period. The Dillow's Ridge faunal assemblage may reflect that the acquisition of certain species of fish was just as important to households as it was to elites.

The role of geography should not be overlooked in the pluralistic creation of Mississippian identities. For instance, the interior location of the Mill Creek chert quarries likely played a strong role in the rural character of the surrounding sites. Not least in this regard is the limited productivity of the region compared with the expansive floodplains of the Mississippi and Ohio rivers, which surely placed constraints on population levels and community size. Restricted access to major waterways also may have reduced access to the more fancy accoutrements of Mississippian material culture. It is notable that blufftop cemeteries containing copper plates and shell gorgets (presumably associated with the Linn site and other floodplain settlements) are not that distant from the Mill Creek locale—less than 10 kilometers—but the easterly flow of fancy goods appears to diminish greatly once the Illinois Ozarks are encountered. This break possibly represents the effective eastern limits of the floodplain-based polities and may reflect a reluctance on their part to trade highly valued symbolic goods for "mere" hoes.

I should emphasize that these thoughts are proffered as a basis for further research on the political economy of identity in the Mississippian world. If this had been the primary thrust of my research, identity would have been a central theme of the first chapters of the study, and I hope not to leave the reader with the sense that I have pulled a "bait and switch." The idea of identity formation is salient to the point raised in the second chapter, where I argued that describing the actual groups who mobilized surplus was an integral part of understanding the class process. It would be of interest to examine whether the Mill Creek locale constituted a community with a sense of material identity that was distinctive in the Central Mississippi Valley and whether the region could even be broken down into distinguishable, constituent subgroups, such as flintknappers.

As this study neared its conclusion, I eventually became just as interested in the idea of why certain forms of production, exchange, and consumption may have occurred as I was in how they occurred. It seems that the reproduction of community and identity in the Mississippian world likely involved an uneasy balance between the more inward-looking relations that fostered autonomy and tradition and the more outward-looking relations that promoted external ties and an expanded scale of social reproduction—and this balance could vary greatly even over short distances. For reasons still poorly understood, sometime around A.D. 1000 widely dispersed groups around the Southeast began to borrow from a shared repertoire of art, technology, monumentality, and subsistence practices in order to forge identities that display broad similarities across space and time at one scale, yet exhibit considerable diversity when viewed at a more minute level of archaeological magnification. In the Mill Creek locale this interplay between agency and structure may have been forged, in part, by the production of agricultural implements and their subsequent exchange for regional and nonlocal goods.

CHIEFDOM REVISITED

It is received wisdom that this larger structure in which the Mill Creek locale participated—that which we call Mississippian—was knitted by interlocking chiefdoms. Yet, it is questionable whether the appellation "chiefdom" is appropriate for the Mill Creek case. This neo-evolutionary category has encountered resistance among many Southeastern archaeologists, not only because of the usual taxonomic problems involved in identifying a chiefdom, but also because many Mississippian communities do not appear to have been strongly hierarchical political-economic entities even if one believes the concept has some validity (Muller 1997:42–43; O'Brien and Wood 1998:344). My interpretation has been that evidence for outside control of the quarries by Cahokia or other nonlocal centers is thin to nonexistent, while social hierarchy locally was weakly developed. What leaders there were in the Mill Creek locale apparently were trying to "talk the talk" with mounds and other forms of signification, but were unable to "walk the walk" when it came to power relations. I doubt if the Mill Creek locale was unique among Mississippian regions in this regard. Whereas hinterlands in some regions may have been under the control of one center or another, or else consisted of small and autonomous communities, I would suggest that the Mill Creek locale was somewhere in between: displaying some evidence of pancommunity integration, but without the development of a clearly differentiated social hierarchy.

Nevertheless, Mill Creek hoes undoubtedly were being consumed by polities that can be construed as chiefdoms, and both objects and ideas were in turn filtering their way back down to the Mill Creek locale. As a result, communities like the Hale site had the material gloss of a chiefdom, but lacked a strongly differentiated social hierarchy. Our models of diversity for Mississippian political economies must pay more attention to these shadow chiefdoms, where the vague trappings of larger polities may be assumed, but the scale, richness, and diversity fall far short in comparison.

Another example of such an entity can be found in southeastern Illinois about 50 kilometers east of the Mill Creek locale. In the upland headwaters of the Bay Creek drainage there is a small ceremonial site known as Millstone Bluff, briefly discussed in chapter 5. The site is perched atop one of the highest hills in the eastern Shawnees, a prominence that appears to have a history of ceremonial use extending at least as far back as the Late Woodland period. The Mississippian component of Millstone Bluff consists of more than 25 house basins arranged around a square plaza. Millstone Bluff also contains a stone box grave cemetery and a sizable corpus of Mississippian rock art (Butler and Cobb 2001). There also is a sprinkling of Mississippian sites along the small drainages around Millstone Bluff (Rudolph 1977).

Radiocarbon dates indicate that Millstone Bluff was occupied in the latter half of the Mississippian sequence, similar to Dillow's Ridge. It appears to have been established at the same time that larger Mississippian polities were fragmenting in the Lower Ohio Valley, sometime in the mid to late 1200s A.D. (Clay 1997; Muller 1986). Millstone Bluff and surrounding sites likely represent splinter groups from the Lower Ohio Valley; perhaps the uplands served as a refuge from the uncertainties of life along the Ohio River. Whatever the reasons for the population movement, the groups that established themselves in the eastern Shawnee Hills do not seem to have attained the level of political complexity and control over labor seen at large centers like Kincaid, or even at moderate sized mound centers along the Lower Ohio. Yet the people who occupied Millstone Bluff adhered to certain regularities and themes that we broadly take as Mississippian: a central plaza for conducting ceremonies; the use of falcons and other important imagery in rock art; and continuity in burial practices, especially in the use of stone box graves.

Such communities, like those in the Mill Creek locale, lived on the margin of Mississippian life as it is popularly conceived. Yet that isolation is more apparent in geography than it is in identity. The notions of identity or "self" assumed by hinterland groups included symbols, aspects of the built environment, and mortuary practices that were common to chiefdoms in the surrounding major river valleys. In this sense the uplands may have embodied an interesting contradiction: an attempt to adhere to a sense of regional identity that we recognize as Mississippian, while at the same time withdrawing (purposely?) from major corridors of Mississippian interaction. Although we do not always know why agricultural groups moved up into more ecologically marginal environments, many of the possible reasons concern power: splintering of social groups among floodplain polities; groups moving to escape the demands of leaders; or warfare.

In this light, it is oversimplistic to view the movement of late prehistoric groups into the chert-rich uplands of southwestern Illinois as merely an economic choice to take advantage of a lucrative resource. It was also a social choice, likely intertwined with political and economic decisions as well. As a result, the production of hoes cannot be understood solely as a manifestation of the organization of technology, at least as that field of study is currently framed in lithic research. Nor can hoe manufacture be reduced to a category of specialization. It was a complex manifestation of labor embedded within the domestic economy, articulated to larger spheres of social reproduction, and linked to regional constructions of identity.

If we can extrapolate from the ethnohistoric sources on gender roles, then adult males were most likely the producers of chert hoes, and possibly those in the best position to take advantage of any immediate benefits accruing from the exchange of hoes (Thomas 1997). But if we integrate notions of identity and community with hoe production, it is difficult to envision the idea of independent producers making tools in a social vacuum. Production demands were likely fueled by pressures from individual family members or groups, who in turn were probably acting on socially constructed needs for objects and comestibles unavailable in the immediate locale. It may be that hoe manufacturers were "attached" specialists, but not in the sense that they were attached to elites. Instead, they were attached to a realm of social obligations and economic realities that dampened the monopolization of surplus at the community level and hindered aggrandizement and the leverage of power relations at the regional level.

But the life history of agricultural implements had only just begun once they left the hands of producers. From there, they moved into an exchange sphere and ultimately ended up in the hands of consumers, who most likely were women. Women may have desired hoes made from Mill Creek chert for any number of reasons, not least of which was their suitability for agricultural tasks relative to most other raw materials in the midcontinent. However, economic rationality is only a partial (and modern) explanation for consumer choice. The popularity of Mill Creek chert for Mississippian hoes may have involved more than the usefulness of this raw material for heavy-duty tasks requiring a durable edge. History and social context also played important roles. The growing panregional demand may have been fueled in part by opportunistic individuals or groups near the source areas who were able to marshal sufficient labor to increase production of a general tool that already had a long and proven history. In part, this strategy may have helped to offset rival technologies or raw materials, although producers of Dover chert hoes from Tennessee appear to have made some headway into the Lower Ohio Valley later in the Mississippian sequence.

From the view of the long term, it is possible that the preference for Mill Creek chert hoes at A.D. 1100 based on technological reasons, may have, by A.D. 1300, evolved into an ingrained and socially natural choice. To reiterate Howard Winters's (1981) insight, by well into the Mississippian period, hoes made from Mill Creek chert may have been *de rigueur* for the average farmer in the Central Mississippi and Lower Ohio valleys—for reasons relating to historical tradition as well as for raw material characteristics.

References Cited

Adair, James
1930 *Adair's History of the American Indians.* Watanga Press, Johnson City, Tenn.

Ahler, Steven A.
1989 Mass Analysis of Flaking Debris: Studying the Forest Rather than the Trees. In *Alternative Approaches to Lithic Analysis,* edited by D. O. Henry and G. H. Odell, pp. 85–118. Archeological Papers No. 1. American Anthropological Association, Washington, D.C.

Althusser, Louise, and Étienne Balibar
1970 *Reading Capital.* Pantheon, New York.

Ammerman, Albert J., and William Andrefsky, Jr.
1982 Reduction Sequences and the Exchange of Obsidian in Neolithic Calabria. In *Contexts for Prehistoric Exchange,* edited by T. K. Earle and J. E. Ericson, pp. 149–72. Academic Press, New York.

Anderson, David G.
1994 *The Savannah River Chiefdoms: Political Change in the Late Prehistoric Southeast.* University of Alabama Press, Tuscaloosa.

Anderson, David G., and J. W. Joseph
1988 *Prehistory and History Along the Upper Savannah River: Technical Synthesis of Cultural Resource Investigations, Richard B. Russell Multiple Resource Area,* vol. 1. Interagency Archeological Services, National Park Service, Atlanta, Georgia.

Anderson, David G., David W. Stahle, and Malcolm K. Cleaveland
1995 Paleoclimate and the Potential Food Reserves of Mississippian Societies: A Case Study from the Savannah River Valley. *American Antiquity* 60:258–86.

Andrefsky, William, Jr.
1994 Raw-Material Availability and the Organization of Technology. *American Antiquity* 59:21–34.
1998 *Lithics: Macroscopic Approaches to Analysis.* Cambridge University Press, Cambridge.

Anonymous
   1973   *Central States Archaeological Journal* 20:39.
Appadurai, Arjun
   1986   Introduction: Commodities and the Politics of Value. In *The Social Life of Things: Commodities in Cultural Perspective,* edited by A. Appadurai, pp. 3–63. Cambridge University Press, Cambridge.
Arnold, Jeanne E.
   1996   Organizational Transformations: Power and Labor Among Complex Hunter-Gatherers and Other Intermediate Societies. In *Emergent Complexity: The Evolution of Intermediate Societies,* edited by J. E. Arnold, pp. 59–73. Archaeological Series 9. International Monographs in Prehistory, Ann Arbor, Mich.
Asad, Talal
   1987   Are There Histories of Peoples Without Europe? *Comparative Studies in Society and History* 29:594–607.
Asch, David L., and Nancy E. Asch
   1985   Prehistoric Plant Cultivation in West-Central Illinois. In *Prehistoric Food Production in North America,* edited by R. I. Ford, pp. 149–203. Anthropological Papers No. 75. Museum of Anthropology, University of Michigan, Ann Arbor.
Bamforth, Douglas B.
   1986   Technological Efficiency and Tool Curation. *American Antiquity* 51:38–50.
Bareis, Charles J., and James W. Porter
   1984   *American Bottom Archaeology: A Summary of the FAI-270 Project Contribution to the Culture History of the Mississippi River Valley.* University of Illinois Press, Urbana.
Bartram, William
   1955   *The Travels of William Bartram.* (Originally published 1791, as *Travels Through North and South Carolina, Georgia, East and West Florida.*) Dover, New York.
Beaudry, Mary C., Lauren J. Cook, and Stephen A. Mrozowski
   1991   Artifacts and Active Voices: Material Culture as Social Discourse. In *The Archaeology of Inequality,* edited by R. H. McGuire and R. W. Paynter, pp. 150–91. Basil Blackwell, Oxford.
Bell, Robert E.
   1947   Trade Materials at Spiro as Indicated by Artifacts. *American Antiquity* 12:181–84.
Belmont, John S.
   1983   Appendix D: Faunal Remains. In *Excavations at the Lake George Site, Yazoo County, Mississippi,* by S. Williams and

J. P. Brain, pp. 451–69. Papers of the Peabody Museum No. 74. Harvard University Press, Cambridge.

Bender, Barbara

1985 Emergent Tribal Formations in the American Mid-Continent. *American Antiquity* 50:52–62.

1989 The Roots of Inequality. In *Domination and Resistance*, edited by D. Miller, M. Rowlands, and C. Tilley, pp. 83–95. Unwin Hyman, London.

1990 The Dynamics of Nonhierarchical Societies: Sociopolitics in Small-Scale Sedentary Societies. In *The Evolution of Political Systems: Sociopolitics in Small-Scale Sedentary Societies*, edited by S. Upham, pp. 247–63. Cambridge University Press, Cambridge.

Bender, D. R.

1967 A Refinement of the Concept of Household: Families, Co-residence, and Domestic Functions. *American Anthropologist* 69:495–504.

Bernbeck, Reinhard

1995 Lasting Alliances and Emerging Competition: Economic Developments in Early Mesopotamia. *Journal of Anthropological Archaeology* 14:1–25.

Billings, Deborah A.

1984 *An Analysis of Lithic Workshop Debris from Iron Mountain, Union County, Illinois.* Research Paper No. 47. Center for Archaeological Investigations, Southern Illinois University at Carbondale.

Binford, Lewis R.

1979 Organization and Formation Processes: Looking at Curated Technologies. *Journal of Anthropological Research* 35:255–73.

1980 Willow Smoke and Dogs' Tails: Hunter-Gatherer Settlement Systems and Archaeological Site Formation. *American Antiquity* 45:4–20.

Black, Glenn A.

1967 *The Angel Site.* Indiana Historical Society, Indianapolis.

Blitz, John

1988 Adoption of the Bow in Prehistoric North America. *North American Archaeologist* 9:123–45.

1993a *Ancient Chiefdoms of the Tombigbee.* University of Alabama Press, Tuscaloosa.

1993b Big Pots for Big Shots: Feasting and Storage in a Mississippian Community. *American Antiquity* 58:80–96.

Bloch, Maurice

1989 *Ritual, History, and Power.* Athlone Press, London.

Bohannon, Paul
  1955   Some Principles of Exchange and Investment Among the Tiv. *American Anthropologist* 57:60–70.
Bourdieu, Pierre
  1977   *Outline of a Theory of Practice.* Cambridge University Press, Cambridge.
Bradbury, Andrew P.
  1997   The Bow and Arrow in the Eastern Woodlands: Evidence for an Archaic Origin. *North American Archaeologist* 18:207–33.
Bradbury, Andrew P., and Philip J. Carr
  1995   Flake Typologies and Alternative Approaches: An Experimental Assessment. *Lithic Technology* 20:100–115.
Bradley, James W.
  1987   *Evolution of the Onondaga Iroquois.* Syracuse University Press, Syracuse.
Bradley, Richard, and Mark Edmonds
  1993   *Interpreting the Axe Trade: Production and Exchange in Neolithic Britain.* Cambridge University Press, Cambridge.
Brain, Jeffrey P.
  1988   *Tunica Archaeology.* Peabody Museum of Archaeology and Ethnology, Cambridge, Mass.
Brain, Jeffrey P., and Philip Phillips
  1996   *Shell Gorgets: Styles of the Late Prehistoric and Protohistoric Southeast.* Peabody Museum Press, Cambridge, Mass.
Braun, David P.
  1983   Pots as Tools. In *Archaeological Hammers and Theories,* by J. A. Moore and A. S. Keene, pp. 107–34. Academic Press, New York.
  1985   Ceramic Decorative Diversity and Illinois Woodland Regional Integration. In *Decoding Prehistoric Ceramics,* edited by B. A. Nelson, pp. 128–53. Southern Illinois University Press, Carbondale.
Braun, David P., and Stephen Plog
  1982   Evolution of "Tribal" Social Networks: Theory and Prehistoric North American Evidence. *American Antiquity* 47:504–25.
Braun, E. Lucy
  1967   *Deciduous Forests of North America.* Hafner, New York.
Braund, Kathryn E. Holland
  1993   *Deerskins and Duffles: The Creek Indian Trade with Anglo-Americans, 1685–1815.* University of Nebraska Press, Lincoln.
Brehm, H. C.
  1981   *The History of the Duck River Cache.* Miscellaneous Paper 6. Tennessee Anthropological Society, Knoxville.

Breitburg, Emanuel

1992 The Faunal Assemblage. In *The Petitt Site (11-Ax-253), Alexander County, Illinois*, edited by P. A. Webb, pp. 295–330. Research Paper No. 58. Center for Archaeological Investigations, Southern Illinois University at Carbondale.

1996 *Faunal Remains from Dillow's Ridge Site (U-635), Union County, Illinois.* Manuscript on file. Center for Archaeological Investigations, Southern Illinois University at Carbondale.

Brown, James A.

1975 Spiro Art and Its Mortuary Contexts. In *Death and the Afterlife in Pre-Columbian America*, by E. P. Benton, pp. 1–32. Dumbarton Oaks, Washington, D.C.

1976 The Southern Cult Reconsidered. *Midcontinental Journal of Archaeology* 1:115–35.

1983 Spiro Exchange Connections Revealed by Sources of Imported Raw Materials. In *Southeastern Natives and Their Pasts*, by D. G. Wyckoff and J. L. Hofman, pp. 129–62. Studies in Oklahoma's Past No. 11. Oklahoma Archaeological Society, Norman.

Brown, James A., Richard A. Kerber, and Howard D. Winters

1990 Trade and the Evolution of Exchange Relations at the Beginning of the Mississippian Period. In *The Mississippian Emergence*, edited by B. D. Smith, pp. 251–80. Smithsonian Institution Press, Washington, D.C.

Brown, Kenneth

1989 A Social Archaeology of Prehispanic Quiche-Maya Households. In *Households and Communities*, edited by S. MacEachern, D. J. W. Archer, and R. D. Garvin, pp. 381–87. Proceedings of the 21st Annual Chacmool Conference. University of Calgary Archaeology Association, Calgary.

Brumfiel, Elizabeth M.

1986 The Division of Labor at Xico: The Chipped Stone Industry. In *Research in Economic Anthropology, Supplement 2: Economic Aspects of Prehispanic Highland Mexico*, edited by B. L. Isaac, pp. 245–79. JAI Press, Greenwich, Conn.

Brumfiel, Elizabeth M., and Timothy K. Earle

1987 Specialization, Exchange, and Complex Societies: An Introduction. In *Specialization, Exchange, and Complex Societies*, edited by E. M. Brumfiel and T. K. Earle, pp. 1–9. Cambridge University Press, Cambridge.

Burton, John

1980 Making Sense of Waste Flakes: New Methods for Investigating the Technology and Economics Behind Chipped Stone Assemblage. *Journal of Archaeological Science* 7:131–48.

1984   Repeng and the Salt-Makers: 'Ecological Trade' and Stone
       Axe Production in the Papua New Guinea Highlands. *Man*
       24:255–72.

1989   Quarrying in a Tribal Society. *World Archaeology* 16:234–47.

Butler, Brian M.

1977   Mississippian Settlement in the Black Bottom, Pope and Massac Counties, Illinois. Ph.D. dissertation, Department of Anthropology, Southern Illinois University at Carbondale.

1991   Kincaid Revisited: The Mississippian Sequence in the Lower
       Ohio Valley. In *Cahokia and the Hinterlands: Middle Mississippian Cultures of the Midwest,* edited by T. E. Emerson and
       R. B. Lewis, pp. 264–73. University of Illinois Press, Urbana.

Butler, Brian M., and Charles R. Cobb

1996   A Tale of Two Villages: Late Prehistoric Life in Upland Southern Illinois. Paper presented at the 53rd Annual Meeting of
       the Southeastern Archaeological Conference, Birmingham, Ala.

2001   The Millstone Bluff Site: A First Approximation. In *Current
       Research in Kentucky,* edited by C. Hockensmith. Kentucky
       Heritage Commission, Frankfort. In press.

Cabeza de Vaca, Alvar Núñez

1993   *The Account: Alvar Núñez Cabeza de Vaca's* Relación. (Originally published 1542.) Translated by Martin A. Favata and
       José B. Fernández. Arte Público Press, Houston.

Callahan, Errett

1979   The Basics of Biface Knapping in the Eastern Fluted Point Tradition: A Manual for Flintknappers and Lithic Analysts. *Archaeology of Eastern North America* 7:1–180.

Canouts, Valetta, Ernest E. May, Neal H. Lopinot, and Jon D. Muller

1984   *Cultural Frontiers in the Upper Cache Valley, Illinois.* Research Paper No. 16. Center for Archaeological Investigations,
       Southern Illinois University at Carbondale.

Carniero, Robert

1981   The Chiefdom: Precursor to the State. In *The Transition to
       Statehood in the New World,* edited by G. D. Jones and R. R.
       Kautz, pp. 37–79. Cambridge University Press, Cambridge.

Carr, Philip J.

1994   The Organization of Technology: Impact and Potential. In *The
       Organization of North American Prehistoric Chipped Stone
       Tool Technologies,* edited by P. J. Carr, pp. 1–8. Archaeological
       Series 7. International Monographs in Prehistory, Ann Arbor,
       Mich.

Carr, Philip J., and Brad Koldehoff
1994 A Preliminary Analysis of Mississippian Lithic Technology at Wickliffe Mounds. *Tennessee Anthropologist* 19:46–65.

Chapman, Carl H.
1980 *The Archaeology of Missouri, II.* University of Missouri Press, Columbia.

Chapman, Jefferson, and Gary D. Crites
1987 Evidence for Early Maize (*Zea mays*) from the Icehouse Bottom Site, Tennessee. *American Antiquity* 52:352–54.

Chase-Dunn, Christopher, and Thomas D. Hall
1991 Conceptualizing Core/Periphery Hierarchies for Comparative Study. In *Core/Periphery Relation in Precapitalist Worlds,* edited by C. Chase-Dunn and T. D. Hall, pp. 5–33. Westview Press, Boulder, Colo.

Cheal, David
1989 Strategies of Resource Management in Household Economies: Moral Economy or Political Economy? In *The Household Economy: Reconsidering the Domestic Mode of Production,* edited by R. R. Wilk, pp. 11–22. Westview Press, Boulder, Colo.

Claassen, Cheryl P.
1991 Gender, Shellfishing, and the Shell Mound Archaic. In *Engendering Archaeology: Women and Prehistory,* edited by J. M. Gero and M. W. Conkey, pp. 276–300. Basil Blackwell, Oxford.

Clark, Gracia
1989 Separation Between Trading and Home for Asante Women in Kumasi Central Market, Ghana. In *The Household Economy: Reconsidering the Domestic Mode of Production,* edited by R. R. Wilk, pp. 91–118. Westview Press, Boulder, Colo.

Clark, John E.
1986 From Mountains to Molehills: A Critical Review of Teotihuacan's Obsidian Industry. In *Research in Economic Anthropology, Supplement 2: Economic Aspects of Prehispanic Highland Mexico,* edited by B. L. Isaac, pp. 23–74. JAI Press, Greenwich, Conn.
1987 Politics, Prismatic Blades, and Mesoamerican Civilization. In *The Organization of Core Technology,* edited by J. K. Johnson and C. A. Morrow, pp. 259–84. Westview Press, Boulder, Colo.
1995 Craft Specialization as an Archaeological Category. In *Research in Economic Anthropology,* vol. 16, edited by B. L. Isaac, pp. 267–94. JAI Press, Greenwich, Conn.

Clark, John E., and William J. Parry
1990 Craft Specialization and Cultural Complexity. *Research in Economic Anthropology* 12:289–346.

Clay, R. Berle
  1976 Tactics, Strategy, and Operations: The Mississippian System
        Responds to Its Environment. *Midcontinental Journal of Ar-
        chaeology* 1:138–62.
  1997 The Mississippian Succession on the Lower Ohio. *Southeast-
        ern Archaeology* 16:16–32.
Clayton, Lawrence A., Vernon James Knight, Jr., and Edward C. Moore
(editors)
  1993 *The De Soto Chronicles: The Expedition of Hernando de Soto
        to North America in 1539–1543.* University of Alabama Press,
        Tuscaloosa.
Cobb, Charles R.
  1988 Mill Creek Chert Biface Production: Mississippian Political
        Economy in Southern Illinois. Ph.D. dissertation, Department
        of Anthropology, Southern Illinois University at Carbondale.
  1989 An Appraisal of the Role of Mill Creek Chert Hoes in Missis-
        sippian Exchange Systems. *Southeastern Archaeology* 8:79–92.
  1991 One Hundred Years of Investigations at the Linn Site in South-
        ern Illinois. *Illinois Archaeology* 3:56–76.
  1993 Archaeological Approaches to the Political Economy of Non-
        stratified Societies. In *Archaeological Method and Theory,* vol.
        5, edited by M. B. Schiffer, pp. 43–100. University of Arizona
        Press, Tucson.
  1996 Specialization, Exchange, and Power in Small-Scale Socie-
        ties and Chiefdoms. *Research in Economic Anthropology*
        17:251–94.
Cobb, Charles R., and Patrick H. Garrow
  1996 Woodstock Culture and the Question of Mississippian Emer-
        gence. *American Antiquity* 61:21–37.
Cobb, Charles R., and Melody Pope
  1998 Sixteenth-Century Flintknapping Kits from the King site,
        Georgia. *Journal of Field Archaeology* 25:1–18.
Cobb, Charles R., and Paul A. Webb
  1994 A Source Area Perspective on Expedient and Formal Core
        Technologies. *North American Archaeologist* 15:181–203.
Cole, Fay-Cooper, Robert Bell, Joseph Caldwell, Norman Emerson,
Richard MacNeish, Kenneth Orr, and Roger Willis
  1951 *Kincaid: A Prehistoric Illinois Metropolis.* University of Chi-
        cago Press, Chicago.
Collins, Jane
  1986 The Household and Relations of Production in Southern Peru.
        Comparative Studies in Social History 28:651–71.
Conkey, Margaret, and Joan Gero
  1991 Tension, Pluralities, and Engendering Archaeology: An Intro-

duction. In *Engendering Archaeology: Women and Prehistory,* edited by J. M. Gero and M. W. Conkey, pp. 3–30. Blackwell, Oxford.

Conrad, Lawrence

1991 The Middle Mississippian Cultures of the Central Illinois Valley. In *Cahokia and the Hinterlands: Middle Mississippian Cultures of the Midwest,* edited by T. E. Emerson and R. B. Lewis, pp. 119–63. University of Illinois Press, Urbana.

Cook, Scott

1975 Comment on "Behavioral Analysis and the Structure of a Prehistoric Industry," by Payson D. Sheets. *Current Anthropology* 16:380–81.

Costin, Cathy Lynne

1991 Craft Specialization: Issues in Defining, Documenting, and Explaining the Organization of Production. In *Archaeological Method and Theory,* vol. 3, edited by M. B. Schiffer, pp. 1–56. University of Arizona Press, Tucson.

1998 Introduction: Craft and Social Identity. In *Craft and Social Identity,* edited by C. L. Costin and R. P. Wright, pp. 3–16. Archeological Papers No. 8. American Anthropological Association, Arlington, Va.

Crabtree, Don E.

1972 *An Introduction to Flintworking.* Occasional Papers 28. Idaho State University Museum, Pocatello.

Crumley, Carole L.

1987 A Dialectical Critique of Hierarchy. In *Power Relations and State Formation,* edited by T. C. Patterson and C. W. Gailey, pp. 155–59. American Anthropological Association, Washington, D.C.

Custer, Jay F.

1987 Core Technology at the Hawthorne Site, New Castle County, Delaware: A Late Archaic Hunting Camp. In *The Organization of Core Technology,* edited by J. K. Johnson and C. A. Morrow, pp. 45–62. Westview Press, Boulder, Colo.

Dalton, George

1977 Aboriginal Economies in Stateless Societies. In *Exchange Systems in Prehistory,* edited by T. K. Earle and J. E. Ericson, pp. 191–12. Academic Press, New York.

DeBoer, Warren R.

1993 Like a Rolling Stone: The Chunkey Game and Political Organization in Eastern North America. *Southeastern Archaeology* 12:83–92.

Deetz, James D.

1977 *In Small Things Forgotten.* Anchor Press, Garden City, N.Y.

DeForest, John W.
  1964 *History of the Indians of Connecticut.* (Originally published
        1851.) Shoestring Press, Hamden, Conn.
Denny, Sidney G.
  1972 The Archaeology of the Big Muddy River Basin of Southern Il-
        linois. Ph.D. dissertation, Department of Anthropology, South-
        ern Illinois University at Carbondale.
Devera, Joseph A., W. John Nelson, and John M. Masters
  1994 *Geologic Map of the Mill Creek and McClure Quadrangles, Al-
        exander and Union Counties, Illinois.* Illinois State Geologi-
        cal Survey, Champaign, Ill.
Dickens, Roy S., Jr.
  1978 Mississippian Settlement Patterns in the Appalachian Summit
        Area: The Pisgah and Qualla Phases. In *Mississippian Settle-
        ment Patterns,* edited by B. D. Smith, pp. 115–39. Academic
        Press, New York.
Dietler, Michael
  1998 Consumption, Agency, and Cultural Entanglement: Theoreti-
        cal Implications of a Mediterranean Colonial Encounter. In
        *Studies in Culture Contact: Interaction, Culture Change, and
        Archaeology,* edited by J. G. Cusick, pp. 288–315. Occasional
        Paper No. 25. Center for Archaeological Investigations, South-
        ern Illinois University at Carbondale.
Dincauze, Dena F., and Robert Hasenstab
  1989 Explaining the Iroquois: Tribalization on a Prehistoric Periph-
        ery. In *Centre and Periphery: Comparative Studies in Archeol-
        ogy,* edited by T. C. Champion, pp. 67–87. Unwin Hyman,
        London.
Dobres, Marcia-Anne
  1995 Gender and Prehistoric Technology: On the Social Agency of
        Technical Strategies. *World Archaeology* 27:25–49.
Dobres, Marcia-Anne, and Christopher R. Hoffman
  1994 Social Agency and the Dynamics of Prehistoric Technology.
        Journal of Archaeological Method and Theory 1:211–57.
Drennan, Robert D., and Carlos A. Uribe (editors)
  1987 *Chiefdoms in the Americas.* University Press of America, Lan-
        ham, Md.
Drooker, Penelope Ballard
  1992 *Mississippian Village Textiles at Wickliffe.* University of Ala-
        bama Press, Tuscaloosa.
  1998 *Fabrics Impressed on Pottery at Millstone Bluff (11-Pp-37)
        and Dillow's Ridge (11-U-635), Illinois.* Manuscript on file.
        Center for Archaeological Investigations, Southern Illinois
        University at Carbondale.

Dumont, Louis
  1977 *From Mandeville to Marx: The Genesis and Triumph of Economic Ideology.* University of Chicago Press, Chicago.

Dunnell, Robert
  1980 Evolutionary Theory in Archaeology. In *Advances in Archaeological Method and Theory,* vol. 3, edited by M. B. Schiffer, pp. 35–99. Academic Press, New York.

Dunnell, Robert C., and James K. Feathers
  1991 Late Woodland Manifestations of the Malden Plain. In *Stability, Transformation, and Variation: The Late Woodland Southeast,* edited by M. S. Nassaney and C. R. Cobb, pp. 21–45. Plenum Press, New York.

Dunnell, Robert C., P. T. McCutcheon, M. Ikeya, and S. Toyoda
  1994 Heat Treatment of Mill Creek and Dover Cherts on the Malden Plain, Southeast Missouri. *Journal of Archaeological Science* 21:79–89.

Durkheim, Emile
  1933 *Division of Labor in Society.* (Originally published 1893.) Macmillan, New York.

Dye, David H.
  1995 Feasting with the Enemy: Mississippian Warfare and Prestige-Goods Circulation. In *Native American Interactions,* edited by M. S. Nassaney and K. E. Sassaman, pp. 289–316. University of Tennessee Press, Knoxville.

Earle, Timothy K.
  1981 Evolution of Specialized Pottery Production: A Trial Model. *Current Anthropology* 22:230–31.
  1987a Chiefdoms in Archaeological and Ethnohistorical Perspective. *Annual Review of Anthropology* 16:279–308.
  1987b Specialization and the Production of Wealth. In *Specialization, Exchange, and Complex Societies,* edited by E. M. Brumfiel and T. K. Earle, pp. 64–75. Cambridge University Press, Cambridge.
  1991a [Editor] *Chiefdoms: Power, Economy, and Ideology.* Cambridge University Press, Cambridge.
  1991b The Evolution of Chiefdoms. In *Chiefdoms: Power, Economy, and Ideology,* edited by T. K. Earle, pp. 1–15. Cambridge University Press, Cambridge.

Edging, Richard
  1990 *The Turk Site: A Mississippi Period Town in Western Kentucky.* Kentucky Heritage Council, Frankfort.

Edmonds, M.
  1990 Description, Understanding, and the Chaîne Opératoire. *Archeological Review from Cambridge* 9:55–70.

218   References Cited

Emerson, Thomas E.

   1982 *Mississippian Stone Images in Illinois.* Circular 6. Illinois Archaeological Survey, Urbana.

   1997 *Cahokia and the Archaeology of Power.* University of Alabama Press, Tuscaloosa.

Emerson, Thomas E., and Douglas K. Jackson

   1984 *The BBB Motor Site (11-Ms-595).* FAI-270 Site Reports, Volume 6. University of Illinois Press, Urbana.

Engels, Friedrich

   1972 *The Origins of the Family, Private Property and the State.* (Originally published 1884.) Pathfinder Press, New York.

Ericson, Jonathon E.

   1984 Toward the Analysis of Lithic Production Systems. In *Prehistoric Quarries and Lithic Production,* edited by J. E. Ericson and B. A. Purdy, pp. 1–9. Cambridge University Press, Cambridge.

Evans, Robert K.

   1978 Early Craft Specialization: An Example from the Balkan Chalcolithic. In *Social Archaeology: Beyond Subsistence and Dating,* edited by C. L. Redman, M. J. Berman, E. V. Curtin, W. T. Langhorne, Jr., N. M. Versaggi, and J. C. Wanser, pp. 113–29. Academic Press, New York.

Feinman, Gary, and Jill Neitzel

   1984 Too Many Types: An Overview of Sedentary Prestate Societies in the Americas. In *Advances in Archaeological Method and Theory,* vol. 7, edited by M. B. Schiffer, pp. 39–102. Academic Press, New York.

Ford, James A.

   1961 *Menard Site: The Quapaw Village of Osotouy on the Arkansas River.* Anthropological Papers Volume 48, Part 2. American Museum of Natural History, New York.

Foucault, Michel

   1980 *Power and Knowledge.* Pantheon, New York.

Fowke, Gerard

   1894 Stone Art. *Bureau of American Ethnology, Annual Report* 13:57–178.

Fowler, Melvin L.

   1975 Pre-Columbian Urban Center on the Mississippi. *Scientific American* 233:92–101.

Fowler, Melvin L., and Robert L. Hall

   1978 Late Prehistory of the Illinois Area. In *Handbook of North American Indians,* vol. 15, *Northeast,* edited by B. G. Trigger, pp. 560–68. Smithsonian Institution, Washington, D.C.

Frankenstein, S., and M. J. Rowlands

   1978 The Internal Structure and Regional Context of Early Iron Age

Society in South-Western Germany. *Bulletin of the Institute of Archaeology* 15:73–112.

Fried, Morton
1967 *The Evolution of Political Society: An Essay in Political Anthropology.* Random House, New York.

Friedman, Jonathan
1975 Tribes, States, and Transformations. In *Marxist Analyses and Social Anthropology*, edited by M. Bloch, pp. 161–202. Tavistock, New York.
1994 *Cultural Identity and Global Process.* Sage, London.

Friedman, Jonathan, and Michael J. Rowlands
1978 Notes Toward an Epigenetic Model of the Evolution of 'Civilisation.' In *The Evolution of Social Systems*, edited by J. Friedman and M. J. Rowlands, pp. 201–76. Duckworth, London.

Fritz, Gayle J.
1990 Multiple Pathways to Farming in Precontact Eastern North America. *Journal of World Prehistory* 4:387–435.

Gallagher, P. A.
1977 Contemporary Stone Tools in Ethiopia: Implications for Archaeology. *Journal of Field Archaeology* 4:407–14.

Galloway, Patricia (editor)
1989 *The Southeastern Ceremonial Complex: Artifacts and Analysis.* University of Nebraska Press, Lincoln.

Gero, Joan M.
1984 Lithics and the Representation of Social Complexity. *American Archaeology* 4:67–70.
1991 Genderlithics: Women's Roles in Stone Tool Production. In *Engendering Archaeology: Women and Prehistory*, edited by J. M. Gero and M. W. Conkey, pp. 163–93. Basil Blackwell, Oxford.

Giddens, Anthony
1976 *New Rules of Sociological Method: A Positive Critique of Interpretive Sociologies.* Hutchinson, London.

Goad, Sharon I.
1978 Exchange Networks in the Prehistoric Southeastern United States. Ph.D. dissertation, Department of Anthropology, University of Georgia, Athens.

Godelier, Maurice
1972 *Rationality and Irrationality in Economics.* Western Printing Services, Bristol, G.B.
1973 *Perspectives in Marxist Anthropology.* Cambridge University Press, Cambridge.

Goodman, Alan H., John Lallo, George J. Armelagos, and Jerome C. Rose
1984 Health Changes at Dickson Mounds, Illinois (A.D. 950–1300). In *Paleopathology at the Origins of Agriculture*, edited by

M. N. Cohen and G. J. Armelagos, pp. 271–305. Academic Press, Orlando.

Goodyear, Albert C.
1979 *A Hypothesis for the Use of Cryptocrystalline Raw Materials Among Paleo-Indian Groups in North America.* Research Manuscript Series 165. South Carolina Institute of Archaeology and Anthropology, University of South Carolina, Columbia.

Gould, Stephen J., and Robert C. Lewontin
1979 The Spandrels of San Marco and the Panglossian Paradigm: A Critique of the Adaptationist Programme. *Proceedings of the Royal Society of London* B205:581–98.

Gramly, R. Michael
1984 Mount Jasper: A Direct-Access Lithic Source Area in the White Mountains of New Hampshire. In *Prehistoric Quarries and Lithic Production,* edited by J. E. Ericson and B. A. Purdy, pp. 11–21. Cambridge University Press, Cambridge.
1992 *Prehistoric Lithic Industry at Dover, Tennessee.* Persimmon Press, Buffalo.

Green, Thomas J., and Cheryl A. Munson
1978 Mississippian Settlement Patterns in Southwestern Indiana. In *Mississippian Settlement Patterns,* edited by B. D. Smith, pp. 293–330. Academic Press, New York.

Griffin, James B.
1985 Changing Concepts of the Prehistoric Mississippian Cultures of the Eastern United States. In *Alabama and the Borderlands: From Prehistory to Statehood,* edited by R. Badger and L. Clayton, pp. 40–63. University of Alabama Press, Tuscaloosa.

Haas, Jonathan
1982 *The Evolution of the Prehistoric State.* Columbia University Press, New York.

Hally, David J.
1993a The 1992 and 1993 Excavations at the King Site (9FL5). *Early Georgia* 21:30–44.
1993b The Territorial Size of Mississippian Chiefdoms. In *Archaeology of Eastern North America: Papers in Honor of Stephen Williams,* edited by J. Stoltman, pp. 143–68. Mississippi Department of Archives and History, Jackson.

Hamell, George
1983 Trading in Metaphors. In *Proceedings of the 1982 Glass Trade Bead Conference,* edited by C. F. Hayes, pp. 5–28. Research Records No. 16. Rochester Museum and Science Center, Rochester.

Hamilton, Henry W.
1952 The Spiro Mound. *Missouri Archaeologist* 14:1–276.

Hammel, E. A.

1984 On the *** of Studying Household Form and Function. In
*Households: Comparative and Historical Studies of the
Domestic Group*, edited by R. M. Netting, R. R. Wilk, and
E. J. Arnould, pp. 29–43. University of California Press,
Berkeley.

Hargrave, Michael L.

1992 A Functional Perspective on the Petitt Site Ceramic Assemblage. In *The Petitt Site (11-Ax-253), Alexander County, Illinois*, edited by P. A. Webb, pp. 183–230. Research Paper No.
58. Center for Archaeological Investigations, Southern Illinois
University at Carbondale.

Hargrave, Michael L., Charles R. Cobb, and Paul A. Webb

1991 Late Prehistoric Ceramic Style Zones in Southern Illinois. In
*Stability, Transformation, and Variation: The Late Woodland
Southeast*, edited by M. S. Nassaney and C. R. Cobb, pp. 149–
76. Plenum Press, New York.

Hargrave, Michael L., Gerald A. Oetelaar, Neal H. Lopinot, Brian M.
Butler, and Deborah A. Billings

1983 *The Bridges Site (11-Mr-11): A Late Prehistoric Settlement in
the Central Kaskaskia Valley.* Research Paper No. 38. Center
for Archaeological Investigations, Southern Illinois University
at Carbondale.

Harn, Alan D.

1975 Cahokia and the Mississippian Emergence in the Spoon River
Area in Illinois. *Transactions of the Illinois State Academy of
Science* 68:414–34.

1978 Mississippian Settlement Patterns in the Central Illinois River
Valley. In *Mississippian Settlement Patterns*, edited by B. D.
Smith, pp. 233–68. Academic Press, New York.

Harris, Olivia, and Kate Young

1981 Engendered Structures: Some Problems in the Analysis of Reproduction. In *The Anthropology of Pre-Capitalist Societies*,
edited by J. S. Kahn and J. R. Llobera, pp. 109–47. Macmillan,
London.

Harris, Stanley E., Jr., C. William Horrell, and Daniel Irwin

1977 *Exploring the Land and Rocks of Southern Illinois.* Southern
Illinois University Press, Carbondale.

Harvey, A. E.

1979 *Oneota Culture in Northwestern Iowa.* Report 12. Office of
the State Archaeologist, University of Iowa, Iowa City.

Hatley, M. Thomas

1989 The Three Lives of Keowee: Loss and Recovery in Eighteenth

Century Cherokee Villages. In *Powhatan's Mantle*, edited by P. H. Wood, G. A. Waselkov, and M. T. Hatley, pp. 223–48. University of Nebraska Press, Lincoln.

Hawkes, C. F.

   1954   Archeological Theory and Method: Some Suggestions from the Old World. *American Anthropologist* 56:155–68.

Hayden, Brian

   1990   The Right Rub: Hide Working in High Ranking Households. In *The Interpretive Possibilities of Microwear Studies*, edited by B. Graslund, H. Knutsson, K. Knutsson, and J. Taffinder, pp. 89–102. AUN 14. Societas Archaeologica Upsaliensis, Uppsala, Sweden.

Healan, Dan M.

   1995   Identifying Lithic Reduction Loci with Size-Graded Macrodebitage: A Multivariate Perspective. *American Antiquity* 60:689–99.

Helms, Mary W.

   1979   *Ancient Panama: Chiefs in Search of Power.* University of Texas Press, Austin.

   1988   *Ulysses' Sail: An Ethnographic Odyssey of Power, Knowledge, and Geographical Distance.* Princeton University Press, Princeton.

   1993   *Craft and the Kingly Ideal.* University of Texas Press, Austin.

Hendon, Julia A.

   1996   Archaeological Approaches to the Organization of Domestic Labor: Household Practice and Domestic Relations. *Annual Review of Anthropology* 25:45–61.

Henry, Don O., C. Vance Haynes, and Bruce Bradley

   1976   Quantitative Variations in Flaked Stone Debitage. *Plains Anthropologist* 21:57–61.

Hickerson, Harold

   1973   Fur Trade Colonialism and the North American Indians. *Journal of Ethnic Studies* 1:15–44.

Hindess, Barry, and Paul Q. Hirst

   1975   *Pre-Capitalist Modes of Production.* Routledge & Kegan Paul, Boston.

Hodder, Ian

   1987   The Contribution of the Long Term. In *Archaeology as Long-Term History*, edited by I. Hodder, pp. 1–8. Cambridge University Press, Cambridge.

   1991   *Reading the Past.* 2d ed. Cambridge University Press, Cambridge.

Hoehr, Peter

   1980   Utilitarian Artifacts from the Cahokia Site. In *Cahokia*

Brought to Life, by R. E. Grimm, pp. 41–44. 2d printing. Greater St. Louis Archaeological Society, St. Louis.

Holley, George R., Rinita A. Dalan, and Philip A. Smith
1993 Investigations in the Cahokia Site Grand Plaza. *American Antiquity* 58:306–19.

Holmes, William H.
1890 A Quarry Workshop of the Flaked-Stone Implement Makers in the District of Columbia. *American Anthropologist* 3:1–26.
1891 Ancient Novaculite Quarries in Garland County, Arkansas. *American Anthropologist* 4:49–58.
1894 *An Ancient Quarry in Indian Territory.* Bureau of Ethnology Bulletin 21. Smithsonian Institution, Washington, D.C.
1919 Handbook of Aboriginal American Antiquities. *Bureau of American Ethnology Bulletin* 60:187–94.

Horberg, Leland
1950 *Bedrock Topography of Illinois.* Bulletin 73. Illinois State Geological Survey, Urbana.

Howard, James H.
1968 *The Southeastern Ceremonial Complex and Its Interpretation.* Memoir 6. Missouri Archaeological Society, Columbia.

Hudelson, C. W.
1938 Aboriginal Agricultural Artifacts, Mill Creek, Illinois. *Illinois State Archaeological Society Bulletin* 1:13–14.

Hudson, Charles
1976 *The Southeastern Indians.* University of Tennessee Press, Knoxville.

Hudson, Charles, Marvin Smith, David Hally, Richard Polhemus, and Chester DePratter
1985 Coosa: A Chiefdom in the Sixteenth-Century Southeastern United States. *American Antiquity* 50:723–37.

Ives, David J.
1975 *The Crescent Hills Prehistoric Quarrying Area.* Museum Brief No. 22. University of Missouri, Columbia.
1984 The Crescent Hills Prehistoric Quarrying Area: More Than Just Rocks. In *Prehistoric Chert Exploitation: Studies from the Midcontinent,* edited by B. M. Butler and E. E. May, pp. 187–95. Occasional Paper No. 2. Center for Archaeological Investigations, Southern Illinois University at Carbondale.

Jackson, H. Edwin, and Susan L. Scott
1995 Mississippian Homestead and Village Subsistence Organization: Contrasts in Large-Mammal Remains from Two Sites in the Tombigbee Valley. In *Mississippian Communities and Households,* edited by J. D. Rogers and B. D. Smith, pp. 181–200. University of Alabama Press, Tuscaloosa.

Jefferies, Richard W.

    1982   Debitage as an Indicator of Intraregional Activity Diversity in Northwest Georgia. *Midcontinental Journal of Archaeology* 7:99–132.

Johannessen, Sissel

    1984   Paleoethnobotany. In *American Bottom Archaeology,* edited by C. J. Bareis and J. W. Porter, pp. 197–214. University of Illinois Press, Urbana.

Johnson, Jay K.

    1981   *Lithic Procurement and Utilization Trajectories: Analysis, Yellow Creek Nuclear Power Plant Site, Tishomingo County, Mississippi,* vol. 2. Publications in Anthropology 28. Tennessee Valley Authority, Knoxville.

    1986   Amorphous Core Technologies in the Midsouth. *Midcontinental Journal of Archaeology* 11:135–51.

    1989   The Utility of Production Modeling as a Framework for Regional Analysis. In *Alternative Approaches to Lithic Analysis,* edited by D. O. Henry and G. H. Odell, pp. 119–38. Archeological Papers No. 1. American Anthropological Association, Washington, D.C.

    1996   Lithic Analysis and Questions of Cultural Complexity: The Maya. In *Stone Tools: Theoretical Insights into Human Prehistory,* edited by G. H. Odell, pp. 159–79. Plenum Press, New York.

    1997   Chipped Stone Artifacts from an Eighteenth-Century Chickasaw Site in Northeast Mississippi. *American Antiquity* 62:215–30.

Johnson, Matthew H.

    1989   Concepts of Agency in Archaeological Interpretation. *Journal of Anthropological Archaeology* 8:189–211.

    1996   *An Archaeology of Capitalism.* Blackwell, Oxford.

Jones, Siân

    1996   Discourses of Identity in the Interpretation of the Past. In *Cultural Identity and Archaeology: The Construction of European Communities,* edited by P. Graves-Brown, S. Jones, and C. Gamble, pp. 62–80. Routledge, London.

    1997   *The Archaeology of Ethnicity: Constructing Identities in the Past and Present.* Routledge, London.

Jones, Terry L.

    1996   Mortars, Pestles, and Division of Labor in Prehistoric California: A View from Big Sur. *American Antiquity* 61:243–64.

Kahn, Joel S.

    1981   Marxist Anthropology and Segmentary Societies: A Review of the Literature. In *The Anthropology of Pre-Capitalist Socie-*

ties, edited by J. S. Kahn and J. R. Llobera, pp. 57–88. Macmillan, London.

Keesing, Roger M.
 1987   Anthropology as Interpretive Quest. *Current Anthropology* 28:161–76.

Kelly, John E.
 1980   *Formative Developments at Cahokia and the Adjacent American Bottom: A Merrell Tract Perspective.* University of Wisconsin-Madison.
 1984   Late Bluff Chert Utilization on the Merrell Tract, Cahokia. In *Prehistoric Chert Exploitation: Studies from the Midcontinent*, edited by B. M. Butler and E. E. May, pp. 23–44. Occasional Paper No. 2. Center for Archaeological Investigations, Southern Illinois University at Carbondale.
 1991a Cahokia and Its Role as a Gateway Center in Interregional Exchange. In *Cahokia and the Hinterlands: Middle Mississippian Cultures of the Midwest*, edited by T. E. Emerson and R. B. Lewis, pp. 61–80. University of Illinois Press, Urbana.
 1991b The Evidence for Prehistoric Exchange and Its Implications for the Development of Cahokia. In *New Perspectives on Cahokia: Views from the Periphery*, edited by J. B. Stoltman, pp. 65–92. Monographs in World Archaeology No. 2. Prehistory Press, Madison, Wis.

Kelly, John E., Steven J. Ozuk, Douglas K. Jackson, Dale L. McElrath, Fred A. Finney, and Duane Esarey
 1984   Emergent Mississippian Period. In *American Bottom Archaeology*, edited by C. J. Bareis and J. W. Porter, pp. 128–57. University of Illinois Press, Urbana.

Kelly, Lucretia S., and Paula G. Cross
 1984   Zooarchaeology. In *American Bottom Archaeology*, edited by C. J. Bareis and J. W. Porter, pp. 215–32. University of Illinois Press, Urbana.

Kelly, Robert L.
 1988   The Three Sides of a Biface. *American Antiquity* 53:717–31.

Kelly, Robert L., and Lawrence C. Todd
 1988   Coming into the Country: Early Paleoindian Hunting and Mobility. *American Antiquity* 53:231–44.

Kimball, Larry R.
 1996   Review of *The Organization of North American Prehistoric Chipped Stone Tool Technologies*. *Southeastern Archaeology* 15:106–8.

King, Adam, and Jennifer Freer
 1995   The Mississippian Southeast: A World-Systems Perspective. In *Native American Interactions*, edited by M. S. Nassaney and

K. E. Sassaman, pp. 266–88. University of Tennessee Press, Knoxville.

Klein, Alan M.
1993 Political Economy of the Buffalo Hide Trade: Race and Class in the Plains. In *The Political Economy of North American Indians*, edited by J. H. Moore, pp. 133–60. University of Oklahoma Press, Norman.

Klein, Joel
1981 The Cypress Citadel and Its Role in the Subsistence-Settlement System of the Late Woodland Lewis Culture of Extreme Southern Illinois. Ph.D. dissertation, Department of Anthropology, New York University, New York.

Knapp, A. Bernard (editor)
1992 *Archaeology,* Annales, *and Ethnohistory.* Cambridge University Press, Cambridge.

Knight, Francis R., and Brian M. Butler
1995 *Archaeological Survey on the Mississippi River Floodplain, Union County Conservation Area, Illinois: Results of the 1994 Southern Illinois University at Carbondale Field School Survey.* Technical Report 1995-3. Center for Archaeological Investigations, Southern Illinois University at Carbondale.

Knight, Vernon James, Jr.
1986 The Institutional Organization of Mississippian Religion. *American Antiquity* 51:675–87.

Koldehoff, Brad
1983 Paleo-Indian Chert Utilization in Southwestern Illinois. *Wisconsin Archaeologist* 64:201–38.
1985 Southern Illinois Cherts: A Guide to Siliceous Materials Exploited by Prehistoric Populations in Southern Illinois. Manuscript on file. Center for Archaeological Investigations, Southern Illinois University at Carbondale.
1986 Lithic Analysis. In *The Bonnie Creek Site,* edited by M. J. Wagner, pp. 145–98. Preservation Series 3. American Resources Group, Carbondale, Ill.
1987 The Cahokia Flake Tool Industry: Socioeconomic Implications for Late Prehistory in the Central Mississippi Valley. In *The Organization of Core Technology,* edited by J. K. Johnson and C. A. Morrow, pp. 151–85. Westview Press, Boulder, Colo.
1989 Cahokia's Immediate Hinterland: The Mississippian Occupation of Douglas Creek. *Illinois Archaeology* 1:39–68.
1990 Household Specialization: The Organization of Mississippian Chipped-Stone-Tool Production. M.A. thesis, Southern Illinois University at Carbondale.
1992 Lithic Analysis. In *The Little Muddy Rock Shelter: A Deeply*

Stratified Prehistoric Site in the Southern Till Plains of Illinois, by C. R. Moffat, B. Koldehoff, W. M. Cremin, T. J. Martin, M. C. Masulis, and M. R. McCorvie, pp. 279–370. Cultural Resources Management Report No. 186. American Resources Group, Carbondale, Ill.

1996   Transportation Corridors and Cahokia's Hinterlands. Paper presented at the 53rd Annual Meeting of the Southeastern Archaeological Conference, Birmingham, Alabama.

Koldehoff, Brad, and Phillip J. Carr

2001   Chipped-Stone Technology: Patterns of Procurement, Production, and Consumption. In *Excavations at Wickliffe Mounds,* edited by K. Wesler. In press.

Koldehoff, Brad, and Mark J. Wagner

1998   *The Archaeology and History of Horseshoe Lake, Alexander County, Illinois.* Report submitted to Illinois Department of Natural Resources. Center for Archaeological Investigations, Southern Illinois University at Carbondale.

Kowalewski, Stephen A., and James W. Hatch

1991   The Sixteenth-Century Expansion of Settlement in the Upper Oconee Watershed, Georgia. *Southeastern Archaeology* 10:1–17.

Kramer, Carol

1982   Ethnographic Households and Archaeological Interpretation. In Archaeology of the Household: Building a Prehistory of Domestic Life, by R. R. Wilk and W. J. Rathje. *American Behavioral Scientist* 25:663–75.

Kreisa, Paul P.

1988   *Second Order Communities in Western Kentucky: Site Survey and Excavation at Late Woodland and Mississippian Period Sites.* Western Kentucky Project Report No. 7. Department of Anthropology, University of Illinois, Urbana.

1991   *Mississippian Sites of the Lower Ohio River Valley in Kentucky.* Western Kentucky Project Report No. 9. Department of Anthropology, University of Illinois, Urbana-Champaign.

Kristiansen, Kristian

1987   Center and Periphery in Bronze Age Scandinavia. In *Centre and Periphery in the Ancient World,* edited by M. Rowlands, M. Larsen, and K. Kristiansen, pp. 74–85. Cambridge University Press, Cambridge.

1991   Chiefdoms, States, and Systems of Social Evolution. In *Chiefdoms: Power, Economy, and Ideology,* edited by T. K. Earle, pp. 16–43. Cambridge University Press, Cambridge.

Lafferty, Robert H., III

1977   The Evolution of the Mississippian Settlement Pattern and Exploitative Technology in the Black Bottom of Southern Illi-

nois. Ph.D. dissertation, Department of Anthropology, Southern Illinois University at Carbondale.

1994   Prehistoric Exchange in the Lower Mississippi Valley. In
Prehistoric Exchange Systems in North America, edited by
T. G. Baugh and J. E. Ericson, pp. 177–213. Plenum Press, New
York.

Latchford, Carl

1984   Mississippian Hoes and Spades. *Central States Archaeological
Journal* 31:157–60.

Lawson, John

1967   *A New Voyage to Carolina.* (Originally published 1709.) University of North Carolina Press, Chapel Hill.

Leacock, Eleanor

1978   Women's Status in Egalitarian Society. *Current Anthropology*
19:247–75.

Lee, Richard B.

1990   Primitive Communism and the Origin of Social Inequality. In
*The Evolution of Political Systems: Sociopolitics in Small-
Scale Sedentary Societies,* edited by S. Upham, pp. 225–46.
Cambridge University Press, Cambridge.

Lemonnier, Pierre

1992   *Elements for an Anthropology of Technology.* Museum of Anthropology Anthropological Papers No. 88. University of
Michigan, Ann Arbor.

Le Page du Pratz, A. S.

1975   *The History of Louisiana.* (Originally published 1758.) Louisiana State University Press, Baton Rouge.

Lewis, R. Barry

1982   *Excavations at Two Mississippian Hamlets in the Cairo Lowland of Southeast Missouri.* Special Publication 2. Illinois Archaeological Survey, Urbana.

1986   [Editor] *Mississippian Towns of the Western Kentucky Border:
The Adams, Wickliffe, and Sassafras Ridge Sites.* Kentucky
Heritage Council, Frankfort.

1990   The Late Prehistory of the Ohio-Mississippi Rivers
Confluence Region, Kentucky and Missouri. In *Towns and
Temples Along the Mississippi,* edited by D. H. Dye and C. A.
Cox, pp. 38–58. University of Alabama Press, Tuscaloosa.

1991   The Early Mississippi Period in the Confluence Region and
Its Northern Relationships. In *Cahokia and the Hinterlands:
Middle Mississippian Cultures of the Midwest,* edited by T. E.
Emerson and R. B. Lewis, pp. 274–94. University of Illinois
Press, Urbana.

1996   Mississippian Farmers. In *Kentucky Archaeology*, edited by
       R. B. Lewis, pp. 127–59. University Press of Kentucky, Lex-
       ington.

Lewis, Thomas M. N., and Madeline Kneberg
1946   *Hiwassee Island*. University of Tennessee Press, Knoxville.

Lopinot, Neal H.
1984   An Environmental Model for the Upper Cache River Drainage.
       In *Cultural Frontiers in the Upper Cache Valley, Illinois*, by
       V. Canouts, E. E. May, N. H. Lopinot, and J. D. Muller, pp.
       44–67. Research Paper No. 16. Center for Archaeological
       Investigations, Southern Illinois University at Carbondale.

Lopinot, Neal H., and Brian M. Butler
1981   *Archaeological Assessment of Exchange Lands in Alexander
       County, Illinois: Shawnee National Forest*. Research Paper No.
       28. Center for Archaeological Investigations, Southern Illinois
       University at Carbondale.

Lopinot, Neal H., and William I. Woods
1993   Wood Overexploitation and the Collapse of Cahokia. In *Forag-
       ing and Farming in the Eastern Woodlands*, edited by C. M.
       Scarry, pp. 206–31. University Press of Florida, Gainesville.

McAdams, William
1895   Archaeology. In *Report of the Illinois Board of World's Fair
       Commissioners*, pp. 227–304. H. W. Rokken, Springfield, Ill.

McAnany, Patricia A.
1989   Stone-Tool Production and Exchange in the Eastern Maya Low-
       lands: The Consumer Perspective from Pulltrouser Swamp.
       American Antiquity 54:332–46.

McBrearty, Sally, Laura Bishop, Thomas Plummer, Robert DeWar, and
Nicholas Conrad
1998   Tools Underfoot: Human Trampling as an Agent of Lithic Arti-
       fact Edge Modification. *American Antiquity* 63:108–29.

McGaw, Judith A.
1996   Reconceiving Technology: Why Feminine Technologies Matter.
       In *Gender and Archaeology*, edited by R. P. Wright, pp. 52–75.
       University of Pennsylvania Press, Philadelphia.

McGimsey, Charles R.
1994   *The 1994 SIU-C Field School Excavations at the Dillow's
       Ridge Site (11-U-635), Preliminary Report*. Report submitted
       to Shawnee National Forest, U.S.D.A. Manuscript on file. Cen-
       ter for Archaeological Investigations, Southern Illinois Univer-
       sity at Carbondale.

McGuire, Randall
1992   *A Marxist Archaeology*. Academic Press, San Diego.

McGuire, Randall H., and Dean J. Saitta

1996 Although They Have Petty Captains, They Obey Them Badly: The Dialectics of Prehispanic Western Pueblo Social Organization. *American Antiquity* 61:197–216.

McNutt, Charles H.

1996 The Central Mississippi Valley: A Summary. In *Prehistory of the Central Mississippi Valley*, edited by C. H. McNutt, pp. 187–257. University of Alabama Press, Tuscaloosa.

Magne, Martin P. R.

1989 Lithic Reduction Stages and Assemblage Formation Processes. In *Experiments in Lithic Technology*, edited by D. S. Amick and R. P. Mauldin, pp. 15–31. International Series 528. B.A.R., Oxford.

Magne, Martin, and David Pokotylo

1981 A Pilot Study in Bifacial Lithic Reduction Sequences. *Lithic Technology* 10:34–47.

Mainfort, Robert C., Jr.

1996 Late Period Chronology in the Central Mississippi Valley: A Western Tennessee Perspective. *Southeastern Archaeology* 15:172–91.

Malinowski, Bronislaw

1961 *Argonauts of the Western Pacific.* (Originally published 1922.) E. P. Dutton, New York.

Mallory, John K.

1986 "Workshops" and "Specialized Production" in the Production of Maya Chert Tools: A Response to Shafer and Hester. *American Antiquity* 51:152–58.

Marcus, George, and Michael M. J. Fischer

1986 *Anthropology as Cultural Critique.* University of Chicago Press, Chicago.

Mark, Robert

1996 Architecture and Evolution. *American Scientist* 84:383–89.

Marquardt, William H.

1992 Dialectical Archaeology. In *Archaeological Method and Theory*, vol. 4, edited by M. B. Schiffer, pp. 101–40. University of Arizona Press, Tucson.

Marquardt, William H., and Carole L. Crumley

1987 Theoretical Issues in the Analysis of Spatial Patterning. In *Regional Dynamics: Burgundian Landscapes in Historical Perspective*, edited by C. L. Crumley and W. H. Marquardt, pp. 1–18. Academic Press, San Diego.

Marshall, Yvonne

1989 The House in Northwest Coast, Nuu-Chah-Nulth, Society: The Material Structure of Political Action. In *Households and*

Communities, edited by S. MacEachern, D. J. W. Archer, and R. D. Garvin, pp. 15–21. Proceedings of the 21st Annual Chacmool Conference. University of Calgary Archaeology Association, Calgary.

Martin, Paul S., George I. Quimby, and Donald Collier
1947   *Indians Before Columbus: Twenty Thousand Years of North American History Revealed by Archaeology.* University of Chicago Press, Chicago.

Marx, Karl
1977   *Capital: A Critique of Political Economy*, vol. 1. Random House/Vintage, New York.
1990   *The Eighteenth Brumaire of Louis Bonaparte.* (12th printing.) International Publishers, New York.

Marx, Karl, and Friedrich Engels
1970   *The German Ideology.* Edited by C. J. Arthur, pt. 1 with selections from pts. 2 and 3. International Publishers, New York.

Mauldin, Raymond P., and Daniel S. Amick
1989   Investigating Patterning in Debitage from Experimental Bifacial Core Reduction. In *Experiments in Lithic Technology*, edited by D. S. Amick and R. P. Mauldin, pp. 67–88. International Series 528. B.A.R., Oxford.

Maxwell, Moreau S.
1951   *The Woodland Cultures of Southern Illinois: Archaeological Investigations in the Carbondale Area.* Publications in Anthropology, Bulletin No. 7. Logan Museum, Beloit, Wis.

May, Ernest E.
1984   Prehistoric Chert Exploitation in the Shawnee Hills. In *Cultural Frontiers in the Upper Cache Valley, Illinois*, by V. Canouts, E. E. May, N. H. Lopinot and J. D. Muller, pp. 68–90. Research Paper No. 16. Center for Archaeological Investigations, Southern Illinois University at Carbondale.

Mehrer, Mark W., and James M. Collins
1995   Household Archaeology at Cahokia and in Its Hinterlands. In *Mississippian Communities and Households*, edited by J. D. Rogers and B. D. Smith, pp. 32–57. University of Alabama Press, Tuscaloosa.

Meillassoux, Claude
1972   From Reproduction to Production. *Economy and Society* 1:93–105.
1978   The Social Organization of the Peasantry: The Economic Basis of Kinship. In *Relations of Production: Marxist Approaches to Economic Anthropology*, edited by D. Seddon, pp. 159–69. Frank Cass, London.

Meltzer, David, and Robert C. Dunnell (editors)
  1992   *The Archaeology of William Henry Holmes.* Smithsonian Institution Press, Washington, D.C.
Merwin, Bruce W.
  1935   An Aboriginal Village Site in Union County. *Journal of the Illinois State Historical Society* 28:78–92.
Michals, Lauren
  1981   The Exploitation of Fauna During the Moundville 1 Phase at Moundville. *Southeastern Archaeological Conference Bulletin* 24:91–93.
Miles, C. C. (assisted by J. W. Scott, B. E. Currie, and L. A. Dungan)
  1979   *Soil Survey of Union County, Illinois.* U.S. Department of Agriculture, Soil Conservation Service, Washington, D.C.
Miller, Christopher L., and George R. Hamell
  1986   A New Perspective on Indian-White Contact: Cultural Symbols and Colonial Trade. *Journal of American History* 73:311–28.
Miller, Daniel, and Christopher Tilley (editors)
  1984   *Ideology, Power, and Prehistory.* Cambridge University Press, Cambridge.
Miller, David
  1958   The Mound Lake Spade Cache. *Central States Archaeological Journal* 4:97.
Milner, George R.
  1984   [Assisted by J. A. Williams] *The Julien Site.* Illinois Department of Transportation, FAI-270 Site Report No. 7. University of Illinois Press, Urbana.
  1986   Mississippian Period Population Density in a Segment of the Central Mississippi River Valley. *American Antiquity* 51:227–38.
  1990   The Late Prehistoric Cahokia Cultural System of the Mississippi River Valley: Foundations, Florescence, and Fragmentation. *Journal of World Prehistory* 4:1–38.
  1993   Settlements Amidst Swamps. *Illinois Archaeology* 5:374–80.
Milner, George R., Thomas E. Emerson, Mark W. Mehrer, Joyce A. Williams, and Duane Esarey
  1984   Mississippian and Oneonta Periods. In *American Bottom Archaeology,* edited by C. J. Bareis and J. W. Porter, pp. 158–86. University of Illinois Press, Urbana.
Mintz, Sidney W.
  1985   *Sweetness and Power: The Place of Sugar in Modern History.* Viking Penguin, New York.
Morrow, Carol A.
  1987   Blades and Cobden Chert: A Technological Argument for Their Role as Markers of Regional Identification During the

Hopewell Period in Illinois. In *The Organization of Core Technology,* edited by J. K. Johnson and C. A. Morrow, pp. 119–49. Westview Press, Boulder, Colo.

Morse, Dan F.
1975 *Report of Excavations at the Zebree Site, 1969.* Research Report No. 4. Arkansas Archeological Survey, Fayetteville.

Morse, Dan F., and Phyllis A. Morse
1983 *Archaeology of the Central Mississippi Valley.* Academic Press, New York.

Morse, George W.
1881 An Inscribed Fragment of Pottery from a Mound in Illinois. *The American Antiquarian and Oriental Journal* 3:331–32.

Muller, Jon
1978 The Kincaid System: Mississippian Settlement in the Environs of a Large Site. In *Mississippian Settlement Patterns,* edited by B. D. Smith, pp. 269–92. Academic Press, New York.
1984 Mississippian Specialization and Salt. *American Antiquity* 49:489–507.
1986 *Archaeology of the Lower Ohio River Valley.* Academic Press, Orlando.
1987 Salt, Chert, and Shell: Mississippian Exchange and Economy. In *Specialization, Exchange, and Complex Societies,* edited by E. M. Brumfiel and T. K. Earle, pp. 10–21. Cambridge University Press, Cambridge.
1989 The Southern Cult. In *The Southeastern Ceremonial Complex: Artifacts and Analysis,* edited by P. Galloway, pp. 11–26. University of Nebraska Press, Lincoln.
1995 Regional Interaction in the Later Southeast. In *Native American Interactions,* edited by M. S. Nassaney and K. E. Sassaman, pp. 317–40. University of Tennessee Press, Knoxville.
1997 *Mississippian Political Economy.* Plenum Press, New York.

Muller, Jon, and Lisa Renken
1989 Radiocarbon Dates for the Great Salt Spring Site: Dating Saltpan Variation. *Illinois Archaeology* 1:150–60.

Myer, W. E.
1928 Indian Trails of the Southeast. *Bureau of American Ethnology, Annual Report* 42:727–857.

Nash, June
1979 *We Eat the Mines and the Mines Eat Us.* Columbia University Press, New York.

Nassaney, Michael S.
1996 The Role of Chipped Stone in the Political Economy of Social Ranking. In *Stone Tools: Theoretical Insights into Human Pre-*

history, edited by G. H. Odell, pp. 181–224. Plenum Press, New York.

Nassaney, Michael S., and Charles R. Cobb

1991   Patterns and Processes of Late Woodland Development in the Southeastern United States. In *Stability, Transformation, and Variation: The Late Woodland Southeast,* edited by M. S. Nassaney and C. R. Cobb, pp. 285–322. Plenum Press, New York.

Nassaney, Michael S., and Kendra Pyle

1999   The Adoption of the Bow and Arrow in Eastern North America: A View from Central Arkansas. *American Antiquity* 64:243–63.

Nassaney, Michael S., and Kenneth E. Sassaman (editors)

1995   *Native American Interactions: Multiscalar Analyses and Interpretations in the Eastern Woodlands.* University of Tennessee Press, Knoxville.

Nelson, Margaret C.

1991   The Study of Technological Organization. In *Archaeological Method and Theory,* vol. 3, edited by M. B. Schiffer, pp. 57–100. University of Arizona Press, Tucson.

Netting, Robert M.

1982   Some Home Truths on Household Size and Wealth. In Archaeology of the Household: Building a Prehistory of Domestic Life, edited by R. R. Wilk and W. J. Rathje. *American Behavioral Scientist* 25(6): 641–62.

Newcomer, M. H.

1971   Some Quantitative Experiments in Handaxe Manufacture. *World Archaeology* 3:85–93.

O'Brien, Michael J.

1991   Review of *The Mississippian Emergence,* by B. D. Smith. *Southeastern Archaeology* 10:147–48.

1994   *Cat Monsters and Head Pots: The Archaeology of Missouri's Pemiscot Bayou.* University of Missouri Press, Columbia.

O'Brien, Michael J., and Thomas D. Holland

1992   The Role of Adaptation in Archaeological Explanation. *American Antiquity* 57:36–59.

O'Brien, Michael J., and W. Raymond Wood

1998   *The Prehistory of Missouri.* University of Missouri Press, Columbia and London.

Oberg, Kalervo

1955   Types of Social Structure Among the Lowland Tribes of South and Central America. *American Anthropologist* 57:472–87.

Odell, George H.

1981   The Mechanics of Use-Breakage of Stone Tools: Some Testable Hypotheses. *Journal of Field Archaeology* 8:197–209.

1988   Addressing Prehistoric Hunting Practices Through Stone Tool
       Analysis. *American Anthropologist* 90:335–56.
1989   Experiments in Lithic Reduction. In *Experiments in Lithic
       Technology*, edited by D. S. Amick and R. P. Mauldin, pp. 163–
       98. International Series 528. B.A.R., Oxford.
1994   The Role of Stone Bladelets in Middle Woodland Society.
       American Antiquity 59:102–20.
1996   Economizing Behavior and the Concept of "Curation." In
       Stone Tools: Theoretical Insights into Human History, edited
       by G. H. Odell, pp. 51–80. Plenum Press, New York.

Oetelaar, Gerald A.
1993   Identifying Site Structure in the Archaeological Record: An Il-
       linois Mississippian Example. *American Antiquity* 58:662–87.

Ollman, Bertell
1976   *Alienation: Marx's Conception of Man in Capitalist Society.*
       2d ed. Cambridge University Press, New York.

Ortner, Sherry
1984   Theory in Anthropology Since the Sixties. *Comparative Stud-
       ies in Society and History* 26:126–66.

Parker Pearson, Michael
1984   Social Change, Ideology and the Archaeological Record. In
       Marxist Perspectives in Archaeology, edited by M. Spriggs, pp.
       59–71. Cambridge University Press, Cambridge.

Parry, William J.
1992   Stone Tools and Debitage. In *The Petitt Site (11-Ax-253), Alex-
       ander County, Illinois*, edited by P. A. Webb, pp. 231–60. Re-
       search Paper No. 58. Center for Archaeological Investigations,
       Southern Illinois University at Carbondale.
1994   Prismatic Blade Technologies in North America. In *The Or-
       ganization of North American Prehistoric Chipped Stone Tool
       Technologies*, edited by P. J. Carr, pp. 87–98. Archaeological
       Series 7. International Monographs in Prehistory, Ann Arbor,
       Mich.

Parry, William J., and Robert L. Kelly
1987   Expedient Core Technology and Sedentism. In *The Organiza-
       tion of Core Technology*, edited by J. K. Johnson and C. A.
       Morrow, pp. 285–304. Westview Press, Boulder, Colo.

Parsons, Lee A., and Barbara J. Price
1971   Mesoamerican Trade and Its Role in the Emergence of Civiliza-
       tion. In *Observations on the Emergence of Civilization in
       Mesoamerica*, edited by R. F. Heizer and J. A. Graham, pp.
       169–95. Contributions No. 11. University of California Ar-
       chaeological Research Facility, Berkeley.

Patterson, Leland W.

  1990   Characteristics of Bifacial-Reduction Flake-Size Distribution. *American Antiquity* 55:550–58.

Pauketat, Timothy R.

  1983   A Long-Stemmed Spud from the American Bottom. *Midcontinental Journal of Archaeology* 8:1–15.

  1989   Monitoring Mississippian Homestead Occupation Span and Economy Using Ceramic Refuse. *American Antiquity* 54:288–310.

  1994   *The Ascent of Chiefs: Cahokia and Mississippian Politics in Native North America.* University of Alabama Press, Tuscaloosa.

  1997   Specialization, Political Symbols, and the Crafty Elite of Cahokia. *Southeastern Archaeology* 16:1–15.

Pauketat, Timothy R., and Thomas E. Emerson

  1991   The Ideology of Authority and the Power of the Pot. *American Anthropologist* 93:919–41.

Paynter, Robert W.

  1989   The Archaeology of Equality and Inequality. *Annual Review of Anthropology* 18:369–99.

Paynter, Robert W., and Randall H. McGuire

  1991   The Archaeology of Inequality: Material Culture, Domination and Resistance. In *The Archaeology of Inequality,* edited by R. H. McGuire and R. W. Paynter, pp. 1–11. Basil Blackwell, Oxford.

Pearson, Harry W.

  1957   The Economy Has No Surplus: Critique of a Theory of Development. In *Trade and Market in the Early Empires,* edited by K. Polanyi, C. M. Arensberg, and H. W. Pearson, pp. 320–41. Free Press, Glencoe.

Peebles, Christopher, and Susan Kus

  1977   Some Archaeological Correlates of Ranked Societies. *American Antiquity* 42:421–48.

Peregrine, Peter N.

  1992   *Mississippian Evolution: A World-System Perspective.* Monographs in World Prehistory No. 9. Prehistory Press, Madison, Wis.

Perino, Gregory

  1963   Tentative Classification of Two Projectile Points and One Knife from West-Central Illinois. *Central States Archaeological Journal* 10:95–99.

Perrine, Thomas M.

  1873   Mounds Near Anna, Union County, Illinois. In *Annual Report of the Smithsonian Institution for 1872*, pp. 418–20. Washington, D.C.

1874   Antiquities of Union County, Illinois. In *Annual Report of the Smithsonian Institution for 1873*, pp. 410–11. Washington, D.C.

Phillips, Philip, and James A. Brown

1978   *Pre-Columbian Shell Engravings from the Craig Mound at Spiro, Oklahoma*, pt. 1. Peabody Museum of Archaeology and Ethnology. Harvard University, Cambridge.

Phillips, William A.

1899   The Aboriginal Quarries and Shops at Mill Creek, Union County, Illinois. *Proceedings of the American Association for the Advancement of Science* 48:361–63.

1900   Aboriginal Quarries and Shops at Mill Creek, Illinois. *American Anthropologist* 2:37–52.

Polhemus, Richard R.

1987   *The Toqua Site: A Late Mississippian Dallas Phase Town*. Report of Investigations 41. University of Tennessee, Department of Anthropology, Knoxville. Publications in Anthropology 44. Tennessee Valley Authority, Knoxville.

1990   Dallas Phase Architecture and Sociopolitical Structure. In *Lamar Archaeology: Mississippian Chiefdoms in the Deep South*, edited by M. Williams and G. Shapiro, pp. 125–38. University of Alabama Press, Tuscaloosa.

Pollack, David, and Jimmy A. Railey

1987   *Chambers (15ML109): An Upland Mississippian Village in Western Kentucky*. Kentucky Heritage Council, Frankfort.

Pope, Melody K.

1997   Stone Tools and Animal Processing Activities at Indian Knoll. Paper presented at the 54th Annual Meeting of the Southeastern Archaeological Conference, Baton Rouge, La.

Pope, Melody K., and Susan Pollock

1995   Trade, Tools, and Tasks: A Study of Uruk Chipped Stone Industries. In *Research in Economic Anthropology*, vol. 16, by B. L. Isaac, pp. 227–65. JAI Press, Greenwich, Conn.

Prentice, Guy

1983   Cottage Industries: Concepts and Implications. *Midcontinental Journal of Archaeology* 8:17–48.

1985   Economic Differentiation Among Mississippian Farmsteads. *Midcontinental Journal of Archaeology* 10:77–122.

1986   An Analysis of the Symbolism Expressed by the Birger Figurine. *American Antiquity* 51:239–66.

Prentice, Guy, and Mark Mehrer
   1981 The Lab Woofie Site (11-S-346): An Unplowed Mississippian
        Site in the American Bottom Region of Illinois. *Midcontinen-*
        tal Journal of Archaeology 6:33-53.

Price, James E.
   1978 The Settlement Pattern of the Powers Phase. In *Mississippian*
        Settlement Patterns, edited by B. D. Smith, pp. 201-31. Aca-
        demic Press, New York.

Price, Mary F.
   1999 All in the Family: The Impact of Gender and Family Con-
        structs on the Study of Prehistoric Settlement. In *Making*
        Places in the Prehistoric World: Themes in Settlement Archae-
        ology, edited by J. Bruck and Melissa Goodman, pp. 30-51.
        University College London Press, London.

Raab, L. Mark
   1982 Expanding Prehistory in the Arkansas Ozarks. In *Arkansas*
        Archeology in Review, edited by N. L. Trubowitz and M. D.
        Jeter, pp. 233-39. Research Series No. 15. Arkansas Archeologi-
        cal Survey, Fayetteville.

Raab, L. Mark, Robert F. Cande, and David W. Stahle
   1979 Debitage Graphs and Archaic Settlement Patterns in the Arkan-
        sas Ozarks. *Midcontinental Journal of Archaeology* 4:167-82.

Rau, Charles
   1864 Agricultural Implements of the North American Stone Period.
        In *Annual Report for 1863,* pp. 379-80. Smithsonian Institu-
        tion, Washington, D.C.
   1869 A Deposit of Agricultural Flint Implements in Southern Illi-
        nois. In *Annual Report for 1868,* pp. 402-4. Smithsonian Insti-
        tution, Washington, D.C.

Rees, Mark A.
   1997 Coercion, Tribute and Chiefly Authority: The Regional Devel-
        opment of Mississippian Political Culture. *Southeastern Ar-*
        chaeology 16:113-33.

Renfrew, Colin
   1973 Monuments, Mobilization and Social Organization in Neo-
        lithic Wessex. In *The Explanation of Culture Change: Models*
        in Prehistory, edited by C. Renfrew, pp. 539-58. University of
        Pittsburgh Press, Pittsburgh.

Resnick, Stephen, and Richard Wolff
   1987 *Knowledge and Class.* University of Chicago Press, Chicago.

Ricklis, Robert A., and Kim A. Cox
   1993 Examining Lithic Technological Organization as a Dynamic

Cultural Subsystem: The Advantages of an Explicitly Spatial Approach. *American Antiquity* 58:444–61.

Riley, Thomas J.

1987 Ridged-Field Agriculture and the Mississippian Economic Pattern. In *Emergent Horticultural Economies of the Eastern Woodlands*, edited by W. F. Keegan, pp. 295–304. Occasional Paper No. 7. Center for Archaeological Investigations, Southern Illinois University at Carbondale.

Riley, Thomas J., Gregory R. Walz, Charles J. Bareis, Andrew C. Fortier, and Kathryn E. Parker

1994 Accelerator Mass Spectrometry (AMS) Dates Confirm Early *Zea Mays* in the Mississippi River Valley. *American Antiquity* 59:490–98.

Robben, A.

1989 Habits of the Home: Spatial Hegemony and the Structuration of House and Society in Brazil. *American Anthropologist* 91:570–88.

Rogers, J. Daniel

1995 The Archaeological Analysis of Domestic Organization. In *Mississippian Communities and Households*, edited by J. D. Rogers and B. D. Smith, pp. 7–31. University of Alabama Press, Tuscaloosa.

Romans, Bernard

1962 *A Concise Natural History of East and West Florida.* (Originally published 1775.) University of Florida Press, Gainesville.

Roseberry, William

1988 Political Economy. *Annual Review of Anthropology* 17:161–85.

1989 *Anthropologies and Histories: Essays in Culture, History, and Political Economy.* Rutgers University Press, New Brunswick.

Rosson, James F.

1973 Structure, Composition, Pattern, and Dynamics of Two Forested Watersheds in the Ozark Hills, Southern Illinois. M.A. thesis, Department of Forestry, Southern Illinois University at Carbondale.

Rudolph, James L.

1977 *Level 2 Investigations in the Bay Creek Watershed (Pope and Johnson Counties, Illinois).* Archaeological Service Report No. 52. University Museum, Southern Illinois University, Carbondale.

1984 Earthlodges and Platform Mounds: Changing Public Architecture in the Southeastern United States. *Southeastern Archaeology* 3:33–45.

Rutz, Henry J.
　　1989　Fijian Household Practices and the Reproduction of Class. In
　　　　　*The Household Economy: Reconsidering the Domestic Mode of
　　　　　Production*, edited by R. R. Wilk, pp. 119–48. Westview Press,
　　　　　Boulder, Colo.
Sacks, Karen
　　1974　Engels Revisited: Women, the Organization of Production, and
　　　　　Private Property. In *Woman, Culture and Society*, edited by
　　　　　M. Z. Rosaldo and L. Lamphere, pp. 207–22. Stanford Univer-
　　　　　sity Press, Stanford.
Sahlins, Marshall A.
　　1963　Poor Man, Rich Man, Big-Man, Chief: Political Types in Mela-
　　　　　nesia and Polynesia. *Comparative Studies in Society and His-
　　　　　tory* 5:285–303.
　　1972　*Stone Age Economics*. Aldine, Chicago.
　　1985　*Islands of History*. University of Chicago Press, Chicago.
　　1990　The Political Economy of Grandeur in Hawaii from 1820 to
　　　　　1830. In *Culture Through Time: Anthropological Approaches*,
　　　　　edited by E. Ohnuki-Tierney, pp. 26–56. Stanford University
　　　　　Press, Stanford.
Saitta, Dean J.
　　1994　Agency, Class, and Archaeological Interpretation. *Journal of
　　　　　Anthropological Archaeology* 13:201–27.
Saitta, Dean J., and Arthur S. Keene
　　1990　Politics and Surplus Flow in Prehistoric Communal Societies.
　　　　　In *Prehistoric Community Dynamics in the American South-
　　　　　west*, edited by S. Upham, pp. 203–24. Cambridge University
　　　　　Press, Cambridge.
Santeford, Lawrence G.
　　1982　Mississippian Political Organization and Chipped Stone Arti-
　　　　　facts: A Typological Model for the Study of a Prehistoric Society
　　　　　in Southern Illinois. Ph.D. dissertation, Department of Anthro-
　　　　　pology, Southern Illinois University at Carbondale.
Sassaman, Kenneth E.
　　1992　Lithic Technology and the Hunter-Gatherer Sexual Division of
　　　　　Labor. *North American Archaeologist* 13:249–62.
　　1993　*Early Pottery in the Southeast: Tradition and Innovation in
　　　　　Cooking Technology*. University of Alabama Press, Tuscaloosa.
　　1994a　Changing Strategies of Biface Production in the South Caro-
　　　　　lina Coastal Plain. In *The Organization of North American
　　　　　Prehistoric Chipped Stone Tool Technologies*, edited by P. J.
　　　　　Carr, pp. 99–117. Archaeological Series 7. International Mono-
　　　　　graphs in Prehistory, Ann Arbor, Mich.

1994b Production for Exchange in the Mid-Holocene Southeast: A Savannah River Valley Example. *Lithic Technology* 19:42–51.

Scarry, John F.
 1996 Stability and Change in the Apalachee Chiefdom. In *Political Structure and Change in the Prehistoric Southeastern United States*, edited by J. F. Scarry, pp. 192–227. University Press of Florida, Gainesville.

Schneider, Jane
 1977 Was There a Pre-Capitalist World System? *Peasant Studies* 6:20–29.

Schwegman, John
 1975 The Natural Divisions of Illinois. In *Guide to the Vascular Flora of Illinois*, by R. H. Mohlenbrock, pp. 1–47. Southern Illinois University Press, Carbondale.

Seeman, Mark F.
 1984 Craft Specialization and Tool Kit Structure: A Systemic Perspective on the Midcontinental Flint Knapper. In *Lithic Resource Procurement: Proceedings from the Second Conference on Prehistoric Chert Exploitation*, edited by S. C. Vehik, pp. 7–36. Occasional Paper 4. Center for Archaeological Investigations, Southern Illinois University at Carbondale.
 1994 Intercluster Lithic Patterning at Nobles Pond: A Case for "Disembedded" Procurement Among Early Paleoindian Societies. *American Antiquity* 59:273–88.

Sellet, Frédéric
 1993 Chaîne Opératoire: The Concept and Its Applications. *Lithic Technology* 18:106–12.

Service, Elman R.
 1962 *Primitive Social Organization: An Evolutionary Perspective.* Random House, New York.

Shafer, Harry J.
 1985 A Technological Study of Two Maya Lithic Workshops at Colha, Belize. In *Stone Tool Analysis: Essays in Honor of Don E. Crabtree*, edited by M. G. Plew, J. C. Woods, and M. G. Pavesic, pp. 277–315. University of New Mexico Press, Albuquerque.

Shafer, Harry J., and Thomas R. Hester
 1983 Ancient Maya Chert Workshops in Northern Belize, Central America. *American Antiquity* 48:519–43.
 1986 Maya Stone-Tool Craft Specialization and Production at Colha, Belize: Reply to Mallory. *American Antiquity* 51:158–66.

Shanks, Michael, and Christopher Tilley
 1987 *Re-Constructing Archaeology: Theory and Practice.* Cambridge University Press, Cambridge.

Sheets, Payson D.

  1975 Behavioral Analysis and the Structure of a Prehistoric Indus-
        try. *Current Anthropology* 16:369–91.

Shott, Michael J.

  1993a *The Leavitt Site: A Parkhill Phase Paleo-Indian Occupation in
        Central Michigan.* Memoirs 25. Museum of Anthropology,
        University of Michigan, Ann Arbor.

  1993b Spears, Darts, and Arrows: Late Woodland Hunting Techniques
        in the Upper Ohio Valley. *American Antiquity* 58:425–43.

  1994 Size and Form in the Analysis of Flake Debris: Review and
        Recent Approaches. *Journal of Archaeological Method and
        Theory* 1:69–110.

Sievert, April K.

  1994 The Detection of Ritual Tool Use Through Functional Analy-
        sis. *Lithic Technology* 19:146–56.

Silverblatt, Irene

  1991 Interpreting Women in States: New Feminist Ethnohistories.
        In *Gender at the Crossroads of Knowledge: Feminist Anthro-
        pology in the Postmodern Era,* by M. diLeonardo, pp. 140–71.
        University of California Press, Berkeley.

Simek, Jan F.

  1994 The Organization of Lithic Technology and Evolution: Notes
        from the Continent. In *The Organization of North American
        Prehistoric Chipped Stone Tool Technologies,* edited by P. J.
        Carr, pp. 118–22. Archaeological Series 7. International Mono-
        graphs in Prehistory, Ann Arbor, Mich.

Singer, Clay A., and Jonathon E. Ericson

  1977 Quarry Analysis at Bodies Hills, Mono County, California: A
        Case Study. In *Exchange Systems in Prehistory,* edited by T. K.
        Earle and J. E. Ericson, pp. 171–88. Academic Press, New York.

Smith, Bruce D.

  1975 *Middle Mississippian Exploitation of Animal Populations.* An-
        thropological Papers 57. Museum of Anthropology, University
        of Michigan, Ann Arbor.

  1978a [Editor] *Mississippian Settlement Patterns.* Academic Press,
        New York.

  1978b Variation in Mississippian Settlement Patterns. In *Mississip-
        pian Settlement Patterns,* edited by B. D. Smith, pp. 479–503.
        Academic Press, New York.

  1986 The Archaeology of the Eastern United States: From Dalton to
        de Soto, 10,500–500 B.P. In *Advances in World Archaeology,*
        vol. 5, edited by F. Wendorf and A. E. Close, pp. 1–92. Aca-
        demic Press, Orlando.

1990   Introduction: Research on the Origins of Mississippian Chief-
        doms in Eastern North America. In *The Mississippian Emer-
        gence*, edited by B. D. Smith, pp. 1–8. Smithsonian Institution
        Press, Washington, D.C.

1992   Mississippian Elites and Solar Alignments: A Reflection of
        Managerial Necessity, or Levers of Social Inequality? In *Lords
        of the Southeast: Social Inequality and the Native Elites of
        Southeastern North America*, edited by A. W. Barker and T. R.
        Pauketat, pp. 11–30. Archeological Papers 3. American Anthro-
        pological Association, Washington, D.C.

1995   The Analysis of Single-Household Mississippian Settlements.
        In *Mississippian Communities and Households*, edited by
        J. D. Rogers and B. D. Smith, pp. 224–49. University of Ala-
        bama Press, Tuscaloosa.

Snyder, J. F.

1910   Prehistoric Illinois: The Primitive Flint Industry. *Journal of
        the Illinois State Historical Society* 3:11–25.

Spence, Michael W.

1981   Obsidian Production and the State at Teotihuacan. *American
        Antiquity* 46:769–88.

1984   Craft Production and Polity in Early Teotihuacan. In *Trade
        and Exchange in Early Mesoamerica*, edited by K. G. Hirth,
        pp. 87–123. University of New Mexico Press, Albuquerque.

Stahle, David W., and James E. Dunn

1982   An Analysis and Application of the Size Distribution of Waste
        Flakes from the Manufacture of Bifacial Tools. *World Archaeol-
        ogy* 14:84–97.

Stephens, Jeanette E.

1995   *An Archaeological Survey of Dogtooth Bend on the Missis-
        sippi River in Alexander County, Illinois.* U.S. Army Corps of
        Engineers, St. Louis District Historic Properties Management
        Report No. 45. Center for Archaeological Investigations, South-
        ern Illinois University at Carbondale.

1996   *Archaeological Mitigation at the Dogtooth Bend Site (11-AX-
        31), Alexander County, Illinois.* Technical Report 1996-1. Cen-
        ter for Archaeological Investigations, Southern Illinois Univer-
        sity at Carbondale.

Steponaitis, Vincas P.

1978   Location Theory and Complex Chiefdoms: A Mississippian
        Example. In *Mississippian Settlement Patterns*, edited by B. D.
        Smith, pp. 417–53. Academic Press, New York.

1983   *Ceramics, Chronology, and Community Patterns: An Archaeo-
        logical Study at Moundville.* Academic Press, New York.

1986   Prehistoric Archaeology in the Southeastern United States, 1970–1985. *Annual Review of Anthropology* 15:363–404.

1991   Contrasting Patterns of Mississippian Development. In *Chiefdoms: Power, Economy, and Ideology*, edited by T. K. Earle, pp. 193–228. Cambridge University Press, Cambridge.

Stoler, Ann L.

1985   *Capitalism and Confrontation in Sumatra's Plantation Belt, 1870–1979*. Yale University Press, New Haven.

Stoltman, James B., Jeffery A. Behm, and Harris A. Palmer

1984   The Bass Site: A Hardin Quarry/Workshop in Southwestern Wisconsin. In *Prehistoric Chert Exploitation: Studies from the Midcontinent*, edited by B. M. Butler and E. E. May, pp. 197–224. Occasional Paper No. 2. Center for Archaeological Investigations, Southern Illinois University at Carbondale.

Sullivan, Alan P., III, and Kenneth C. Rozen

1985   Debitage Analysis and Archaeological Interpretation. *American Antiquity* 50:755–79.

Sullivan, Lynne P.

1995   Mississippian Household and Community Organization in Eastern Tennessee. In *Mississippian Communities and Households*, edited by J. D. Rogers and B. D. Smith, pp. 99–123. University of Alabama Press, Tuscaloosa.

Sussenbach, Tom, Paul P. Kreisa, and Charles B. Stout

1986   Redefining the Late Woodland Ceramic Assemblage in the Northern Lower Valley. Paper presented at the Southeastern Archaeological Conference, Nashville, Tennessee.

Swanton, John R.

1928   Religious Beliefs and Medical Practices of the Creek Indians. *Bureau of American Ethnology, Annual Report* 42:473–62.

1946   *The Indians of the Southeastern United States*. Bureau of American Ethnology, Bulletin 137. Smithsonian Institution, Washington, D.C.

Tankersley, Kenneth B.

1995   Seasonality of Stone Procurement: An Early Paleoindian Example in Northwestern New York State. *North American Archaeologist* 16:1–16.

Telford, Clarence J.

1926   Third Report on a Forest Survey of Illinois. *Illinois State Natural History Bulletin* 16:1–102.

Teltser, Patrice A.

1991   Generalized Core Technology and Tool Use: A Mississippian Example. *Journal of Field Archaeology* 18:363–75.

Terray, Emmanuel

1972   *Marxism and "Primitive" Societies.* (Originally published 1969.) Translated by Mary Klopper. Monthly Review Press, New York and London.

Thing, L. H.

1882   Letter to Cyrus Thomas. On file with the Anthropological Archives. Smithsonian Institution, Washington, D.C.

Thomas, Cyrus

1894   *Report on the Mound Exploration of the Bureau of Ethnology.* Annual Report of the American Bureau of Ethnology, vol. 12. Smithsonian Institution, Washington, D.C.

Thomas, Julian

1987   Relations of Production and Social Change in the Neolithic of North-West Europe. *Man* 22:405–30.

Thomas, Larissa A.

1997   Hoe Production and Household Production at Dillow's Ridge: Gender Division of Labor and the Place of Production for Exchange in Mississippian Economy. Ph.D. dissertation, Department of Anthropology, State University of New York at Binghamton.

Thompson, E. P.

1966   *The Making of the British Working Class.* (Originally published 1963.) Vintage, New York.

Throop, Addison J.

1928   *Mound Builders of Illinois.* Call Printing, East St. Louis, Ill.

Thurston, G. P.

1897   Engraved Shell Gorgets and Flint Ceremonial Artifacts. *American Antiquarian* 19:96–100.

Tilley, Christopher

1984   Ideology and the Legitimation of Power in the Middle Neolithic of Southern Sweden. In *Ideology, Power, and Prehistory,* edited by D. Miller and C. Tilley, pp. 111–46. Cambridge University Press, Cambridge.

Titterington, P. F.

1938   *The Cahokia Mound Group and Its Village Site Materials.* Cahokia Mounds Museum Society, St. Louis.

Tomka, Steven A.

1989   Differentiating Lithic Reduction Techniques: An Experimental Approach. In *Experiments in Lithic Technology,* edited by D. S. Amick and R. P. Mauldin, pp. 137–62. International Series 528. B.A.R., Oxford.

Torrence, Robin

    1986 *Production and Exchange of Stone Tools: Prehistoric Obsidian in the Aegean.* Cambridge University Press, Cambridge.

    1989 Re-tooling: Towards a Behavioral Theory of Stone Tools. In *Time, Energy and Stone Tools,* edited by R. Torrence, pp. 57–66. Cambridge University Press, Cambridge.

    1994 Strategies for Moving On in Lithic Studies. In *The Organization of North American Prehistoric Chipped Stone Tool Technologies,* edited by P. J. Carr, pp. 123–31. Archaeological Series 7. International Monographs in Prehistory, Ann Arbor, Mich.

Tosi, Maurizio

    1984 The Notion of Craft Specialization and Its Representation in the Archaeological Record of Early States in the Turanian Basin. In *Marxist Perspectives in Archaeology,* edited by M. Spriggs, pp. 22–52. Cambridge University Press, Cambridge.

Trigger, Bruce G.

    1989 *A History of Archaeological Thought.* Cambridge University Press, Cambridge.

    1990 Maintaining Economic Equality in Opposition to Complexity: An Iroquoian Case Study. In *The Evolution of Political Systems: Sociopolitics in Small-Scale Sedentary Societies,* edited by S. Upham, pp. 119–45. Cambridge University Press, Cambridge.

Tuden, Arthur

    1979 An Exploration of a Pre-Capitalist Mode of Production. In *New Directions in Political Economy: An Approach from Anthropology,* edited by M. B. Leons and F. Rothstein, pp. 19–32. Greenwood Press, Westport.

Walker, Winslow M., and Robert McCormick Adams

    1946 Excavations in the Matthews Site, New Madrid County, Missouri. *Transactions of the Academy of Science of St. Louis* 31(4).

Wallerstein, Immanuel

    1974 *The Modern World-System: Capitalist Agriculture and the Origins of the European World-Economy in the Sixteenth Century.* Academic Press, New York.

    1978 Civilizations and Modes of Production. *Theory and Society* 5:1–10.

Walthall, John A.

    1981 *Galena and Aboriginal Trade in Eastern North America.* Scientific Papers 17. Illinois State Museum, Springfield.

Walthall, John A., and George R. Holley

    1997 Mobility and Hunter-Gatherer Toolkit Design: Analysis of a Dalton Lithic Cache. *Southeastern Archaeology* 16:152–62.

Waring, Antonio J., and Preston Holder
 1945 A Prehistoric Ceremonial Complex in the Southeastern
 United States. *American Anthropologist* 47:1–34.
Webb, Paul A. (editor)
 1992 *The Petitt Site (11-Ax-253), Alexander County, Illinois.* Research Paper No. 58. Center for Archaeological Investigations,
 Southern Illinois University at Carbondale.
Webb, William S.
 1974 *Indian Knoll.* (Originally published 1946.) University of Tennessee Press, Knoxville.
Weiner, Annette B.
 1992 *Inalienable Possessions.* University of California Press,
 Berkeley.
Welch, Paul D.
 1991 *Moundville's Economy.* University of Alabama Press, Tuscaloosa.
Welch, Paul D., and C. Margaret Scarry
 1995 Status-Related Variation in Foodways in the Moundville Chiefdom. *American Antiquity* 60:397–420.
Weller, J. Marvin
 1940 *Geology and Oil Possibilities of Extreme Southern Illinois.*
 Report of Investigations 71. Illinois State Geological Survey,
 Urbana.
Wells, Peter S.
 1998 Culture Contact, Identity, and Change in the European Prov-
 inces of the Roman Empire. In *Studies in Culture Contact: Interaction, Culture Change, and Archaeology,* edited by J. G.
 Cusick, pp. 316–34. Occasional Paper No. 25. Center for Archaeological Investigations, Southern Illinois University at Carbondale.
Wesler, Kit W.
 1985 *Archaeological Excavations at Wickliffe Mounds, 15BA4:
 Mound A, 1984.* Wickliffe Mounds Research Center Report
 No. 1. Murray State University, Murray, Ky.
 1991 Ceramics, Chronology, and Horizon Markers at Wickliffe
 Mounds. *American Antiquity* 56:278–90.
 1997 The Wickliffe Mounds Project: Implications for Late Mississippi Period Chronology, Settlement, and Mortuary Patterns
 in Western Kentucky. *Proceedings of the Prehistoric Society*
 63:261–83.
Wilk, Richard R.
 1989 Decision Making and Resource Flows Within the Household:
 Beyond the Black Box. In *The Household Economy: Reconsider-*

ing the Domestic Mode of Production, edited by R. R. Wilk, pp. 23–52. Westview Press, Boulder, Colo.

Wilk, Richard, and William Rathje
    1982 Household Archaeology. *American Behavioral Scientist* 25:617–40.

Williams, Stephen
    1990 The Vacant Quarter and Other Late Events in the Lower Valley. In *Towns and Temples Along the Mississippi,* edited by D. H. Dye and C. A. Cox, pp. 170–80. University of Alabama Press, Tuscaloosa.

Williams, Stephen, and John M. Goggin
    1956 The Long Nosed God Mask in Eastern United States. *Missouri Archaeologist* 18:4–72.

Winters, Howard D.
    1981 Excavating in Museums: Notes on Mississippian Hoes and Middle Woodland Copper Gouges and Celts. In *The Research Potential of Anthropological Museum Collections,* edited by A. E. Cantwell, J. B. Griffin, and N. A. Rothschild, pp. 17–34. Annals of the New York Academy of Sciences 376, New York.

Wittry, Warren L.
    1969 The American Woodhenge. In *Explorations into Cahokia Archaeology,* edited by M. L. Fowler, pp. 43–48. Bulletin No. 7. Illinois Archaeological Survey, Urbana.

Wolf, Eric R.
    1966 *Peasants.* Prentice-Hall, Englewood Cliffs, N.J.
    1982 *Europe and the People Without History.* University of California Press, Berkeley.
    1990 Distinguished Lecture: Facing Power—Old Insights, New Questions. *American Anthropologist* 92:586–96.

Wong, Diana
    1984 The Limits of Using the Household as a Unit of Analysis. In *Households and the World Economy,* edited by J. Smith, I. Wallerstein, and H. Evers, pp. 56–63. Sage, Beverly Hills, Calif.

Woods, William I.
    1987 Maize Agriculture and the Late Prehistoric: A Characterization of Settlement Location Strategies. In *Emergent Horticultural Economies of the Eastern Woodlands,* edited by W. F. Keegan, pp. 275–94. Occasional Paper No. 7. Center for Archaeological Investigations, Southern Illinois University at Carbondale.

Woods, William I., and George R. Holley
    1991 Upland Mississippian Settlement in the American Bottom Region. In *Cahokia and the Hinterlands: Middle Mississippian*

Cultures of the Midwest, edited by T. E. Emerson and R. B. Lewis, pp. 46–60. University of Illinois Press, Urbana.

Yanagisako, Sylvia J.

1979 Family and Household: The Analysis of Domestic Groups. *Annual Review of Anthropology* 8:161–205.

Yerkes, Richard W.

1983 Microwear, Microdrills, and Mississippian Craft Specialization. *American Antiquity* 48:499–518.

1989 Mississippian Craft Specialization on the American Bottom. *Southeastern Archaeology* 8:93–106.

Index

Cache River, 102, 106, 111, 160, 182, 194

Cahokia, 13–15, 41–42, 44, 56–57, 60, 62–64, 68–69, 105, 108, 117, 120, 122, 179, 185, 193, 203

Cairo Lowlands, 102–3

Cannel coal, 39

Capital, 10, 22, 26, 85; symbolic, 34

Capitalism, 3, 5, 7–8, 10, 21–22, 26, 30, 35, 200

Celt, 50, 72, 120, 122, 167

Centralization, 21, 33, 41–45, 96, 101, 123, 145, 154, 157, 191, 194–95

Central Mississippi River Valley, 4, 13, 38, 40–41, 58, 60, 66–67, 102–103, 106, 109, 120–121, 123, 136, 178–179, 192, 201–202, 206

Chaîne de travail, 76, 192

Chaîne opértoire, 76, 82

Chambers site, 177

Charleston, 90

Chenopod, 12, 183

Cherokee, 90–91

Chickasaw, 88–89

Chiefdom, 3–4, 54, 98; economic classes in, 26–28; political economy of, 39–40, 42, 45, 80, 187, 190, 197; size, 43; traits, 11, 17–21, 29, 31, 203

Chisels, 50, 167

Choctaw, 45, 90–91

Chunkey, 185

Class (economic), analysis, 17, 22, 202; defining, 9, 23–28, 92; fundamental, 44; Mississippian, 42; subsumed, 27–28, 44, 193

Cobden chert, 170–71, 201

Cofitachequi, 74

Coles Creek, 12

Colha, 81, 129

Commodity, 10

Community, 2, 8, 11, 18, 38–39, 75, 103, 161–62, 181, 186–88, 192–95, 197, 201–3, 205

Confluence (Mississippi and Ohio Rivers), 67, 102–4, 106, 108–10, 118, 121, 178–79, 186

Consumption, 28, 35–36, 46, 78, 84,

97, 124, 176; fur trade, 89; hoes, 3, 5, 17, 54, 65, 72, 75–77, 92, 145, 150, 167, 189, 199–200; identity and, 200–202; Neolithic axes, 96; obsidian, 96; political economy of, 47, 186–87, 198; Ramey knives, 171

Coosa, 43

Copper, 1, 3, 14, 34, 37, 40–41, 58–59, 71, 77, 154, 155, 190, 197, 202

Cortex, 51, 136–38, 141–42, 175–76

Cottontail rabbit, 182

Crescent quarries, 120. See also Burlington chert

Crosno, 102

Cucurbits, 55

Dart, 147

Daub, 1, 160, 162

Deer, 53, 55, 89–91, 136, 179, 181

Denticulate, 151, 168

De Soto, 54, 60, 75, 109

Dillinger phase, 107

Dillow's Ridge, 18, 132, 136–38, 149–50, 156–90, 192–93, 197, 201, 204

Discoidal, 184–85

Division of Mound Explorations, 100, 112

Dog, 133, 179

Dogtooth Bend, 105

Douglas phase, 108

Dover, chert, 53, 56, 67, 122, 205; quarries, 121, 123; workshops, 148, 150, 171–72

Drills, 92, 167

Drumfish, 181

Duck, 182

Duck River style (chert swords), 50, 70

East St. Louis site, 69

Egalitarian, 157

Elco chert, 116

Elco site, 130–31, 154, 197

Elites, 21, 43, 52, 54–55, 73, 86, 93, 99, 222, 224, 227–28

Emergent Mississippian, 55–56, 65–66, 107, 150, 166, 177

About the Author

Charles R. Cobb is Associate Professor of Anthropology, State University of New York at Binghamton. He received his B.A. from the University of Arizona in 1980 and his Ph.D. from Southern Illinois University at Carbondale in 1988. He is the co-editor of one book and author or co-author of numerous articles on methodological and theoretical issues in archaeology. Currently, he is the editor of *Northeast Anthropology*.